Living
By
Modern Myths

(In a World of 'Maverick' Values)

Pushpangadan Mangari

CONTENTS

INTRODUCTION

Traditional, classical myths are omnipresent. Study of these myths or 'Euhemerism,' is very much a part of our life, as in many ways, we live by myths. They are, by definition, fictional. This book is about some views, beliefs, theories, norms, concepts, and practices that modern societies broadly follow, which can be considered as bordering on myths. They are real social narratives and experiences, but illusory in some sense or other.

Societies of all shades in the world have always been living with beliefs of various types, origins, and longevities and they will continue to do so. These beliefs were possibly created or developed primarily to justify the then prevalent social arrangements and to facilitate the acceptance of social norms, rituals, and traditions. Over a period, these beliefs or myths got retold, rewritten, and sometimes even forgotten. Many of them also got entrenched deeply in societies.

Societies traverse through unknown paths all the time. Hence, questions arise, as to whether the recordings and interpretations of their historical trips are truthful, and whether the paths believed to have been travelled by them were factual. These recordings, understandings, and questions become more relevant when they relate to existing nations, to live cultures, to practiced traditions, and to real human beings. Many of these histories and social beliefs might then lack conviction.

The saying that "I am a human being, and nothing human is alien to me" is critically valid in any community at any point in history, and more so in our current, chaotic one. Though we call ourselves civilized, conflicts are emanating due to different perceptions of our origins, ethnicities, races, religions, political ideologies, nationalities, and other identities. The situation is likely to get worse, as all imaginable types of social supremacies are increasingly getting planted in societies. The very social worth of an individual is being doubted in many situations. The silent majority seems to be resigned to the fact that they have no other option but to live with these enigmatic phenomena. They are either complicit in it, or indifferent or merely helpless.

The social world of human beings is a complex one and people always had social crises of some sort ever since they started living as a society. Societies are made of competing and conflicting internal and external forces, aided, and guided by man-made norms, regulations, and institutions. The value systems of human beings therefore cannot escape some degree of complexities as they are destined to be shaped and reshaped continuously by these mysterious, diverse influences. The fact that social sciences are born out of postulations, unsupported by any concrete scientific evidences, does not help explain the phenomenon either. In a world that is still looking for convincing answers for the unpredictable social and individual behaviour, the combined, mystical, and questionable impacts of faiths, values, ideologies, philosophies, traditions, and cultures will continue to provide both comforts and conflicts. And some of these will have a mythical aura around them.

The social evolution of human beings has another dilemma in-built. Human evolution is a dynamic process, creating continuous social differentiations. The change in equations happen due to economic, cultural, or political factors, to name a few. In line with such differentiations, the social rankings, and roles of individual members in societies keep changing. The continuous shifts in perceived societal status, power positions, competencies, and weaknesses of members in a community will have impact on its inter-relational models, making the social equations highly unstable. A near perfect blending of such roles of all players, at the individual or group level within a society becomes almost impossible or unpredictable, as even the new roles and differentiations will keep shifting. Gaps in social integration as above will inevitably lead to disharmony and frictions in societies. Thus, all dynamic societies would, by default, have internal conflicts and they would be fragmented always, to some extent.

Some of the ideas that keep emerging in societies will have relatively longer lives. They would persist, and would become part of human values, traditions, and culture. Other ideas may either get abandoned or redeveloped. In such a transitional society, a citizen must always be prepared to face unknown experiences. People will encounter newer, unknown concepts and outcomes on a regular basis. Logical understandings in respect of human values and key drivers of social behaviour are, however, missing in many societies. People are generally floating with the current. In the process, man is becoming more isolated, self-centered, and is being told not to trust other human beings. Social welfare has become a burden which no one wants to carry or look at. People have too many temporary, working relationships without any deeper bondages. Convincing, non-controversial solutions for social problems do not seem to be materializing.

Can societies tackle these issues? Some of these could certainly be. Governments can and must endeavour to elevate the values of citizens to higher levels. Such a level would help him or her to become an informed participant in a society, as a citizen with a sense of personal efficiency. That will also allow him or her to understand the societal dynamics and complexities better. He or she would then be able to recognize and counter the sources of influences in society, and to ward of its trappings.

The world faces a problem of real vs artificial. Many social events are simulated. Social players project them as real. These are hyper-realities, in the make belief category, that pervade all walks of life like arts, literature, and social activities. Many of them are possibilities created by commercial entities, offering newer experiences and relationships. *This book is about some of the current day hyper-realities, in the realm of values, culture, economics, religion, politics, etc. Given the fact that all these areas are interlinked, there would admittedly be some overlaps in the narratives in different chapters.*

The book begins with an examination of universal human values. The second chapter brings a national perspective to such values. Third chapter dwells on the religious orientations and obsessions of various groups. The fourth chapter is on cultural purity, cherished by many communities. The fifth chapter narrows it down to national celebration of some of the legacy cultures. Chapter six is about the social ladders in societies, both visible and invisible. Social welfare is the key thread in the entire book, and an attempt to cover some of its characteristics is made in the seventh chapter. A Hindu epic character, 'Mahabali,' known for his fair and just rule, is recalled in chapter eight, to focus on the increasing menace of inequality in societies. Chapter nine discusses few issues related to the much celebrated, democratic 'self-rule.' Chapter ten talks about current political set ups in democracies and their misplaced functional logics. The final chapter, eleven, talks about the pros and cons of globalization and its likely future.

The combined domino effect of actions pursued by powerful, entrenched players and social systems, on the lives of common men, is the central theme in the book. Societies can significantly minimize these adverse effects, if they collectively opt for some unconventional policies and approaches. *Few such approaches are put forward and discussed in each chapter. It is hoped that most of these would be seen as actionable by policy makers.*

Chapter 1

<u>MYTH OF UNIVERSAL VALUES</u>

Social order is the rule of the world that gets evolved over a prolonged period, by way of reinforced norms and regulations of human conduct as per certain prevailing social values. Societies create and uphold these values categorizing them as appropriate or otherwise, which then become the social norms. These values in any community evolve from a set of ethical guidelines or standards that indicate perceived desirable behaviour fit for a civilized life. The process of socialization typically nudges the members towards a set of conditioned responses meant to respect the social order, enforcing, and defending it. More critically, during the process of growing up, people in a society would typically develop a behavioural framework that creates for them, a stake in the smooth, orderly functioning of the society. The social orders provide meaning and legitimacy for the members' social behaviour. The conditioned social responses are therefore pre requisites in any society, as many vital attributes of members' personal and social identities get linked to it.

Human values are critical to the conceptions of what are good behaviour and desirable road maps, for a meaningful life. The roles such values are expected to play in shaping one's character and his overall personal identity, are equally critical. These concepts primarily shape and define the kind of person he or she wants to become. The 'structure' of values broadly refers to the relations of conflict and congruence among different values. They help characterize individuals, cultural groups, societies, and even nations. They form the core identifiers of human groups.

Changes in these values over a longer period can be studied to understand their evolving patterns, disagreements in norms, underlying social conditions, inter relationship between different values, causes for conflicts in value systems, etc. There could be ideological divisions as well.

Values differ from other concepts used to explain behaviour like attitudes, beliefs, norms, and traits. They compel a person to behave in a certain manner, consistent with the socially accepted norms. At all stages of growth, these values in a way, dictate the road to be taken, like which educational or vocational path to take, which job market to enter, which talents to be sharpened, which circle of friends to develop, when to marry, what type of family structure and bonding is ideal, what extra-curricular options to pursue, what kind of challenges and experiments to be taken in life, etc. Though there are common or shared values, there are substantial differences in the value systems of individuals and communities.

A social value differs from an individual value in the sense that it contains a concern for others' welfare. The western values are generally dominated by a greater belief in material progress, and they are more focussed on individuals. Therefore, it becomes easier for the westerners or Anglo Saxons to transcend their own cultures or embrace alien cultures. The Asian values, on the other hand, are traditionally marked by a domination of spiritualism. These arguably fading values advocate the forgetting of self, abandonment of personal desire and elimination of all sorts of personal, material ambitions. There is an inner quest, a search for finding the ultimate truth, the real human value, in life. It is therefore difficult for Asians to break away from traditions. The Eurasian Economic Union (EAEU) countries consisting of Russia, Belarus, Kazakhstan, Kyrgyzstan, and Armenia generally consider themselves as a single cultural group, one that is not fully culturally aligned with either Europe or Asia, but with higher levels of community orientation. These differences in social values found in different nations get reflected in each community's social structures. These norms are not mere representations arising out of some imaginary constructs. They are operating norms and those who disobey these are typically penalized by the group.

There are universal or shared values, or a set of values shared by all people across nations. The shared value concept warrants some critical reflections. Human behaviour is highly complex and, in many cases, hidden from public gaze. The model public behaviour therefore, is mostly a mental construction. Beliefs themselves are different for different people, given their different levels of civilizations, standards of education, exposures to media, interactions with others, reading habits, etc. Another way of looking at shared value is not to search for an existing, permanent set of shared values in a community. Instead, we could look at a *shareable* set of values, a combination of both past, present, and future values. Thus, these values could include the past values cherished by the community itself or the ones that could be considered desirable and worthy of emulation.

Devaluation of Values

Social value is many times measured in terms of the monetary value derived by inhabitants of a community. Such measurements confine the value to just a few economic concepts like business profits or Gross Domestic Product (GDP). Human beings themselves are very often evaluated based on their financial assets or liabilities, or in terms of their future earning capacity or their net estimated financial position. This tendency to value everything in life in terms of its economic benefits, is driven by the market concepts like demand and supply for a product in a commercial space. Human beings are seen as mere commodities under this approach and factors like human happiness and general well-being are ignored. Objects for which there is no market price like a beautiful sight of a landscape or an art work or a sunset or a caring mother, are deemed to have no value. These are invaluable objects and experiences and their values cannot be brought down to the level of a mere price.

Ethical practices, political morality, freedom of expression, etc., are all values in themselves which must be based on socially desirable norms. Given the current situation, there is a case for reimaging the whole set of human values. The concept of value must move away from comparisons and rankings in society, to betterment of human lives in terms of relative equality, peaceful coexistence, empathy and caring. An obsession with social rankings based on economic and political power is destructive for mankind. It is a devaluation of human values.

There are 'Anti Values' as well. They typically have a negative impact on societies. Cheating someone, deliberately spreading misinformation, unduly dominating someone, starting a war, or killing innocent people, are all considered as anti-values.

Shared Values

Globally, human values have evolved from the shared wisdom of various civilizations, nations, intellectuals, and individuals. Some of these are considered universal values, which are broadly agreeable to the whole humanity. Some values cannot be considered as perfectly universal, but they have been adopted by a significant percentage of global population, like the democratic values. Prolonging the average life span of a citizen by scientific methods, using modern medicines, is considered as a good value proposition by many. But spiritually oriented people, contemplative mystics, and monks might consider the quality of life a better value barometer, than the number of years lived. Technological development, rapid communication, globalization, travel, internet, etc., are all values for many, but not accepted by some. Many believe that living in harmony with nature is a great value, but a significant number of others do not agree.

Values transcend generations and they have evolved differently in different societies. Human beings and societies historically had divergent values. When people migrate to new places and start interacting with 'alien' social traditions, many of these values get mixed up, some get discarded, and new values take birth. It is a moot point as to whether in a world where millions of people are in extreme poverty, any value other than survival is worth arguing about. However, human existence cannot be meaningful if it is restricted to mere survival. There should be some higher levels of quality attached to life, like enjoying the wonders of nature, exploring the unknown, experiencing the unseen, and generally extending the use of one's physical and mental health to the maximum. Some of the universally accepted human values address these aspects. People hold numerous values like the sense of achievement, security, benevolence, understanding the life itself, etc., with varying degrees of importance. Of these, some values like benevolence and power conflict with one another whereas others like empathy are compatible.

The socialization hypothesis states that people's basic values change very little after adulthood. Family values inculcated right from the childhood lasts for entire life. People who have experienced poverty in childhood generally value economic needs more, and those who have experienced sustained material comforts in childhood value personal expressions, use of technology, freedom, justice, participation in governance, environment protection, etc., more.

Universal value objectives include the values of unity, social justice, peaceful co-existence, respecting fellow living beings, equality, preservation of nature and its aesthetic attractions, respect for globally accumulated intellectual and received wisdom, protection of the environment, promotion of mental or inner peace, etc. They also cover inter and intra group harmony, caring, and the like. Human welfare is not limited to material comforts alone. Mystic aspects of life are extremely comforting to a lot of people and form a part of human well-being. Spiritual values, with their transcending meanings, coherences, and inner harmonies, are realities in the lives of many. If finding ultimate meaning is a basic human need, then spirituality might as well be an important and distinct value required in all societies. However, spirituality does not have a consistent, sharable meaning across cultures.

At the global level, there are values that are shared and opposed. Nature is seen by people in different ways. Many of us get lost in the serene valleys of mountains or aesthetic wilderness of an enchanting forest. However, a significant number of people are against the concept of preservation of nature, at the cost of human material comforts. Taking care of natural gifts is an important value for many of us. But there are people who see these places as sources of valuable raw materials and resources, and they want to extract these resources from nature, for survival and prosperity. Some are interested in carrying out mining, farming, or fishing in these natural places whereas some others prefer to do trekking, farming, or swimming. It is a tough case to argue that a land used for just sight-seeing is more valuable than when it is used for farming. There are alternate options of consumption for most of the natural objects. A value judgement, at best, can be a personal preference.

Climate change, environment protection, homosexuality, same sex marriage, etc., are modern values that many nations share, which can be categorized as universal as they are getting increasingly accepted. There are other values relating to business, international laws and regulations, technological standards and procedures, political and institutional frameworks, etc. There are broad agreements in the logic and methodology adopted for various national performance indices like the ones that measure economic progress, freedom, human poverty, happiness, etc.

Some values are highly shared, but are too vague. We can say that all people love their homeland, or are fond of their culture, or that they all love their mother tongue, or that most of them are religious, or that almost all of them are committed to diversity, or that all are forward looking. These are mostly true for all human beings across the globe. They only create an illusion of sharing a value.

In 2003, the United Nations issued the Universal Declaration of Human Rights, in which the ideal universal human values are stated as *peace, freedom, social progress, equal rights,* and *human dignity* (United Nations 2003). Human rights have become globally accepted social benchmarks and goals, as embodied in the UN Sustainable Development Goals.

A good society with ethical or moral values is a basic social objective. An ideal society, however, is a utopia. People in general would always tend to maximize their personal desires, even if that requires imposing their values on others. Such a biased behaviour by a human being is a natural phenomenon. What distinguishes one value from another is the type of goal or motivation that it expresses. Universalism is basically a care-for-all approach, with an in-built, broadminded outlook, but its universal acceptance is almost impossible due to the self-interests and traditions of people. Hence, human values are bound to be controversial and they often lead to lose-lose situations. Since these are universal practices followed by virtually all, who in turn are similarly conditioned, the dilemma continues.

Rousseau, the Genevan philosopher, felt that human beings are naturally dependent on and inclined to cooperate with others. Individuals who live alone are expected to perish. But when they cooperate, use the strength of team, and develop common goals, they can not only ensure their own survival, but also promote the happiness and well-being of all. In order to achieve this objective, a political establishment is necessary. A strong political leadership that is both willing and capable of implementing a set of fair policies, aimed at the good of all, is warranted in all nations. In politically weak, unstable nations, or in states where certain segments are appeased for political considerations, these options would be virtually non-existent.

Universal values derive from the critical, survival needs of individuals and groups. However, people many times do not recognize them until they meet up with others who are different from their basic group or until they badly need essential natural resources which are under the control of such alien groups. Their failure to protect say, a territory or a common natural environment, may lead to destruction of shared resources on which they all depend. When these situations arise, people are forced to accept other groups or at least have working relationships with them, to avoid life-threatening situations. Under such circumstances, special interests give way to universalism, which addresses the concerns relating to the welfare of a larger society and the world as one entity.

Valuable Theories

Anthropology as a social science, postulates that cultural and social values are relative. It has many theories that are supported, ignored, and opposed by people. The value theory of Schwartz adopts a set of values with six main features that are implicit in the writings of many theorists: They are: 1. Values are beliefs, 2. Values refer to desirable goals, 3. Values transcend specific actions and situations, 4. Values serve as standards or criteria, 5. Values are ordered by importance, and 6. The relative importance of multiple values guides action. Walter Goodnow Everett classified values into the following eight categories; 1. Economic values, 2. Bodily values, 3. Value of recreation, 4. Value of association, 5. Character values, 6. Aesthetic values, 7. Intellectual values, and 8. Religious values.

One could add cultural values, social and moral values, political values, educational values, etc., to the list. Values normally get prioritized and ranked based on the value systems inherited by individuals and societies.

Values have been categorized as individual and cultural standards by the German philosopher and psychologist, Eduard Spranger (1914) in his book 'Lebernsformen' (Types of Men). There are values based on social fulfillment, as per the List of Values by Kahle, and those based on fulfillment of basic needs, as suggested by Galtung's capability approach. Galtung identifies a hierarchy of three basic needs comprising of survival needs, welfare needs and identity needs. Amartya Sen's capability approach claims that individual well-being rises with increased freedom and opportunities that individuals value. An example of this capability is like getting higher levels of education, which enables people to get better jobs and supportive social relationships. As per Daniel Hojman and Alvaro Miranda[1], our understanding of human well-being and development has shifted from a traditional focus on income and consumption towards a richer multidimensional approach.

There are higher level values[2] as per Tong-Keun Min, that are typically categorized as those involving 1. Absolute values such as absolute truth, absolute goodness, absolute beauty, and absolute holiness; 2. The act of contributing to the development and happiness of humankind; 3. The act of contributing to the nation or the state; 4. The act of contributing to the regional society; and 5. The act of cultivating oneself and managing one's family well.

Max-Neef's Model of Human Scale Development, Narayan's values based on the poor, Social Role Valorization by Wolfensberger, the Intergovernmental Platform on Biodiversity and Ecosystem Services (IPBES), Triandis' Universal Values, and Nussbaum's ten 'central human capabilities' are all well recognized. So are the value theories by Allport-Vernon-Lindzey, Rokeach, and by Schwarz. The idea of Social Role Valorization was introduced by Wolfensberger and his associates, which is a social science concept to create or support socially valued roles for people in their society.

Some values are achieved by individuals alone, whereas some are realized by team work. Values can be based on cultural differences, as per Hofstede's work-related values. Values could also be based on motivation, social norms, fulfillment of basic needs, etc., as indicated in Erik Allardt's Scandinavian sociology. Universal good things of life proposed by Wolfensberger, Thomas, and Caruso (1996) include ideas like affiliations to family, home, sense of belonging to a tribe or closely-knit village, or fraternity or religion, etc.

The Social Progress Index (SPI) measures the extent to which countries provide for the social and environmental needs of their citizens. It comprises of Fifty-four indicators relating to various areas like the basic human needs, foundations of well-being, and opportunities to progress. The index is published by the non-profit Social Progress Imperative, and is based on the writings of Amartya Sen, Douglass North, and Joseph Stiglitz.

One major categorization of values is into traditional values and secular-rational values. Traditional values emphasize on the importance of religion, respecting parents and other authorities, traditional family values, etc. People who belong to this group normally value traditional institutions like marriages. They show higher levels of patriotism. Secular-rational values have different inclinations and they tend to relate to liberal approaches, such as accepting higher levels of freedom of expression, homosexuality, and abortion. The move from traditional to secular-rational values is marked by the development of science and political interventions that help replace religious beliefs and myths (Inglehart 1990).

Yet another categorization is survival values vs self-expression values. The survival value believers recognize the economic, physical, and safety needs of individuals. Nations that prioritize survival values generally have low levels of trust and tolerance. They are more conservative in their approach and outlook. Self-expression values, on the contrary, give higher priority to enhancing the quality of life. They generally promote ideas like environmental protection, tolerance towards other people and unknown cultures, gender equality, globalization, freedom of expression, etc. The move from survival to self-expression in a way signifies the transition from an industrial society to a post-industrial society, and the promotion democratic values[3] (Inglehart and Flanagan 1987; Inglehart and Welzel 2005).

One more categorization would be Anthropocentric or 'instrumental' values, non-anthropocentric or the 'intrinsic' values, and relational values. Of these, anthropocentric values are those that focus on people and which aim to create benefits for people. The more natural objects are appreciated by people for their intrinsic value, the more instrumental value it gains. In contrast, non-anthropocentric values are those that include values of entities and objects in nature, and the ecosystems which are values in themselves, irrespective of their utility to humans. Relational values are different types of valued relationships between humans, and between humans and nature, which lead to a good quality of life. Relational values include purity-sanctity, authority-respect, in-group-loyalty, fairness-reciprocity, harm-care, etc.

Ethical and Mythical Values

Despite these excellent theories, the universality and acceptability of the whole set of human values appear to be questionable. Most of the human values are based on ethical concepts and beliefs. However, the material world of today has a workable social theory that looks mainly at measurable economic growth, whereas the qualitative and moral aspects are ignored. An ethical value-based society continues to be elusive. There is more of noise and drama, and less of real intention in pursuing fair human values. Many values are constantly contested and debated, yet remain unsettled.

Value theories, as above, have virtually been relegated to the back stage by the so-called civilized, modern-day intellectuals and citizens. Societies globally, are driven generally by financial capitalism, knowledge capitalism and social capitalism. An important factor impacting our value system today is the 'market,' critical principles around which societies organize people and businesses. The obvious end-result is that market has become the dominant determinant of social values now. Most market players want to take care of their own self-expressions and brand images. In order to achieve these narrow objectives, a whole new set of values have been invented. These include social rankings based on one's income, wealth, power exercised, etc. Such rankings are widely published so that the concerned individual can bask in its glory. The means of achieving the rankings are mostly ignored, and the focus is only on the end-results. Money could be amassed and power positions achieved by anyone, by any means. The results presumably justify the means.

How do we explain this phenomenon? There is a strong argument that societies world over, under the influence of capitalism, are preserving the economic order and benefits enjoyed by certain segments. They believe that laws and regulations are deliberately made and maintained to ensure continuation of the unequal social rankings, and value preferences of the richer sections in the communities. This is done obviously with the active support of the political class. While this is a convincing argument, the phenomenon is not new. It is well known that in the 3rd and 4th century AD, Rome had rich people who were unabashedly displaying their wealth while there were extremely poor people, including slaves, who toiled. So, the situation is similar.

Given the above realities, the very concept of a universal values looks like a beautiful myth. The story tellers of the world are doing just that; telling stories. Even though the human history has always been full of societies mingling and sharing their values, the world seems to be unsure of its own core values and their directions. Apparently, we have lost our power of critical reasoning.

Social values of nations change over a longer period. In vast countries like India, while there would be many similarities in cultures and traditions, it is natural to have significant differences in approach to life itself and beliefs. Some of these values get converged over a longer period due to inter-state movements, migration of people, common governance, etc. At the same time, there are valid reasons to suggest that active persuasion of value convergence can be counter-productive as some segments may view it as an indirect attempt of cultural invasion. The attempts to converge language across India was a classic case, which faced a lot of resistance, especially from some south Indian states. This is because there is a high level of perceived threat of loss of identity for the affected groups, should such convergence become a reality. So, while people accept themselves as a part of the broad national framework and share the identity, they would still like to hold on to some unique attributes applicable only to their smaller group, so that they can feel proud of them, and differentiate themselves from others. These cannot be strictly viewed as divisive.

Value Divergence

People have divergent views on 'shared' values. There are controversial values as well like the duels of religious vs secular outlook. Many values fall in the category of grey, with unclear and changing support bases. Capital punishment is supported by some, and opposed by many. Wars are considered unethical by many, while some justify them in the name of self-defense. Using atomic bombs to destroy human lives and property is perfectly justified by some while vehemently opposed by many. Killing people belonging to alien faiths is acceptable to some. Some believe that a domestic guerilla war within a nation is justifiable. Mercy killing is both justified and opposed by many. Denying liberty to women is considered unethical by many, but justified by some. Abortion is a hotly debated issue with strong arguments favouring and opposing it. Use of force by elected governments or social institutions or by powerful people to ensure 'orderly behaviour' is argued for and against. Many consider offering a 'puja' to please a God as a selfish and unethical act, but many indulge in it. Economic equality as a human value is still a hotly contested line of thought. Elimination of social vices like tax evasion, black money, bribing to get things done, lying, holding back truth for personal gains, are all agreed publicly but resisted privately.

The world is divided in many ways. As per one classification based on shared values, there are nine clusters of countries, not based on their geographical proximity. These are the English-speaking, Latin America, Catholic Europe, Protestant Europe, African-Islamic, Baltic, South Asian, Orthodox and Confucian clusters. The countries can also be clustered based on wealth they have. Nations can be classified based on religion, race, etc., as well.

A major divisive global force is religion. The religious and personal values are increasingly getting metamorphized into social and political values. The European wars in the last few centuries were broadly based on lack of shared, mainly religious, values. Value-pluralism makes understanding of real values tough, when rulers interpret them as per their perception of what is good for their society. This invariably leads to conflicts, as could be learnt from the history of many civil wars in Europe. When Aryans came to India, they thought that their ways of life and thinking were far superior to that of the native Indians. They reportedly tried to impose their beliefs and religion, on Indians. Something similar happened when North Indians came to South India. The lesson to be learnt is that people do have divergent and even opposing value systems and as such the concept of a 'good value' need not be universal or unique.

Our value standards are significantly determined by our traditions and received knowledge. Culture is a great divisive, conflict prone value. It sometimes leads to conflicts on meaningless positions like say, appropriate 'greeting manners.' It either extends the individual's value on to the society or organization or creates a mental model of a culture that captures the societal or organisational consciousness that exists or presumably existed in the past.

Value perceptions change due to differences in linguistic, cultural, or ideological background, or religious beliefs. However, since the social institutions in a particular country are same, it is generally expected that the personal values of all individuals in a nation would be same, as they are influenced by similar cultural and other macro factors unique to a nation. But this is a myth. There is very less evidence of a value convergence across different segments in a nation. It is often observed that the set of values preferred by different sections of a particular nation or society are not identical. The business men in a country typically have a set of preferred values, the ruling political class may have another set of values, common men may have another, rich may have their preferred list, poor would have their own, etc. There are language-based, gender-based, religion-based, and working class-based set of preferred values in a community or nation. Some of these admittedly overlap.

As per Harry C. Triandis (2001), people in collectivist cultures tend to see themselves as part of identified groups, give priority to in-group goals, and focus more on context than on the content in communicating. They pay less attention to internal rather than to external processes as determinants of social behavior. They define relationships generally with in-group members as communal. In contrast, a person in an individualist culture neither assumes nor values such a connectedness among individuals. The individualists seek to maintain their independence from others by attending to the self and by discovering and expressing their unique inner attributes.

Value systems get affected by self-interests. The late 19th century economic theories and postulations had popularized the idea that unbridled self-interest, under the influence of the invisible hand of the market, would ensure both social order and prosperity. Selfishness in a man was supposed to be the best thing for society. Greed was considered good for community. The argument was that, given the basic set of rights to property and personal liberty, people would select and establish their own stable set of cooperative relations, without much external guidance. The problems emerged later. With the given set of rights, a satisfactory social order was achievable. But getting the rights was not easy. It was difficult to persuade people to respect the rights of others. The sources of self-interest came from one's family, as also from the primacy of his or her ethnic group, race, religion, community, nation, etc. In addition, individuals could get potential material benefits by indulging in use of force, misrepresentation, and cheating. The value systems got distorted in the process.

Seven studies, related to ethics, were conducted using experimental and naturalistic methods[4] which revealed that upper-class individuals behave more unethically than lower-class individuals. It was observed that upper-class persons were more likely to break laws while driving, relative to lower-class persons. In follow-up laboratory studies, upper-class persons were found to have more unethical decision-making tendencies, like taking valued goods from others, lie in a negotiation, cheat to win, and endorse unethical behavior at work. They compromise values. Mediator and moderator data show that upper-class individuals' unethical tendencies are partly due to their greed.

There must be a sense of orderliness in social interactions by way of our willingness to abide by a set of shared rules of conduct, even if these conditions result in some level of individual discomfort or loss or disadvantage. The consequential issue is as to how the society could motivate its people to act in a manner that could be perceived as against their very own personal interest. The society cannot detect all crimes and certainly not punish all criminals. Therefore, social penalties were imposed on members or groups or nations (in the case of wars) based on perceived values of some. But they often do not provide any meaningful deterrence to unfair or disorderly practices. This is because many individuals and nations anticipate these sanctions, and prepare to bypass them. In the final analysis, people ended up compromising their stands on many values in the wider interest of so-called societal harmony. This has created the 'practical' societies that people own today. These are reasonably stable societies, where majority of the population obey the rules, regardless of whether they are benefitted from them or not. Rest of them go with their own interpretations and practices.

Value Induced Divisions

Many civil wars were and are fought allegedly due to absence of shared values. There are cases where, despite having strong shared values, secessionist trends appear in countries. In India, the Khalistan movement was based on an identified different set of shared values for the Sikhs. Various sub-segments like the Catalonians in Spain, the Quebecers in Canada, all aspire for sovereign states status, on the same logic. Many African countries are suffering from long drawn secessionist agitations. There are many on-going and potential wars in the world, triggered by divergent 'national' values.

Humans tend to be ethnocentric, a belief that one's culture is unique and better than others. Therefore, people judge others through their own cultural lenses. To avoid ethnocentrism and cultural relativism, Triandis suggests adherence to a set of universal values that can be widely shared across cultures and can be used to evaluate the success of societies. But the concept of shared values is an intrinsically problematic one, and many of these problems are not even identified, let alone getting addressed.

Values try to seek truth, uphold the self-respect of people, are useful in life, and have religious, moral, and spiritual support. They regard empathy and love for fellow human beings, and are beneficial in terms of creating a sense of belonging, a sense of achievement, and communal harmony. They also help political outfits and individuals to get and hold on to power positions. However, when the political system becomes the dominant determinant of values, the repercussions are different. Given the fact that there is always a conflict between the interests of self and broader society in any community, frictions relating to perceived values are natural. It needs active institutionalized interventions as most societies are not organically united. Here the governments must strive to uphold the centrality of society's interests.

When a belief system is inconsistent with reality there is a discord. A person who neglects his parents would be isolated in a society where parental care is a basic core value. The immigrant population that imbibes or reluctantly assimilates an alien culture, many a times fall victims of this phenomenon. One of the questions that arises in sociological theory and social behaviour is as to what force can hold human societies together. This is more critical as there are, ever present, evident and no-so-evident forces that keep dividing the societies, rather than holding them together.

The World Values Survey (WVS) is an international research program devoted to the scientific and academic study of social, political, economic, religious, and cultural values of people in the world. WVS studies patterns in cultural values, attitudes and beliefs towards gender, family, religion, poverty, education, health, and security. It considers the social tolerance, trust, attitudes towards multilateral institutions, cultural differences and similarities between regions and societies, justice, moral principles, corruption, migration, national security, global governance, etc. WVS data captures cultural changes, and value orientations in different societies.

In various World Value Surveys, it was found that factors of economic development like rising education, information, mobility, etc., have tilted mass attitudes and world views towards more assertive, independent, and self-seeking attitudes.

Mad, Maverick Values

Most of our traditional values are non-controversial. But some new entrants are not. They are, in a way, *'value delusions.'* We can consider these as *'maverick'* values. They are the new 'destination' values for the so-called winners in a modern society, who get ranked based on the material resources they hold, skill sets or intellect they possess, formal educational levels they have achieved, celebrity status they enjoy, wealth they amass, leadership positions they are in, powers they use, etc. The ethical, conventional social values have become *'herd'* values in comparison to these *'maverick'* values. *'Herd'* values do not count much today, in most societies.

Visible Mavericks; Invisible Humanists

Maverick values are on a non-stop, on-stage performance now. They try to mesmerise the masses by creating and sustaining sensational perceptions of social rankings. They force each human being to do a continuous self-evaluation based on certain highly visible, observable, and measurable attributes and parameters. These *'endowment'* values are related to superior status of persons in terms of their material achievements. These values are highly noticeable, thereby generating, promoting, and perpetuating mad races in societies. Under the system, the paths and byways used for the achievements are irrelevant. The concept of using clean, ethical or 'instrumental values' is not invoked. Only end results matter in the scheme of things.

Powers linked to values are being rediscovered, reinterpreted, and redefined under the new system. Traditional values have become powerless, as they are no more strong or useful in generating top-of-the-table material gains. Instead, power is believed to be emanating from and resting with material wealth and comforts. Pursuing common goals by cooperation and team work has been replaced by ever expanding individual cravings to achieve personal goals in terms of authority and resources. The moral, ethical, and qualitative attributes of '*herd*' values like honesty, integrity, compassion, etc., have got marginalized, and relegated to the background. The noble concept of being a 'good human being,' first and foremost, has been virtually confined to rhetoric.

The prime determinants of value under this phenomenon have got changed to harvesting and accumulating wealth and achieving positions of power and fame. Human beings have become extremely selfish and egoistic in the process. Markets and communities are seen by these wealth and fame seekers as instruments to achieve their personal targets, not as platforms to offer a range of services to communities and consumers for a living, or for a reasonable return. Monetary values are replacing and destroying humane values. As a result, the humane values have gone underground and genuine humanists have become an endangered species.

A maverick's solo performance is always lauded. But when such an achievement is made possible by exploiting some, or by pushing down or subjugating others using unfair means, the success stories lose their charm and sheen. Here the mavericks really go down in society, with their misplaced values.

Value About-Turn

As per the Hindu 'Upanishads,' the 'value' of a human action must be generally based on the degree of personal sacrifice involved in it. In the verse 47 of chapter 2 of Hindu '*Bhagavad Gita*', there is a highly popular teaching that says: *"Karmanye vadhikaraste Ma Phaleshu Kadachana, Ma Karmaphalaheturbhurma Te*

Sangostvakarmani. " It says that one has the right to work only, and not to its fruits. Let not the fruits of action be one's motive, nor let one's attachment be to inaction. This is a noble concept of human value, which is conspicuous by its absence today. Selfless contributions to society are hardly appreciated today by the 'enlightened' world, where human performances have become synonymous with efforts to generate wealth.

Buddhism has similar teachings. Gauthama Buddha's Dhammapada promotes human values and ethics and it suggests an eight-fold path consisting of 1. Right View or Right Understanding of the true nature of reality, 2. Right Intention to realize enlightenment, 3. Right Speech, 4. Right Action, 5. Right Livelihood, through ethical means, 6. Right Effort, 7. Right Mindfulness, and 8. Right Concentration, or meditation. These are basically supportive of the '*herd*' values and against the '*maverick*' values.

Buddhist thoughts are in line with Article 1 of UDHR (Universal Declaration of Human Rights of United Nations) which is considered a model for all human rights, based on the principle that "all human beings are born free and equal in dignity and rights."

As per Hindu 'Bhagwat Gita,' a man must lift himself by his own self. Austerity in living, renunciation of material comforts, and self-knowledge are key for the same. But a lot has changed over the past centuries in the understanding, interpretation, and promotion of human values. Values are making an 'about turn.' The materialistic, production-oriented world of today, is obsessed with 'concrete' human values that manifest themselves in various forms of social dominations related to one's wealth, political power, race, etc. Finding value by pushing down the fellow human beings, in order to achieve a higher social ranking for oneself is the new game in town. Images are deliberately built and destroyed in order to create hegemonies. The material values have also migrated to museums, modern day caves and corridors of academic institutions, where they display the social rankings and status of these hegemonic mortals, both past and present. The social rankings as per the maverick values, is essentially a paradox and it badly needs a course correction.

Encourage Empathy; Not Jealousy
The world will continue to change, and with it, the value systems will also get transformed. The values, however, would continue to be

constructions of mind based on man's hopes for a better life for both himself and for those he cares for. Our brains are trained to believe what it already believes is true. Hence, it is important to impart good values to members of a society in their early stages in life.

Values get refined and reformed over time, leading to their acceptance by societies in line with the evolving awareness levels of its inhabitants. On the non-material front, an increasingly complex world will continue to keep a vast majority of its population ignorant of human rights, obligations, and opportunities, among others. They are at a stage of development where their mere existence and survival itself is a big question mark.

The world order is being misrepresented and misguided by distorted values. The '*maverick*' values are encouraging creation of jealousy in the minds of people rather than empathy or compassion. This dangerous trend needs immediate correction.

Unlearn 'Modern' Values
The modern societies use different types of filters to select and deselect values. These filters are also apparently different for different segments of society. Therefore, certain values get filtered out in some segments. The end-result is that we have one set of values for the elites, another set of values for workers; we have one set of values for the fair skinned, another set of values for the coloured, etc. We use a set of filters to measure material progress, which completely filters out certain fundamental non material human values. Monitoring systems also use different yardsticks to measure the compliance of various segments. They are typically stricter with the lower segments of society and lenient with the elites. A vast majority of the population gets reduced to the status of mere commodities in such a distorted social order.

People need to be alert with each transition of values. We need to mind the values that get thrown out of a society, and the ones that get kicked in, and the net gain or loss to humanity in this on-going process. There is a case for unlearning some of the dubious 'progress' in value transformation. For example, bio-electronics is being seen as a future human value by some. Installing a chip in a person's brain is a value enhancing process. However, we need to carefully analyse the consequences of such a revolutionary value 'upgrade,' and try to understand the likely impact on human values due to say, the generation and spread of synthetic lives. There are many fake values floating around, created, and maintained possibly for polarising people by shrewd politicians, religious fanatics, and sectarian advocates, which must be recognised and discarded. Society also needs to be mindful of the anti-values of various sorts.

Let us come back to the idea of '*maverick*' values. The future is more likely to see stronger, wealthier nations and individuals, along with poorer and economically weaker nations. The concentration of wealth in few countries, in top businesses, and select groups would continue to put pressure on the governing systems. Nations under democracies would try to bridle the inequality, but with very little success. The national wealth would continue to be a myth, with the wealth of persons, families, and corporates remaining ground realities. A value shift is highly suspect.

The coming few decades will also change the way human beings live in the world. It may not resemble the clash of civilizations as predicted by Samuel P Huntington. But it would be more polarized, based on money power and skill sets. The most prosperous nations in future would willingly welcome and create space for rich and skilled people, irrespective of their culture, value systems or places of origin. The main criteria would be their perceived ability to generate still more wealth for their adopted nations, by helping them outsmart other nations in innovations. This would aggravate the rich poor divide, by the skilled-unskilled split. At the same time, solidarity of weaker nations would remain a dream as most of them would be relatively less educated and led by divisive leaders, primarily focussed on retaining their political power. They will also face huge challenges in keeping their skilled and knowledgeable young people at home.

Values are moral guides. However, if the trend continues, values that uphold basic human dignity would be victims of human material progress and greed. Most humane values would cease to be universal, as they would not be favouring a segment or working against other segments. The members supporting humanity in societies, who want a cleaner society with a good set of values, would be hugely outnumbered and marginalized by those who want to promote narrowly defined, material and sectarian values. We badly need a 'successful retreat.'

Adopt the Laggards

Values can change due to change in living standards. *It should also be possible to change the living standards of people, with a change in values.* Considering all living beings as part of the supreme 'Atman,' which is an ability to feel for others as we feel for ourselves, is an important human value, that can change the living standards of people. Question is, can the *'maverick'* values be elevated to this grand level? Of course, with a strong commitment to real human values.

At present, the maverick values are not driven by their usefulness to masses. A change in this outlook can be revolutionary. To begin with, the corporate social responsibility can be invoked globally and extended to all humanity. It would be great if the top 500 business firms in terms of profitability globally, can take a collective initiative to identify and adopt say, 500 poorest districts or identified locations in the world, and offer their entire population below an economic level, free education, and healthcare for say, ten years. That would be an elevation of the maverick values of the elites, in the real sense. The super rich individuals can also adopt say, poor villages for similar help. More such activities can be added to the list.

Media can play a big role in this effort, by questioning the value systems of elites and suggesting a repositioning. For that to happen, the value system of media itself must change first.

Let ethical values lead the world.

Chapter 2

<u>MYTH OF NATIONAL VALUES</u>

Trust and solidarity between members of a nation are essential for social cohesiveness in a community. This calls for certain common, shared national values. As per the 'national identity argument,' societies whose members are united by national identities are likely to achieve a range of desirable ends that would otherwise be unobtainable. This argument has strongly influenced nationalistic concepts in many countries. Application of this argument is primarily meant to position a nation as a single, culturally homogeneous, and integrated political entity. Such a positioning is considered critical in the sense that a value-based oneness of a nation can be a strong binding force behind a stable nation state. The idea of national pride is emotionally appealing, and can be effectively used for achieving a nationwide political integration. Many mass agitations against ruling colonial empires were successfully organized around this shared-value argument in the past. Freedom from colonization was achieved by most nations with the help of this weapon. The shared national identity argument is also used to explain how multi-nation states and large, multi-location empires tend to be highly unstable.

Based on this view, it is argued that global political integration would always remain elusive, due to strong nationalistic concepts. According to the shared value principles, national political institutions create a unique set of home-grown values that are shared by the citizens. Citizens identify themselves with the community with the help of these values.

The national values are reinforced by way of reciting national anthems, celebrating national festivals, remembering national heroes, and the like. Efforts are also deliberately made to differentiate one nation with others. Due to this strategy, people are generally not willing to accept the sharable values of other nations. There is no incentive to undertake an integration of common values beyond one's home state. Consequently, the world not only remains divided, but also faces wars driven by cultural differences, as warned by Samuel Huntington, in his 'Clash of Civilizations.'

Mega Inheritances

Nationalistic segments in nations talk about their mega inheritances including their history, religious, racial, and cultural superiority, common values, natural resources, languages, philosophical and literary achievements, political, military, and economic domination, wealth advantage, etc. Many of these are just myths, based on the understandings handed down over generations, or reinterpretations of such understandings, which may or may not be factual.

There could be many bonding factors in a nation. Religious or ethnic tribes, and castes (in countries like India) are some of them. A villager in a remote location in say, Kerala, a state in India, may consider a person in another village in say, Assam, a distant, different state in India, as part of his community, under the influence of the concept of India as a single nation or based on the understanding that both share the same faith. These shared values are, however, not uniform. People differ in their tastes and preferences even with in a small community. The question of shared values in a nation therefore becomes trickier, when the nation is a pluralistic one. People differ fundamentally in their approach to what constitutes a 'human value.' In most countries, where democracies are functional, the political institutions just give platforms where all these differing values are 'accommodated.' Even within a single community, persons may have their own style of lives, both out of choice, and out of choiceless-ness. To ensure a peaceful co-existence, they are forced to make compromises.

There must be a set of common minimum policies and values in any society, on which members need to agree. This is a critical social necessity. Issues like an optimal level of power that a government can exert on its citizens and the degree of freedom and choice a citizen is allowed to enjoy in the society, are all matters of debate. An important factor related to good governance is the question of government interfering or taking sides when there are genuine, different perceptions on values among its diverse groups of citizens. Governments can take an indifferent or neutral stance as well, leaving the navigational responsibility to people themselves.

Pluralism is the basic feature of any modern community, and as a conglomerate of communities, a nation is no different. In India, for example, the Keralites believe they have their own set of values. So do others. An interesting case is that of the Khasi community in Indian state of Meghalaya, and the Nair community in the Indian state of Kerala. They both are matrilineal communities, where the ancestral property traditionally belonged to the youngest daughter of the family. Children born into these communities receive the last name from the family name of mother. The inheritance laws have since changed. However, the systems in both states allow and prefer matrilocal residence, where, after marriage, the husband of a girl belonging to a Khasi or Nair community comes to reside with the wife's family. Thus, *Khasis* of Meghalaya and *Nairs* of Kerala have a different value system, as compared to other communities in different Indian states.

Value shifts keep happening in societies. Reports suggest that noticeable changes take place in the value systems of people over longer periods. For example, as per one survey, the Confucian cultures of Japan and South Korea were found to be gradually shifting to stronger self-expression values due to sustained political involvement.

Documented National Values

Documentation of shared values by a nation is not so common. The government of Singapore chose to legislate a set of 'Five Shared Values,' in the form of five statements introduced by the government on 15 January 1991 for Singaporeans of all ethnic groups to embrace. The aim of introducing them was to create a Singaporean identity that incorporates various aspects of the nation's multicultural heritage with the attitudes and values that contributed to Singapore's success. The concept came up as a result of the recognition that Singaporeans had become more exposed to Western lifestyles and values, risking their own core values like hard work, thrift, and sacrifice, along with the erosion of their Asian values.

In a bid to preserve these core values among Singaporeans, government proposed the creation of a national ideology that would encapsulate the core values of Singaporean society and develop a Singaporean identity. It was also felt that a national ideology would be useful to bond Singaporeans together by preserving the cultural heritage of the various communities, and by upholding certain common values that would capture the essence of being a Singaporean. These values include 1. Nation before community and society above self, 2. Family as the basic unit of society, 3. Community support and respect for the individual, 4. Consensus, not conflict, and 5. Racial and religious harmony.

In Kenya, the Articles of Constitution distinguishes a set of everyday values as National Values and relates them to globally acknowledged principles of governance. These values include patriotism, national unity, human dignity, non-discrimination, integrity, etc. Similar, formal, and informal guidelines can be observed across various nations.

Inventing Common Platforms

Any general theory that claims to explain human nature is either false or trivial. However, all types of cultural myths do impact people's values, beliefs, convictions, and critical life preferences. They, in a way, limit the horizons of their mental travel. Indeed, there are certain basic, personal, or social values that are recognized across cultures which broadly form the set of universal or national values. An interesting observation is the fact that both the conflicting and unifying factors in different values are mostly universal, culturally.

Cultural relativism, a concept that emerged in 1887 through the research of Franz Boas, is an anthropological approach. It is based on the principle that all cultures are of equal value, and that an individual's beliefs and actions need to be appreciated through his or her own culture, studied from a neutral point of view. This virtually meant that there are no universal rules of conduct since each culture is different.

The unique social values of a nation, as a concept and driver of nationalistic feelings, is under threat now. In the modern era, money and power are dominating values for most people. These values are more universal than nationalistic or traditional values. With so much of divergence in outlook, it is difficult to have universal human values even for a nation. Politically, however, the identification of a community based on its past glory, or a common platform, is the emerging trend. These identities, considered more critical for a nation, are replacing the old core values in many places. In the absence of a shared set of national values, the political independence is projected to be unclear or insufficient, or both.

Human beings have various associational linkages which create different identities for the same individual. One can identify himself by his family, religion, ethnicity, nationality, mother tongue, race, gender, class, culture, profession, etc. Affiliations could also be linked to different groups like the office one works for, college one studied, sports and arts clubs where he is a member, activist groups, and the like. In a nutshell, there could be many layers of identities. All these identities, including apparently conflicting ones, can and must survive together. Thus, an Indian can keep his village level, state level and national level social values intact, while allowing himself to be a global citizen.

The case for common platforms or shared values as a determinant for independent nations is a very dangerous one for a country like say, India which has so many different languages, ethnic groups, traditions, and cultures. The whole country could possibly be fragmented if we are to go by unique, shared values for all different groups. A broader, inclusive set of national policy framework, embracing all divergent shades and colours of its cultures, is therefore a must. All sub groups and sub cultures must learn to co-exist and navigate their differences within that framework, to ensure stability of nation.

It is often said that human beings create values first and then those values reshape human beings. We cannot force all people to think or behave alike. Given the fact that people are all equal and are free to decide their own fate, the natural result would be a wide spectrum of views and behavioural patterns. This must be acceptable to the wider society, as pluralism is a social reality. As per Nietzsche, there are only interpretations, and no truths. In line with that, societies must allow for multiple interpretations of perceived truths and values.

Multiple identities are a norm, rather than an exception, for any person and in the absence of such an understanding, the human values will get fragmented within a community, across a nation and across the globe. The concept of 'own' social values become relevant for each such identity, as people in each category tend to accept or reject standards of behaviour, according to the conduct judged right-or-wrong, for each of them. The norms applicable to judgement of each category may also vary from nation to nation, group to group, culture to culture, between communities, and between religions. These value judgments have historically been handed down to newer generations and have become very much a part of the social culture over a longer period. Most of these values are neither universal nor eternal. Some of them get re-examined, revalidated, and even abandoned.

Glimpses of these can be found in the works of renowned psychologist Sigmund Freud, and the famous sociologist Emile Durkheim. A synthesis of two traditions was achieved by American sociologist Talcott Parsons in the early 20th century. Parsons used the term value to describe elements of the personality structure that are both essential to one's personal identity as also one that is functional for the creation of social institutions. In Parsons's view, each social institution is associated with some set of values. Social integration is achieved when members broadly accept and internalize these values. It is this process of internalization that gives the members in a society the incentive to fulfill the duties and obligations that the social institutions impose upon them. A culture, in Parsons's view, is essentially a set of shared values. These shared values are reproduced over generations by becoming, in Parsons's classic phrase, "institutionalized in society and internalized in personality." Parsons's theory later acquired wide acceptance, and became the cornerstone of 'folk sociology.' This theory in a way justified the notion that values are the glue that holds societies together.

New Water in Old Rivers

National value systems are intrinsically linked to immigration. Countries that are relatively liberal with immigration typically tend to be more inclusive when it comes to promoting multi culturalism. European nations historically have been multi-cultural and they have also encouraged external migration of their people to other continents. People today migrate to developed, industrialized and prosperous locations, mainly for economic reasons. These movements create both negative and positive experiences and social conditions. Social values get impacted by immigration due to assimilation of alien values, cultures, and other hitherto unknown practices, customs, and traditions.

Highly race conscious nations restrict immigration or are selective in allowing migrants. Some nations do a racial filtering before allowing migration of foreigners. Some other nations create immigration policies based on the principle of assimilation. They consider it important that the potential immigrants come from a similar or related cultural background. For example, the Canadian immigration policy was earlier dominated by what was referred to as 'Anglo-conformity' model. Immigrants were expected to integrate themselves into the basic institutional framework of Canadian society and be a part of it. In order to achieve this, the immigrants were broadly directed to assimilate the Canadian cultures and values, and conform. The former Swedish Prime Minister, Magdalena Andersson, reportedly held the view that social integration in Sweden had failed and therefore they did not want immigration.

Population growth, unemployment levels, internal and external migrations, multi-culturalism are all inter related. In a modern society, the idea of co-existence of multiple identities must percolate down to the lowest strata of society. Else, the society can get agitated by noises of 'my values vs their values.' In India, in the 1970s, there was a strong 'sons of the soil' movement, in certain relatively prosperous states. That was primarily driven by high level of unemployment in India, which the local politicians conveniently blamed on internal migrants. The issue was then taken over by vested interests and activists who initiated agitations aimed at driving away migrants, who were essentially Indian citizens. Today, many members of well to do nations pursue a similar strategy. They add the cultural contamination aspect to strengthen the arguments against immigrants. Growing religious intolerance and exaggerated fears of terrorism also ignite the sentiments.

Value Pluralism

In the nineteenth century, Friedrich Nietzsche introduced the concept of 'transvaluation of values.' He was talking about the way different groups in the society viewed moral values and how, over a period, some of the segments redefined and repositioned societal values. The process, Nietzsche thought, ultimately leads to a higher kind of man, who will have the vision to rise above mediocrity and traditional value systems.

In the decades that followed, we saw the concept getting applied to business situations. Behind every successful invention or innovation, there is a subtle process of revaluation of existing process mechanisms involved in product or service offerings. Nietzsche had argued that the strong willed are responsible for every human creation in every sphere of life, whether it be philosophy, art, religion, or politics. We could easily extend this list to other areas including commercial activities and social spheres, where a maverick's unchartered path often becomes a national highway in no time.

Social objectives and targets keep moving. To meet these shifting targets, societies need to challenge their existing systems and push them to newer levels regularly. The basic requirement for this is that the hope values for such changes must exceed their fear values. Value pluralism is arguably a good option that nations can seriously look at and implement when economies are increasingly getting connected.

Monolithic identities in societies are highly problematic. They need to slowly but surely, create space for multiple identities. In any case, these identities are many times, as Yuval Noah Harari says, based on certain unproven stories that repeatedly get handed down to new generations. In the process, they undergo huge changes in their original objectives, contents, and narratives.

Australia is a nation that actively encourages multi-cultural values and beliefs. Singapore, Canada, etc., also promote a blended value system. Australia has a ministry for inter cultural integration (Ministry of Immigration, Citizenship and Multicultural Affairs). Australians share the benefits and responsibilities arising from the cultural, linguistic, and religious diversity of their society. The Government promotes social cohesion through structured programs that embrace Australia's cultural diversity. The idea behind the policy is the recognition that in order to become a law-abiding citizen of a nation, one need not get affiliated to any specific religion, or group or any special value systems. He or she can simply adhere to the socio-political institutional structures and regulations applicable to them. This is a social integration model sans the cultural assimilation. Many sociologists however, believe that such a model, which does not have the backing of a solid shared-value system, may not be a sustainable one. The jury, of course, is out on this. The fear is that differences in value sharing can and will lead to conflicts. But the supporters of integration without assimilation policy argue that it may not happen. They quote the reports that suggest that Toronto, arguably the most culturally diversified city in the world, is also well known for its extremely low levels of crime.

These values must overcome the divisions inherent in multi-language, multi-cultural systems like India. Otherwise, instead of having a united nation, it will result in a broken nation, with negative consequences. Ossification of any culture into an inflexible format or form is bad for any society. In one sense, people in a nation should be neither too united nor too divided as both are dangerous for a society, in different ways. Both extremes have adverse political, economic, and cultural ramifications.

Value Fragmentation

Human beings are unique in many respects. They can work together to achieve a common good for mankind by exploring the nature, expanding the knowledge base, enlarging scientific advancement, etc. In such a scenario, a nation must accept different shades of group behaviour. A blended culture that is manageable and enriching, with a healthy mix of dissimilar ingredients, must be the nation's preferred staple diet.

There are perceived conflicts between certain values. There could also be conflicting views on values related to a particular segment. Values related to political power, for example, are considered by many as legitimate only if they serve the common good. But the concept of common good itself is often unclear, with conflicting inter and intra group interests. The welfare of one segment could be at the cost of another, in many cases. In military conflicts, the interests of soldiers are risked to ensure the safety of general public. Construction of huge infrastructure projects like dams, requires evacuation and rehabilitation of residents. Same is true with taxation, reservation in jobs for some segments of society, etc.

The world is today fragmented in many ways and a major divider is the set of values that individuals and groups consider as their own. This divergence of human value concepts leads to formation of group solidarities, based on real or imaginary values. Value systems and norms display wide differences across regions, built over centuries. In multi-cultural societies, these differences weaken nations by creating situations ranging from social vacuum to civil conflicts.

Human creativities and their interpretations are both biased and unpredictable. Hence it will lead to differing judgments on what are pursuable values, irrespective of a person's level of intelligence or knowledge or education. Pursuing achievement values typically conflicts with pursuing benevolence values. Seeking success or benefits for self can create hurdles in the welfare of others or obstruct others from seeking their success or prosperity. Pursuing innovation, improvement and change in a society can challenge or undermine preservation of some time-honored traditional values. Some values could also be complementary. Values pursued by the members of cooperative societies, NGOs, etc., complement each other. Pursuing success in career or business in a regulated framework can lead to greater economic value for multiple segments. Pursuing traditional societal values can tantamount to honouring conformity values.

There are questionable practices as well, that are considered values by some segments of people in certain nations, but considered extremely undesirable by some others. The practice of infibulation, widely prevalent in East African nations and few other regions, is considered a highly inhuman treatment by many. The concept of a single God, and rejection of all other Gods, is also a value that is seen by many as perfectly acceptable, but as highly restrictive and questionable by many others.

So, do we require a core set of shared values to work together as a single nation? Can people with admittedly no shared values not come together as a nation and live peacefully? Are communities threatened by the fact that different groups in their nation have different religious faiths or social practices, and traditions? And more importantly, are we super-sensitive to certain core personal or group values and insensitive to the public good? Abject poverty and high levels of unemployment are certainly against public good. High unemployment levels, homelessness, etc., are all major setbacks to national well-being and attached values. There are relatively less controversial practices as well, like celebrating festivals by different sections of the community. Nations can and must concentrate on giving better nationwide security, education, industrial development etc., that improves the lives of all its citizens, rather than hunting for a set of ambiguous and questionable shared values, which in any case are moving targets. Social integration can indeed be achieved, albeit with a set of differences in beliefs and traditions.

Majoritarianism

Shared value, in any society, is the value shared by most people or by majority. However, one of the serious problems with shared value in a multicultural society is that it is vulnerable to use of majoritarianism. Discussions on 'value' under majoritarian regimes tend to transform themselves into majority views, with tastes and preferences of the majority becoming the default or standard norms. This is a highly divisive and dangerous trend, which can easily slip into a situation leading to tyranny of the majority. Such moves in a multi-cultural society can be seen as efforts to push the agenda of majority in the guise of preserving and promoting national, traditional cultures and values. Such situations warrant critical course correcting agents or institutions. Anti-social activities in any society must be stopped primarily by preventive and corrective activities and interventions of a society's own enlightened members and institutions.

Most societies are controlled and ruled by few powerful people. The policy makers are generally in the category of politicians or businessmen. Hence, in the absence of intervention by neutral intellectuals, societies, by default, would be led by the business class or other interested parties who would redefine social values to suit their self-interests. Unfortunately, the so-called 'intellectuals,' in most cases, play an insignificant societal role in this critical area. The role of intellectuals in judging or condemning undesirable events in, or elements of, a society is conspicuously missing. As a result, anti-social activities and cultural decay become acceptable, indirectly.

No Valueless Nations

All nations would be unique and valuable in some sense or other. The special features of any nation would therefore be ideal uniting factors and they must be respected and preserved. However, when the inhabitants of a nation are led to believe that their legacy or culture is supreme, and others are worthless, it is the beginning of human degradation. There are no valueless nations. Human imagination is varied and limitless. Therefore, the historical experiments and discoveries made by them are not just fascinating but also intriguing in many ways. Deeper analysis of some of them can certainly lead us to newer meanings and values.

Nations have millions of people. Two nations as of now have more than a billion people. A vast majority of these people rarely understand the culture of other regions of their own nation. But they come under the umbrella of a nation ignoring their regional cultural differences. If over billion people can overcome regional cultural differences and unite under a banner in two nations, is it not possible for eight billion to overcome similar hurdles across the globe?

Future-Fit Values; Value-Fit Nations

The theory of what is good or bad is called axiology. And the theory of what is right or wrong is known as deontology. Both these theories are relevant for nations. Axiological variations or value changes are historical realities. Values, including moral values, evolve over a period. Therefore, the value systems of future generations would be different from those of current generation. Theorists call the study of such changes as 'axiological futurism.'

Deontology believes that human beings have an innate dignity, based on their very nature. It suggests that human beings must follow the morally right thing by not 'using' fellow human beings as commodities or treating them as mere resources for production. They are not 'means' for attaining one's material goals.   The concepts of what is right or wrong, also change over time. In the past, the rights of winners of wars and their heirs to rule a nation was an accepted value. No more, in democratic nations.

An active inquiry into the future of national values is both critical and necessary. A question that arises is on the possibility of reimagining a set of new or revised, future-fit national values. The concept of 'future-fit' brings with it an air of uncertainty over its longer time fitness. It is more about designing value systems that would relatively be more durable, and which could in turn make the future nations more peaceful and cohesive. An obvious concern would naturally be the integration of fragmented, prevailing value systems within a nation itself, to ensure that internal conflicts are minimized.

Nations that are focused on welfare of its citizens can figure out their future value trajectories, in line with their long-term objectives. This would need examination of policy options requiring 'value shifts,' based on the stage of a nation's development. Few challenges and possible policy options relating to the current value paradigms could include the following:

Bonding with Parents: In many nations, especially in the developed nations, children become totally independent after adulthood and they hardly return to live with parents. Many parents also get divorced, and lead separate lives. In such a scenario, the natural bonding between children and their parents get weakened. Parents, in such environments, do not typically expect their children to take care of them in their old age. This trend is one of the major factors behind the lower birth rates in many nations, as parents increasingly find 'parenting' a worthless engagement.

In the absence of an inter dependence between parents and children, the existence of human race itself is under threat. The world must rediscover the values and benefits of bonding between blood relations, which need not necessarily be financial. It could be emotional.

Sharing Economy: Another likely shift in values could be the way possessions are treated in future. There is a human desire to own and use physical assets. These could include houses, cars, wearables, etc. People use rented assets as well, due to unaffordability or to meet temporary needs or due to other reasons. However, there is a realization now that physical assets like these can be shared, and there is no need to 'own' them. There is no need to get emotionally attached with such 'usable' physical assets. In a shared economy, there is less pressure to produce and consume more as idle and available products can be used by those in need. It preserves natural resources and if majority of people follow sharing, it would be for the greater good of mankind.

World Peace as a Shared Value: Human race is fighting each other for territorial, ideological, religious, and other imaginary spaces. This obsession leads to diversion of scarce resources for production of negative goods like arms and ammunition. A peaceful atmosphere can eliminate or reduce conflicts and wars. Humans can preserve resources or use them for the betterment of the lives of millions of people. This is a value system that global leaders must consciously create.

Cross Cultural Tourism: This has critical impact on a nation's future value systems. Multiple cultures are a norm in many nations, and more so in their urban settings, where the personal identities do not have a settled character. There is a broad working unity, without a full-fledged uniformity. An Indian citizen living in an Indian city could be a Hindu, a Maharashtrian, a poet, an activist, a worker, a husband, son, political party supporter, etc., all rolled into one. Today, many western cultural events and festivals are celebrated in eastern world and vice versa. Globally, multi culturalism is aided by factors like new forms of knowledge, high end technologies, global telecasts, mega advances in data storage and retrieval, faster information networks, and social media platforms. These should be taken advantage of, for creation of communities that are more tolerant towards alien cultures and values.

Collective Intelligence Efforts: The human progress will be faster if their efforts are collectively used. This would critically need mutual trust and respect, which must be built between nations and among institutions, over a period. A roadmap for the same must be created and made operational as early as possible. One of the major hurdles in this could be the issue of patents and ownership of 'inventions,' which needs to be addressed.

Technological Progress: Many technologically advanced products and services affect our values significantly. These involve use of say, Internet of Things (IOT), Artificial Intelligence (AI), Brain - Computer interfaces, Genomics, Robotics including take-out carrying robots, Block Chain technology, Delivery Drones, Virtual reality (VR), Nano technology, 3D printing, etc. Machine assisted elderly lives have become a reality in greying nations and that brings with it a new set of value systems. The education systems will have to undergo major changes to make the learning process itself a technology driven one, and to meet the requirements of a tech driven future work space.

Emerging Societal Rules: The future societies could be different in many ways. The urbanisation trend could be reversed, due to lower population, or in response to trends like remote working, virtual meetings, development of satellite cities, etc. Elder people could be working, due to better health conditions, or due to economic reasons or due to de-population induced pressures. Above all, a post privacy society dominated by data, will have its own issues and likely solutions. Our value systems would require major changes to address these issues.

Social Integration: One goal that nations must pursue, is the development of academic networks in their various locations. These institutions must promote new ideas in not just business segments, but also in areas relating to integration of social values, including different religious beliefs. Finding common identities and values is the key in this approach. A society in which different segments cannot agree on concepts like the meaning of life, God, etc., will be at a loss to agree on concepts like morality, sin, love, salvation, etc. Empathy towards other fellow human beings can lead to sharing of each other's feelings.

A cooperative approach can result in societies benefitting from human knowledge, learning, scientific discoveries, etc., and thereby expand the library of common human cultural heritage. In order to promote social integration and uphold human and civic values, the forms of higher education must also undergo major changes. The curriculum could include community-based functions like taking care of elders, environment protection, etc. The focus needs to change from individual welfare and social ranking to creation and maintenance of social unity. Individuals pursuing these goals must get the same level of social respect that academic achievers get. A range of social contributions made by individuals currently go without any social recognition or honour. Craft and vocational trainings must have same perceived value and social standing, as academic education.

Technology could help in social integration, if it is aligned with the way of life. Living with smart objects must be encouraged, especially for the older people. This is a knowledge-based economy which demands a basic minimum level of digital skills from all citizens. But while making the best use of human knowledge and technology for living smartly, care can be taken to balance it with other human needs like the aesthetic and spiritual aspects of life.

Deontological Question: A society that wants a future-fit culture needs a combination of different players who complement each other. It needs people who can take fair and sensible decisions, and those who can implement them efficiently. This calls for less of power-based governance which relies on brutal exercise of power to control people, and more of tolerance that requires acceptance and understanding of those who are different from oneself. If everyone had the same set of values, society would indeed be more stable, but that stability would come at the cost of shortage of people who would think differently. And that could lead to non-diversity of experiences and services, which come with innovation. Attempting to resolve these complex challenges can lead us to search within our cultural, religious, and mythological understandings to arrive at the deontological question of what is right and what is wrong.

Doctrine of Honey: There is a concept of 'doctrine of honey' (*madhu kanda*) in 'Satapatha Brahmana' (of Hindu *Brihadadaranyaka Upanishad*). It is about the knowledge that holds the secret of oneness of life and the interdependence of all forms of life. This is equally applicable to nations, which must be driven by good values, irrespective of their origins, as all nations and living beings are interdependent. There is a commonality of support and sustenance between nations. The future-fit values of all nations must therefore include the best ones for all, like being humane, inclusive, nature caring, culturally tolerant, just, fair, etc. Major national values must always be *shared* values, and *shareable* values.

Let the national values unite the world.

Chapter 3

<u>MYTH OF RELIGIOUS BLISS</u>

Religions are some of the oldest and probably the longest surviving, binding power sources known to human beings. They are 'puzzle' games for which the creators apparently have not documented or ensured any unique, convincing solutions. Hence the games are being played by the participants in all imaginable ways, pronouncing 'own' solutions and victories. The puzzle continues, with human beings in bewilderment, reaching nowhere. Possibly, the Athenian Sophist, Critias (460-403 BCE) was right, who considered religion to have been invented with the objective of frightening humans and forcing them to accept morality and justice.

Pre modern societies virtually all over the globe believed in super spirits of various descriptions, around them. Some of these beliefs and imaginations arguably gave births to Gods. Most city states in pre-Christiane Europe had their own Gods and temples. Today, God is either a concept of supreme power, or super consciousness, or an occupational reality or an unbelievable concept or a mix of all these. God is also seen as an ideal, immortal, 'perfect being,' a wishful concept, for the human mortals. A scientific, knowledge-based explanation for God is missing in almost all religions. However, the mythical images generated by religions around God, the social norms based on them, the rituals built around them, all have a huge impact on billions of people, irrespective of the religion, type of society, or governance. Religious leaders ruled many societies in the middle age and they continue to wield huge power in many nations. Kings were considered as the chosen representatives of God for a very long time. Temporal power and spiritual power were inter changeable for a major part of human history. Mr Han in the film 'Enter the Dragon' correctly observes that 'old empires worshipped strength.' Religion was a source of strength for them and possibly a pastime for the common man in the earlier era.

Religion is an important part of human evolution. Inventions of languages, fire, energy, elements, etc., were more revolutionary and, in many ways, more beneficial to human beings. In contrast, religious beliefs evolved slowly, and most of them have no common history, as the major religious traditions of Asia, Middle East and Europe were confined to certain geographies for very long periods. There were and are attempts to attack religious postulations and practices, based on emerging human knowledge. Yet, religions continue to be supported by many believers, despite the rising, scientific way of thinking.

Human beings have a dual nature, of matter and spirit. Plato argued that the body is matter which belonged to earth, but the soul, being spirit, belonged to a different dimension. Socrates extrapolated the idea to suggest that the body is of lesser value, whereas the soul is of superior value. The Hindu philosophy considers all living beings as part of the 'Supreme' God.

In the real world, religions have outgrown their initial scope. Issues related to the material existence typically belong to the realm of political systems, and players. Unfortunately, religion is into this space now in a big way. Probabilities of acceptance of a God, or a Prophet, or a political leader are all today linked to their perceived charisma, which in turn, are carefully built on grand stories and epics. These are reaffirmed in an institutionalized framework, by means of regular rituals, blessed by both spiritual and political power centres. In a multi-divine world, each God is being projected differentially by 'His' own set of believers and advocates. These processes and related myths are going on for generations, with no end in sight.

A religion or a culture, is an experience. A religion is also unproductive, in a material sense. Religions help us create or imagine a transcendent world beyond our natural senses, aided by the concept of an all knowing, omni present God. Once this process is completed, the Almighty becomes a source of moral values. It then embodies and defines the very history of the mankind. Many philosophical concepts that offer and elucidate alternative visions of life, and which provide new insights and meanings for human beings, have borrowed reason from religious models. Some have even built their very philosophies on religious logic, systems, and doctrines. Religious beliefs are important in understanding and defining what it means to be a person in a social setting. It helps one to position oneself as a good cultural member of a given community, which is important for a smooth, friction less living.

Different religions focus on different aspects of life and they differ in their degree and mode of interferences with their devotees. There is a general lack of focus on material life in four major Eastern traditions of Hinduism, Confucianism, Buddhism, and Taoism. The self is decentered in them. Hinduism does not talk much about specific ways of living in a society. It does not focus on societies and their behavioural issues, though there is a stress on advancing social welfare by way of performing one's duties or *dharma*. It is centered on immortal self, and talks about how an individual should conduct himself / herself. More specifically, it is about how, by one's conduct, an individual can attain *'moksha'* or salvation. It is assumed that if all individuals do their jobs sincerely and perfectly, social welfare would be a natural outcome.

The situation is entirely different in some other religions. The Buddha Religion focusses on group (*'Sangha'*). The social arrangement in Africa creates the perception that religion is enmeshed with politics. Traditional African Religion includes a wide variety of rituals and myths and believes in the 'idea' of Africa, along with the idea of Supreme Being.

Religions, many believe, have helped people fight fear and awe from their minds. They arguably gave people the courage to face unpleasant incidents in life. However, religion cannot be the main or only source of intellectual authority in a society. It can even be a backward looking one, and an antithesis for a modern society, though there are no shortages of intellectuals in any religion. There is a strong view that religion and culture can only lead an individual or a group to a 'make belief' world. Temples, churches, and mosques can at best, as per the line of argument, be regarded as hubs for social interactions. Any such place cannot by itself improve the living standard of the citizens. However, life is, many times, interpreted as meaningful with religion and incomplete with just scientific or received knowledge.

Political Driver

Religion is a part of the heritage of people, that attempts to connect man to the sacred. At the same time, religion as a social activity causes it to be viewed as possessing a communal character. Politicians use this personal identity to polarize voters. Imaginary fears are created in society about both lack of faith in one's 'own' God or faith in 'alien' Gods or religions. Such fears are then reinforced and perpetuated to polarize people.

A religiously attuned society is a must for using religion for political benefits. The history of human race is full of theocracies, with priests of all colors and beliefs wielding a great degree of political power. It is debatable whether the religious leaders were primarily interested in seeking or holding on to power, or in spreading the divine messages. In any case, religious practices and beliefs have impacted the cultural and political transformation of most nations. Religious cult is highly institutionalized now and it is cohabiting with politics in many nations, including the democratic ones.

Recent events in many democracies show that religion is an extremely effective tool to bring about social and political change. Religious gatherings are excellent platforms for politicians to make an appeal on social issues. By addressing religious gatherings politicians create the impression that they are not only religious, but are also moral, pious, and trustworthy. The logic behind this is the simple understanding that religion and politics form a core identity marker of human existence. Religion is a cultural and political identifier. Nationalistic sentiments can be reinforced through religion. Invoking religious elements can trigger the collective memory of a society to call in remembrance the unity of a particular tradition. Affiliation to a religion also gives a claim of divine approval for political decisions. Opposing political ideas can be discredited by hinting at the violations of religious traditions.

Religion can take a country backwards as well, as recycling the past is a favourite game of religious leaders. It is difficult for the fundamentalists to appreciate or recognize the welcome changes in society brought about by human knowledge and innovations. Therefore, they tend to discredit technological and scientific achievements or simply ignore them. The question that needs to be asked is as to whether such a trip backwards can be rewarding psychologically or economically, for communities.

Religious communities are present in virtually all societies and they are seen as fixed, stable, and trusted entities. They typically have an effective network of communication and functional infrastructure within the local community. Moyser (1991) indicates that the relationship between religion and politics can play out in three different forms: (a.) Political authorities controlling religious institutions, (b.) Religious leaders prescribing to political authorities and (c.) Existence of a symbiotic relationship between politics and religion. There have been examples of all the above forms in different nations.

The inseparability of religion from everyday political and cultural life continues. In Japan the national identity is closely connected to Shinto religion. In South Africa Zuma makes religious references in the political domain recognizable to fundamentalists, causing them to support or oppose the political decisions. In many states of Africa, religion is a critical part of politics. India, the birth place of Hinduism, Jainism, Buddhism, and Sikhism now have a significant number of Muslims and Christians, many of whom are converts from Hinduism. When culture and religion are intertwined, political considerations tend to be based on religious considerations, akin to pre-modern societies.

Will religious influences wither away anytime soon? As per Pew Research Center's Forum on Religion and Public Life, the number of people actively practicing religion is declining in the world. However, sociologists believe that the historical effect of religion on traditions, practices and their related institutions may persist over many more centuries. The current trend suggests that religious heritages continue to influence people's cultural and moral values, even where religiosity is low.

It is often said that the seed of any concept or invention contains its own destruction. If so, there is a distant possibility of a sunset for religion. However, such seeds of destruction will have to overcome the deep-rooted beliefs, reinforced over centuries by epics, myths, and narratives, which is not an easy task. In the meanwhile, the current civilization can and must prevent the religion induced conflicts and genocides. Societies may encourage the religious spirit, but certainly not the frenzy.

Escape Valve for Rulers

By controlling the minds of people and social norms, religion plays a critical role in any society. Religions are embedded with their own self-styled functionaries of various status and forms. They mediate between the transcendental and the earthly, set morality norms, interpret the aesthetics involved in social rituals and beliefs, and are considered supreme in many societies. Hence the relevance of religion in politics is quite significant.

Religion is seen as acting either in a supporting or opposing role to other spheres such as politics, economics, science, or law. Religion and politics have had a long history of reciprocal collaboration or disagreement. The relationship between religion and politics in pre-modern society can be described as one that affected many aspects of life [Moyser (1991)]. It included beliefs such as the sacred is present in social institutions, laws are divine commands, social classes are arranged hierarchically as determined by divine order, education needs to be religious, economic behaviour must be regulated by the sacred, kings are divine, religion and kingdoms are parts of an integrated system, etc. Some of these continue still, in different formats, even in democratic countries.

The objectives of a religion in the eyes of a group are different from the objectives seen by an individual. Thinkers described them differently. Marx thought that the function of a religion was to provide a 'flight from the reality of inhuman working conditions' and to make 'the misery of life more endurable.' Nietzsche considered it to be the refuge of the weak. Today, religion is partly spiritual, partly business and partly a political mass mobilization tool.

Religion is an effective platform to over stimulate fear likely to befall on the non-believers among people, especially the poor and ignorant sections. The religion-based conflicts induced by the power-seeking groups can be highly destructive for any nation. Politicians who are behind such conflicts believe that by creating a sense of injustice in a multi-cultural society, they can derive political gains.

Religion is a part of humanity. It has been projected to possess magical solutions for problems of individuals. The typical tools used for the achievement of this objective are few sets of worship related rituals, that are at best postulations, and most probably invented by creative minds and interested parties. When these rituals in any religion expand unbridled, faith gets replaced by superstitions, scientific logics disappear and knowledge banks are abandoned. When situation deteriorates even further, the salvation of economy becomes impossible. Then the magic happens. Religious leaders then replace the salvation of society with salvation of individuals, which is a simple change in concept. For that divine individual salvation to happen, the spiritual leaders smartly replace the concern for welfare in this life with concern for life after death. Unknown unverifiable welfare in after life is positioned as more desirable than the known and experienced pains in the earthly life.

Religions typically escape the questioning or critical examination of its credentials by the doctrine of 'non-knowability.' Religious dogmas are not normally included in the segment of pure knowledge, but are in the area of so called, unproven, 'possibility spectrum.' These possibilities include both promises and threats like the 'salvation by deity,' and 'penalisation by deity,' unprovable beliefs, drilled into the common people deeply, from birth.

This is a convenient tool in the hands of rulers who are unable to provide social welfare. When living standards of people go under, or when people face miseries, religion comes to the rescue of inefficient rulers. They can shake off their responsibility for the miseries by blaming the people themselves. All sufferings of the people can be attributed to their own past sins, committed in unknown, unknowable, past lives. The remedy is to worship God even more. The rulers cannot be blamed for the miseries. An excellent anticipatory bail for all mis-governance of politicians.

Rationalising Crimes

When religions become too intolerant, it turns morally corrupt. As a result, values are either distorted or a value vacuum is created in societies. One such distortion can be seen in the story of Parasurama, a God in Hindu epics. As per the epic, Parasurama was born to the sage Jamadagni of Brahmin class, and the princess Renuka, belonging to the Kshatriya class. When Jamadagni suspected Renuka of an unchaste thought, he ordered Parasurama to cut off her head.

Parasurama obeyed his father. Later, to avenge the murder of his father by a Kshatriya, Parasurama killed all the male Kshatriyas on earth 21 successive times and filled five lakes with their blood. He then conducted the 'Ashvamedha,' a sacrificial rite of horse, and gave all his conquered possessions to the Brahmin priests of the world. Parasurama is believed to be the founder of Kerala, a southern state in India. There are temples dedicated to Parasurama throughout India.

The moral of the story is that killing of enemies or even close relatives is perfectly justified. The story tells that the supreme God of Hindus, Lord Vishnu, incarnated himself as Parasurama in this world to avenge arrogant Kshatriyas (kings) who were suppressing the Brahmins (priests) in the world. So, the God was evidently siding with a particular caste or class. One of the key messages contained in the well-known Hindu text, the 'Bhagwat Gita' also gives the message that killing one's enemies including close relatives is justifiable.

Such stories, presumably created by a particular upper class, in a way, try to justify class wars and extremely heinous murders. Similar episodes are available in other religions as well. These mythical stories dilute and distort the value systems of devotees.

Invisible Walls

Religions are highly divisive and it has not been possible for the mankind to get out of it over the past several centuries. There are strong warring sub groups within some major religions as well. Robert Frost said 'good fences make good neighbours' in his 'Mending Wall.' Going by that, one option to avoid social frictions emanating from religions is to create strong fences around them. There could be a better option under which, walls can be created with pores. Such walls can then allow transmission of cultural values, so that over a period, there are agreements on, and assimilations of, good religious concepts.

Religious intolerance has always been and continues to be a critical aspect of human life and history. Religious-faith propelled hate speech and violence have been a part of human societies, ever since religions took birth. In India it also got extended to different castes, where people got identified in separate boxes of 'in-groups' and 'out-groups.' based on their birth. The damages they inflict on societies take many generations to repair, if the hostilities stop during that period. The situation has often led to religion induced holocausts, across the globe.

The United Nations had stepped in and created a 'Fez Process,' to tackle religion induced crimes. This process refers to a series of consultations, organized by the United Nations Office on Genocide Prevention and the Responsibility to Protect, between April 2015 and December 2016, with religious leaders, faith-based and secular organizations, regional organizations, and subject matter experts from all regions of the world. The recommendations contained in the Plan of Action were developed by the religious leaders and actors who participated in these consultations.

Tatwamasi

Religion would be a bliss if it is used to purify oneself. The mind can be detoxicated by means of good deeds and thoughts, or by meditation. Though meditation is considered an excellent method for seeking knowledge and for self-purification, it is not an effective tool for controlling others. It is a discipline to control ourselves and understand our inner self. As per Hindu concepts, meditation could also be used as a mirror to see our own images in other living beings and the divine presence in them. Religion, in that sense, could help a person differentiate the devilish and compassionate voices within him and empathize with fellow human beings. This is the message of 'Tatwamasi.' or 'Tat Tvam Asi.' It is a Sanskrit mantra from the Indian Chandogya Upanishads, meaning 'I am that' or 'Thou Art That.' It is one of the four principle Mahavakyas, or 'Great Sayings' from the ancient Hindu teachings.

'Tat Tvam Asi' refers to the unity of *Atman* (the individual self or soul) with *Brahman* (universal consciousness or the Absolute). To understand the meaning of Tat Tvam Asi, one needs to have a mental revolution of sort, to realize that all living beings are part of the same supreme God. Hence, all living beings are to be loved and respected. Such a change can be brought about only by deep self-analysis.

Tolerance towards other religions is not such a big deal. Hinduism, as per some beliefs, has 330 million Gods. A few more should not be worrisome. The issue can become less complicated, and a lot easier to grasp, if we all can agree that the Super God is nature itself. Nature is omni present, though not visible to our external eyes as a separate, concrete entity. Nature does not discriminate living beings based on their place of birth or group characteristics or physical makeup. We can also understand God as an experience. Different Gods do not matter then, as all of them would be part of that unknown, unknowable super power.

Religious-neutral NGOs and spiritual leaders can enlighten the masses on this noble, higher-level concept. They can also spread the non-controversial teachings and philosophies of all religions to the entire humanity. Time has come for people to stand up and get united, for entire humanity. Let the nationalistic prayers be changed from 'God save my country' to 'God save humanity.'

Attention Deficit

What kind of attention do human beings get from the Almighty? As per estimates, human beings account for just 0.01% of biomass upon Earth. It would be a smaller share if we take the absolute number of living beings, as smaller ones have larger populations, but lower organic mass. Biomass is measured in tons of carbon as it is a key building-block of life. Plants, mainly trees, dominate life on Earth. They account for more than 82% of biomass. Then comes bacteria at 13%. Animal kingdom accounts for only 0.4%. Human beings account for just 0.01% of biomass. So, if we consider the number of individual, human 'souls' in the planet, we are just a miniscule in the scheme of things, with God's attention obviously more on the other 99.99%. There is a case for a potential 'divine attention' deficit.

The other view is to consider that the Supreme God is all knowing and all caring. That goes with the Hindu 'Tatwamasi' concept, where all living creatures are part of the God himself. He has access to, and attends to the needs of every living being, human or otherwise. Hence comparisons as above, and related anxieties have no place in the world order or relationships between living beings. In such a situation, different religions do not obviously make any sense.

Alternate Models

In a world of multiple religions, one needs to use more than one identity to effectively communicate and smoothly navigate his or her social interactions. A wider domain of human experiences must be understood and at least partly assimilated, as this process continues. There must also be a genuine respect for different views and freedom of choice for all, irrespective of where they come from. A sustainable social model is one that allows development of identities based on a freely chosen set of values. No nation or group or community must impose their will on their current or future members. Norms and values should be allowed to be questioned, reviewed, and revalidated as the human perceptions, aspirations, and possibilities change.

A society must be in tune with the times. One's affinity with a particular religion or group as a part of his personal identity should not decide or limit how one considers his place in the broader society or the possibilities of how he might live. All cultural identities are dynamic. When moral and cultural views constantly change, finding a common path for all may not be easy. Efforts must be made to create a cosmopolitan ethic, showing human diversity in line with the times.

Sociological research reveals that cultures including religions cannot be seen as fixed, indivisible wholes. The manifestations of social belonging exhibit a "constructed and pliable nature." Cultural resiliency has much to do with heterogeneity, assimilation of outside ideas, and the capacity to adapt. Lisen Stenberg[5] quotes the political scientist Seyla Benhabib: "We should view human cultures as constant creations, recreations, and negotiations of imaginary boundaries between *we* and the *others*." The focus of such creations and recreations must be on uniting people across the religions.

However, such an orientation is clearly missing, going by the actions of religious leaders and practitioners, in our current day societies. Indifferent or parochial approaches work against social progress and cohesion. The value of variety and differences in view points and faiths in a modern society cannot be ignored or dismissed as immaterial. At the same time, all differing views and value systems must have a peaceful and to the extent possible, complimentary existence. Unity is critical for human survival and it has a creative power. So, efforts must be made to create a global human identity across religions.

One can accept the fact that all human beings are members of one family (*vasudaiva kudumbalam, as per Hindu concept*). Let us celebrate the 'oneness' of human race, the divinity in each living being, and the global 'brotherhood.' While respecting traditional loyalties and identities related to individual religions, there must be an acknowledgement of a higher-level loyalty, one that considers the common destiny of all global human beings. Lower-level loyalties must make way for a superior, selfless approach. In order to avoid conflicts and to change the culture befitting a modern nation, people can reimagine the set of religious rituals and approaches for themselves and for their fellow citizens. Here are few sample approaches that could be considered by believers.

Horizontal Worship

People need mental strength to face unpleasant events in life and growing turbulence in societies. Spirituality arguably helps in this process. But while the mind can indeed be conscious of the presence of Gods, the physical body and energies of most people should be made productive in the economies they live or used for expanding the knowledge base of mankind. In order to optimise such a living for the believers, we need new models of religious practices in the coming years. Such models will have to consider smoother, better organised, non-intrusive, and quieter ways of worships. These revised models of worship should ideally help navigate and negotiate potential inter religious differences, and preferably assist a believer in learning from alien beliefs and cultures. Above all, it must help cultivate a scientific, rational, and logical approach to religious beliefs. This would be tough as religion, by definition, does not follow any rationality or logic.

The current model of worship is a vertical, pyramidal one in almost all religions with the devotees at the bottom, layers of administrators in the middle and priests and interpreters at the very top. This model creates hierarchies and hierarchies always tend to keep top positions as coveted seats of power to hold on. These seats therefore become symbols of supremacy. Supremacies can be maintained only if these positions are revered by maximum number of followers or devotees. Therefore, the functionaries of religious institutions create strategies to build faith by promoting their brands of beliefs and rituals, creating festivals rooted on religious epics and myths, reading and narrating religious classics publicly, and conducting other events. Simultaneously, they try to eliminate opposing faiths. These actions and strategies create social tensions, violence, and even genocides.

An alternate model for worship is worth considering. The worship could be in a *horizontal* model, where all believers are treated equally, with no hierarchies. They all can worship independently in a self-service model. This can remove the barriers of high-low members in a religion. There could be free, common worship places, where worships could preferably be in silent mode. This is an initiative that all peace-loving governments can undertake and implement. Since these are to be self-service models, necessary physical (infrastructural), or digital support could be provided by religious institutions themselves, or by NGOs or even by governments.

A virtual platform for worship is an effective one. Here, technology can facilitate virtual divine places where devotees can pray. Virtual worship centres could be at home, on a river side, in a hospital room, in a park, and in any relatively quiet place, where devotees can silently assemble and pray. Such a system can decongest temples, mosques, churches, and other places of worship. This would bring places of worship to people. The dialogues could be direct, virtually. An omnipresent God will certainly love the change.

Many long running religious conflicts have their roots in disputes relating to the history and ownership of physical places of worship. These abodes of worship are attacked by religious fanatics based on their contested origins. A horizontal model of worship, as suggested above, defocuses on the physical nature of places of worship. Therefore, it can minimise such conflicts. It can also discourage the devotees who go to such places of worship for 'optical' and 'networking' objectives.

Aurobindo Model

An attempt to reimagine the spiritual world resulted in the setting up of the Aurobindo Ashram in India. The philosophy of Aurobindo that emphasizes on concentration and meditation, aims to make a person conscious of his own true self or soul or the divine spark inside one. In 1950 the Sri Aurobindo International Centre of Education was opened which receives students from all over the world for kindergarten through college level. It has a large library of English, French, German and Indian literature, a theatre for drama and dance, and a comprehensive program for physical education. The Ashram has a full spectrum of activities including agricultural farms, dairies, poultry, bakery, laundry, flower gardens, food and clothing services, engineering and construction, hand-made paper and other cottage industries, high-quality furniture production. It has two large printing presses issuing publications in 14 languages. It is a self-contained region of sort.

Auroville is located five miles north of Pondicherry, in India. It was founded in 1967 when students from all over the world came with soil from their native countries. UNESCO adopted it as the first international city on earth. Designed to eventually contain upwards of 50,000 citizens, at present there are about 400 residents from over 20 different countries living and working in the first communities.

The idea of setting up the Centre was to establish a viable, self-sufficient community of individuals where each man has freedom to follow his own line of development while at the same time contributing to the general upliftment of the community and the larger body of humanity. With great foresight, 'the Mother[6]' prepared for the future by founding a new city, Auroville, which is designed to enlarge on the experiment begun in the Ashram, and extend it to embrace a broader field of worldly life.

The centre does not want to become another religious institution espousing a dogma, seeking followers. It ensures that it does not degenerate into a cult of personality worship that dies with the passing of its founders. The Ashram has the reputation of refusing to become a small isolated group of devotees following their own quiet way of life, to the exclusion of the outer world.

Auroville has been established as an experiment in Human Unity where an individual is expected to be freed from the bondages of social conventions creating cravings for material possessions. It is a highly dynamic institution spread throughout and integrated with the larger city of Pondicherry.

There is no religion practiced, and no ownership of property in Auroville. The emphasis is on each man discovering his own inner center behind the social, moral, cultural, and racial heredity and appearances and actively living from that center, expressing it in outer work for the community. The Auroville Charter reads:

1. Auroville belongs to nobody. It belongs to entire humanity, but to live in Auroville one must be a willing servitor of the Divine Consciousness.

2. Auroville will be the place of an unending education, of constant progress and a youth that never ages.

3. Auroville wants to be the bridge between the past and the future. Taking advantage of all discoveries from without and from within, Auroville will boldly spring towards future realization.

4. Auroville will be a site of material and spiritual researches for a living embodiment of an actual human unity.

There are several other active groups radiating out from the Ashram. Various societies have been designed to further Sri Aurobindo's vision of the ideal of Human Unity. The Mother's Service Society is working to extend the application of yoga to the field of economic and social development through its project at Mother Estates and to extend Sri Aurobindo's philosophy of spiritual evolution into all areas of man's intellectual pursuit.

Let the religious spirit make people humble.

Chapter 4

<u>MYTH OF CULTURAL PURITY</u>

The societal culture of any community is a cumulative library of its surviving values and traditions, built over a long period. These libraries are never in a 'steady state,' as they keep getting modified by various events and thought processes that evolve in their social eco systems. New ideas always emerge in a society, from its members like professionals, thinkers, scholars, scientists, and other knowledge seeking outfits belonging to different segments, categories, shades, and beliefs. Therefore, by their very nature, cultures are always facing revalidations and consequently, they are constantly under transition. Mega trends in culture are normally irreversible in the short to mid-term. However, in a longer-term perspective, all trends, including the mega rends, are always 'in between.'

Over the centuries societies have faced multiple social changes and challenges. And they will certainly have to face still more of hitherto unknown societal shifts and threats in future. Human beings have witnessed Tribal Wars to modern day Infowars, and inventions of stone tools to wheels to artificial intelligence. They have seen communities shifting focus from heroic values in the older era to economic, civil, social, and cultural values. In the next stage of evolution, there could potentially be a transformation into higher level human values, as cultural progress, going forward, is expected to elevate human beings to higher, more civilized levels. The question is whether we are on right track for such a noble change, as many societies apparently want to cling on to their imaginary 'pure' and homogeneous culture, rather than a universal one.

Mythical Undercurrents

Only human beings can boast of a cumulative culture that involves a collection of common group behaviour in certain locations, in each period. Culture means many things to many. They are part of values for some, which must be adhered to, always. At the other extreme, some consider cultures as just pastimes of the elites and privileged.

The term 'culture' itself is not easily understood. It reportedly has as many as 164 different definitions. The commonly used one is "Culture is that complex whole which includes knowledge, beliefs, arts, morals, laws, customs, and any other capabilities and habits acquired by a human being as a member of a society[7]." Culture consists of tangible and intangible objects. The tangible objects or belongings form a part of material culture. Non-material or intangible culture mainly consists of ideas, attitudes, and beliefs of a society.

Social aspects of one's life describe a person, and they create the context and structure for a person in an organized society. There is a wider human inheritance, that provides the basis for a meaningful, civilized, collective life. Those inherited traditions which survive in a society form part of its culture, and they typically get inculcated in a person in a natural way. Thus, people are born into certain social situations and they get their initial set of inherited identities virtually imposed on them by society. These identities then get strengthened by the practices of everyday life. Later in life, socialization allows people to further develop these acquired identities.

Assimilation of a culture involves learning, understanding, recognizing, and accepting or rejecting a belief, including one's pre-existing beliefs. It is not a one-time exercise, but a life-long process that continues to work in every social interaction. A person's own diversified cultural outlook can include his pre conceived notions as also the mis-conceptions on them.

Culture influences society's behaviour, norms, practices, and traditions including religious beliefs. In turn, these social practices also impact culture. An unaffiliated or unrooted person in a society finds himself isolated due to this human obsession for social conformity. Deep-seated cultural affinity can turn ugly if they become unreasonable, when certain powerful sections in a society start dictating their dogmas and terms on others who are less powerful. This then could result in situations where non adherence to certain values or norms are treated as unacceptable, leading to social conflicts. In the international scene, such conflicts between cultures lead to intra and inter-civilizational clashes.

Cultures get identified in groups, small or large, like in a village or in an office or in a religious class. In a country like India, if one travels from Kanyakumari in the south to Kashmir in north, or from Gujarat in the west to Assam in east, after every few miles, one can encounter a different society, may be with a different language, or a different tradition or a different type of food. Specifically identifiable cultural groups exist across Indian land masses with different set of population, like in a nation. Belonging to a particular cultural group does not, however, necessarily mean that a person fully agrees with or follows all aspects of that culture.

Culture is arguably not unique to human beings. Species of monkeys, apes, bees and possibly others can transmit information and behaviour from one generation to the next. The classic examples often quoted are those of termite-fishing or nut breaking by chimpanzees. Bees use strong signaling systems like our languages. According to Professor Andrew Whiten[8] of the University of St Andrews, there are evidences of culture among a variety of animals, including mammals, fish, birds, and insects. The young of many species first learn these from their parents, and then from the group members.

Almost all cultures have mythical connections. They have created and used myths and stories as vehicles for narrating and describing the happenings of their time and showcasing their glorious heritage. Myths can be invented for virtually anything, as could be seen from the mythical stories found across regions and religions. They try to provide answers to perennial human fears and doubts and explain logic for traditions. Myths create divine icons for worship based on their super human feats, which then produce symbols of bravery, love, care, etc. Cultural myths create deities, many of whom co-exist. Hindu religion has millions of gods and goddesses who are interlinked mythologically through various stories. Myths help in communicating complex and abstract ideas, themes, rituals, and traditions, and provide logical support for culture. For many, they supposedly fill the 'void' in human life.

Myths and their perceptions undergo changes over time. New knowledge and experience often generate curiosities, additional learnings, and understandings in men which enable them to assess the world around them differently. As a result, people learn to question old paradigms. Technologies and emerging scientific possibilities help in this process. With some of the technological innovations in the anvil likely to lead to better or hitherto unknown interpretation of human mental imagery itself, this process of questioning is now likely to stir the cultural perceptions much deeper.

Since most cultures are built using certain myths, there is almost always an aura of myths around a person who is identified as part of a cultural group. Such an aura could just be an illusory one. Members of a typical group are supposed to live in a manner that respects and upholds such a mythical aura. This is akin to the way in which all group members get defined by character archetypes. In order to treat one as a part of a group or of a particular culture, he or she must behave in a manner that is close to the 'normal' behaviour of the group members. Any major deviation in this makes one 'abnormal,' and he is then pushed out of the group. The society, using such a penal procedure, forces all members to fall in line and behave properly, irrespective of the logics applied for such behaviour. Many a times, this force is applied by the self-appointed jury within the society, who may or may not have a political or religious agenda behind such an enforcement.

Culture as an Illusion

Cultures, for many, are merely abstract notions, in the 'make belief' category, more like some of the myths themselves. Nietzsche felt that cultures often replace old illusions with new ones. As per Nietzsche, life has no meaning, and it is only thanks to culture, itself a form of illusion, that existence has the semblance of meaning, and is thereby being made bearable. According to him, culture cannot demonstrate to people that life is not absurd. Culture, as per Nietzsche, can merely distract us from the fact that it is absurd, imposing a semblance of meaning in the chaos. Nietzsche's nihilist philosophy can extend these arguments and reduce the very human existence itself to nothing and proclaim all human values as baseless.

Culture is not defined exclusively by race and ethnicity and it includes a varied spectrum of identities. Cultures keep 'mutating' or evolving in response to factors like environmental conditions, emerging social challenges, contacts with other cultures, technologies, etc. Culture is generally believed to be unique, but such a belief is disputed by many. As per Amartya Sen, in *'Identity and Violence,'* the presumption of a "unique and choiceless identity," that people are what they are because they have been born into a certain ethnic, cultural, or religious inheritance, is an 'illusion' that underlies many of the "conflicts and barbarities in the world." Given the complexity of human life and varied nature of its experiences, the relationships between human beings belonging to various groups cannot be considered as just mirror images of the respective relationships between their civilizations. That would be illogical as civilizations themselves are dynamic and diverse in many ways.

The society in general learns, unlearns, and relearns continually. Given this situation, the cultural values give an impression of being unstable, constantly evolving, transforming, illusory set of concepts. Modern societies also create such illusions in cultural identities through policies relating to say, citizenship or nationalism.

Homegrown Cultural Disorders

The domestic disorder in an individual nation is not an exception. Nations have emerged from tribes and in the process, they have inherited many cultures and sub cultures which have unique or different world views. In World War I, as per estimates, 14 percent of all deaths were civilian. That figure rose to 67 percent in World War II, and in the 1990s, where most wars were internal rather than between nations, civilian deaths totalled 90 percent of all deaths[9]. Nations are, however, trying hard to achieve satisfactory, if not sustainable, political integration of various ethnic groups.

Some modern societies are more tolerant, and inclusive. Some are less. Historically, many people have also migrated from their home countries or were forced to take refuge in foreign countries. These were propelled by reasons including domination of a particular culture in their home country at a particular period, that was against their own values and practices. Cultural conflicts are also deliberately promoted by certain groups in some places, to politically benefit from them. Political relevance of a particular cultural identity in a nation can be weakened by not legitimizing it or supporting it by state institutions. On the other hand, if the state institutions themselves are weakened, such unfair or oppressive institutions can directly or indirectly promote internal conflicts in societies.

Exploiting cultural cleavages, using their perceived levels of purity, is a popular game politicians play, especially in nations with weaker institutional framework. The culture of remembrance of ethnicity is identified as a political winner in democracies, as it contributes to the formation of a group conscience with collective memory. Such a play of the ethnic card helps build a different identity, which can polarize a society or nation. But when such culture of identity politics leads to resource allocations based on say, ethnicity and religion, the society will see turbulence. Resource allocations and power distributions based on cultural criteria lead to inter group conflicts and clashes.

One of the major reasons attributed to the increase in civil wars in some states is the degree of domination of certain deep-rooted hierarchies in those nations. These dominations could vary both within and among different societies. No culture can today afford not to listen to other philosophies and traditions, without creating social friction. This is more so when these divergent views are strongly rooted in dominant or major groups, within a nation.

Inevitable Idioculture

Cultural identities are normally fixed and non-negotiable. At the same time, identities are not all about diversity, though they do showcase their differences. There are common values of humanity of which these are just parts. At the central or national level, therefore, an inward-looking policy is counter-productive as the practice of identity politics increases the odds of cultural violence. Cultural trends also do not generally obey border related rules. Cultures and identities interact continuously with alien cultures and identities, and in the process, they keep getting modified. The island view of identities leads to fragmentation of societies which can only be destructive for the mankind.

A unidimensional understanding of human beings is incomplete and distorting. As Amartya Sen says "The hope of harmony in the contemporary world lies to a great extent in a clearer understanding of the pluralities of human identity, and in the appreciation that they cut across each other and work against a sharp separation along one single hardened line of impenetrable division." This warrants newer ways of living. Human beings have a shared future and shared destiny. The earth is just one country, and entire mankind are its citizens, a philosophy enshrined in Hindu philosophies.

Cultures are cumulative, and are typically designed and documented by many central powers, including imperial powers over the years. But they are hardly universal or timeless. The struggles for self-preservation of own cultures happen at various levels at different points in time, in each society. Culture normally does not become more homogeneous over a longer period. People tend to get exposed to globalization, trades, wars, etc., which end up hybridizing his or her cultures.

The pre modern societies were mostly organised around tribal culture and religion, and they were mainly under the influence of Gods and myths. Their lives were simple, though hard. Modern man is more complex, more open to new experiences, and he uses tools like structured higher education, science, technology, etc., to enrich life with new values and experiences. The exposure to media, urbanization, and the like facilitate faster transmission and spread of new knowledge.

The cultural shift during agrarian, manufacturing and knowledge-based societies were built around production of goods and services. Education systems have since undergone major changes. For example, the ancient '*Gurukula*' education system in India, with its focus on epics and military skills, got changed to western style of education. Child marriages are mostly off in modern India. These changes are more prominent in an increasingly urbanized environment where migration is an economic necessity. A 'pure' culture is just unimaginable there.

The overlapping of identities, social norms, relations, and working arrangements in a community cannot be avoided in many cases, and are welcome in some other cases. One person can be a citizen of one country, but may speak the language of another country and work in a third country. An artist may perform in a country where his language is not popular or taught. The learnings from various philosophies and spiritual insights may be attractive to persons who do not share the culture of their originating places. Modern world has transformed identities in a way that one must today view himself or herself as being not just in a state of dependence or independence but also in a continued state of interdependence.

The international nature of economic production involves critical supply chains in multiple nations and locations. Communities are also seamlessly connected today by electronic means. The concept of citizenship, or membership in a relatively small geographic group is no more ideal for a person in such a connected world, to effectively express himself or be fully creative. Therefore, a cultural overkill is a self-destroying mechanism.

John Stuart Mill (1806-1873), the British thinker, was against homogenization of human culture. He held the view that each person is unique and that such diversity is beneficial to the society. Mill's theory of diversity is however, individual diversity and not cultural diversity. Today, in the fight for power and resources, some want to use culture as a political tool. Social structures that support use of such tools aim to impose dominant views and cultures, based purely on race or ethnic factors. The fact, however, remains that there are large scale internal and external migrations across the globe due to economic reasons or wars, or due to other social or civil disorders or due to natural calamities. In addition, there are illegal migrations, and forced migrations. These create multi-cultural societies and in such diversified democratic societies, some smart politicians look at majority groups as critical winnable factors. They prefer to promote the welfare of selected aligned groups, instead of common welfare, just to grab power.

Continuous interactions with alien cultures lead to creation of an 'idioculture,' a combination of multiple cultures. This is virtually inevitable in a progressive, dynamic society and citizens in such situations need a new mental software in tune with the changing times, to experience, appreciate and internalize this development. It calls for some level of personal literacy to understanding oneself, social literacy to interact meaningfully with others, and a reasonable level of cultural literacy to navigate cultural differences, among others.

Cultural conflicts with in an individual or between individuals or between groups are all dangerous situations when we are global citizens first. As per American geneticist, and anthropologist Spencer Wells' DNA theory, all human beings living today are progenies of same blood, who have inherited the same set of chromosomes. It is possible today to determine the composition of genes of any individual from genetic materials like say, saliva and the chances are that each one of these individuals might belong to many nations. All of us will have a certain percentage of genes from say, Middle East, Africa, etc., and we are all, by default, multi-race.

Elusive 'Pure' Culture

Human evolution has historically been involved with both competition and cooperation. We have not learned anything from the likes of other life forms like bees, birds, wild animals, fish, etc., who do not have the concept of a nation or own dedicated or exclusive space. They have a borderless living place and we have our own dark caves. In the process, we have also invented enemies within our own group, and created battlegrounds, flags, swords, chains, and weapons of mass destruction. And we describe them as part of our 'culture.'

'Pure' cultures lose their purity when the main stream cultures get entangled with other cultures, and adopt some of them, thereby leading to creation of mixed cultures. Advances in human knowledge reduce distances, and increase global interchanges, making the world smaller. As a result, the sphere of social interaction of an average person, globally, is expanding. In this scenario, various parts of one's identity must serve as forces for unification. Such unification can in turn lead to coherence in diversified experiences of an individual.

Though almost all human groups claim to have 'home grown' unique and pure cultures, the human history is full of cases that confirm that all cultures have borrowed and exchanged ideas with one another. The spread and reach of most of the religions was made possible by borrowing and assimilating alien cultures. In the past, merchants from different countries exchanged not just goods, but also their languages, norms, practices, and traditions. Then trade got mixed up with religion which irretrievably changed the world cultural landscape.

Alien food culture, art forms, languages, institutional models, businesses, economic models, etc., all have been copied and recreated in various parts of the world. The Baroque style of paintings and sculptures are all over Europe. Pablo Picasso was reportedly hugely influenced by African sculpture. Art and architecture were at its peak in India during the Mughal period, and the Mughal architecture itself was an amalgamation of Islamic, Persian, Turkic, and Indian architecture. In the modern world, many countries have accepted same sex marriages, a big cultural change, copied from the early adopter countries.

As per a Washington Post article[10], based on data collected by Harvard Institute of Economic Research, African countries are the most diverse. Uganda had the highest ethnic diversity rating, followed by Liberia. World's 20 most diverse countries are all African. A major factor that contributed to this diversity is the continent's colonial legacy. Japan and Korea are the most homogeneous.

People are multi layered. They have layers of identities that make them complex entities to understand and predict. Many of these identities overlap. The polygenists believed that each race has been created separately with their own roots, unique social properties, strengths, and weaknesses. This belief is getting hard coded in many societies and groups now. Creation of super tribes by demolition of social identities of smaller tribes is the game in such societies. Contrary to this, there is a strong view by many anthropologists that race itself was invented by a few in powerful positions, in order to categorize certain segments as inferior classes so that people belonging to those classes could then be made to work as slaves. History tells us that categorizations as above helped societies to deny a variety of basic human rights like education to them, on the ground that they did not deserve it. The Indian caste system was one such grand categorization, that was used to divide people economically, politically, and culturally, a classification that continues to be a group identifier even today.

Thought processes of all philosophies contribute to public knowledge in any society. One can cherry pick from these thoughts. While this is a clear possibility, history of mankind points out the opposite. Human beings always had a good measure of conflicting beliefs and warring tribes in their history. Their opposing doctrines have always created mistrust of other people who did not share same beliefs or skin colour or nationality, to name a few. People seem to be naturally hard wired not to trust strangers, even with effective communication lines open. This approach has been mostly destructive, weakening the social structures. As a result, the mental distance between members of same communities and between communities is increasing. People do not apparently understand each other. Opponents' theories and doctrines are not acceptable to many intellectual groups simply because they are from a different ethnic group. Ego satisfaction appears to be more important.

Today, dividing people based on their culture has itself become a culture. The belief in 'unique' or 'pure' culture creates hate politics, which is prevalent in many nations, including the developed world. This can relate to different aspects of a nation's culture. In the United States of America, critical race theory (CRT) is a hot topic. CRT, a social movement, considers race as an unnatural, socially invented categorization of people, primarily aimed at exploiting the people of colour. Critical race theorists target elimination of all sorts of racism. Transgender is a big dividing issue in UK. Extreme expressions of religiosity or spiritual hunger, is a major bone of contention in many countries. The thirty-year war fought in Europe was a war fought by groups within a major religion. The Peace Agreement of Westphalia (1648) that followed, is considered a milestone in the progress toward religious tolerance. It also broadly helped European nations keep religions away from politics.

The 'cancel culture,' so widely prevalent in America, is also catching up in many other places. This concept relates to a virtual ban on all sorts of free expressions and speech. Some sections of the society simply want to 'cancel' all persons whose opinions they feel are controversial or unacceptable. In India, there have seen similar protests not just against specific movements or speeches, but also against artists, writers, films, novels, poems, etc., that could be seen as part of a 'cancel' culture where some creative or artistic expressions are labelled as attacks on the 'purity' of a belief or culture. It is the new weapon in the socio-political war game. People want cancellation of ethnic and religiously sensitive topics, left-wing ideas, related institutions, etc. There is a virtual ban on discussing 'sensitive' topics.

Leaders in religion and politics generally use emotions and fears to polarize. The cynical, publicity seeking media also fan the conflicts and try to benefit from 'spicy' stories that would be generated with escalation of divisions and conflicts. People appear to have forgotten the perils of Nazi Germany's state-sponsored persecution and holocaust of millions of Jews. Ultimately, when a nation becomes unlivable, the citizens either opt for a backward escape by withdrawing to oneself or resort to a physical escape by migrating outside. There could also be a forward escape by removing the 'unlivable' regimes. The primary requirements for such an escape plan include the timely recognition of artificial polarizations, and an executable strategy for change in regime.

We have knowingly or unknowingly boxed people into groups not just based on culture, but also using the binaries like capitalist vs worker, proletariat vs bureaucracy, low vs high income classes, etc. Most nations are aggregations of such diverse groups today and we have created fragmented nations virtually everywhere. If we consider each of the religions, their castes, sub castes and tribes in India as separate classes of people with own traditions and 'pure' cultures, then India is just a conglomeration of many cultures. Existence of different groups paves the way for strong divisions, extreme positions, and dangerous polarizations. It is a moot point whether the basic nature of human beings, one that believes in loving and caring each other, will ever come back. For that to happen, humanity needs to encourage trust more than mistrust.

Multiculturalism, therefore, is the only way forward in an increasingly globalized world. People with multiple cultures need to peacefully co-exist. Neither a cultural isolation nor a cultural leadership could be an ideal way forward, in a dynamic world. Excessive interventions by ethnic or racial groups can be counterproductive. A shared history and shared culture for entire humanity is obviously preferable. The very idea of a national culture, a permanent pure identity, is becoming more and more irrelevant, and in many ways undesirable, in a world with diversified, and differentiated societies.

Many major nations have accepted this fact as a part of life. However, conservatives in certain countries continue to consider their cultures as 'rich' and do not like to equate their culture with the immigrants' or 'alien' cultures. Some of them allot space and geography to minorities and expect them to live in that space as second-class citizens. Some others make acceptance of their code of conduct a basic requirement for awarding citizenship to outsiders.

Purity by Default

Religion is an imagined reality. But it is an important part of our culture. While religions are always considered as 'pure,' the individual purity of its members can differ across them. The ancient Hindu traditions based on its caste system had two basic types of purities. These were the permanent purity and the temporary purity. The caste system considered a person born into a 'brahmin' family, the top most caste, as one with highest permanent purity, while one born into the lowest, or 'Shudra' caste, as one with highest level of permanent impurity. Hindu religion believes in rebirth and as per its beliefs, the caste status of every living person is a cumulative result of his general conduct in his past lives, including the virtuous and sinful deeds committed by him, in those lives. The low status in this life is therefore a punishment for bad moral performances in past births. Let it be clarified here that the Hindu laws also indicate that a person born into a highly rated caste could lose his purity, if he indulges in impure or immoral acts. As per the ancient law books of Hinduism, higher level jobs and engagements like priesthood, learning, teaching, etc., were duties of 'permanently pure' persons, and menial jobs were the duties of the 'permanently impure' persons.

The personal purity can get temporarily polluted due to contacts with lower castes, non-performance of one's duties, etc. Many of these concepts are getting vanished from Indian Hindu societies. However, even today, a woman under menstruation cannot enter many places of worship, as menstruation is considered highly polluting. In many sub segments of Hindus, no person can enter a temple for few days, if a woman in his family, including a far relative, gives birth to a new born, as giving birth is also considered polluting, temporarily.

An interesting aspect to the whole saga of purity vs impurity as per above Hindu traditions is that there are escape valves for all kinds of cultural pollutions. Temporary impurities due to contacts, etc., could be removed by purifications involving bath, or shaving of head, or using cow products etc. Where there is a cultural pollution, there is a traditional remedy.

Culture Gazing

Evolution of a culture is not linked to human genes. In the past millennia, many cultures and traditions got developed, and a lot of them perished. Cultures got evolved due to continuous interactions between members of the groups, often guided by tribal leaders, religious practitioners, and social thinkers. They reflect the collective, cumulative experiences and traditions of societies. However, they were not primarily intended to create a sense of tribal or national pride. Cultures, like languages, were also not specifically owned by anyone. Certain ideologies and religions were actively promoted by its proponents. Their wider acceptance depended on many critical factors, including patronage from ruling classes. The principle of 'survival of the fittest' was applicable to cultures; the stronger ones survived and prospered.

The theoretical chemist Leslie Eleazer Orgel's 'Rules' on evolution of living beings are relevant here. Orgel's widely quoted Second Rule is, "Evolution is cleverer than you are." Evolution is a better 'designer' than any so-called 'intelligent designer.' This is relevant in the realm of culture as well. The twists and turns of evolution are difficult to predict, let alone outwit. Culture is no different.

Death of Creators

'The Death of the Author' is a highly influential essay by the French literary theorist Roland Barthes. It makes a strong argument about the way a work of literature has meaning in relation to its readers rather than its author. Words convey different meanings to different readers and over time. The textual meanings are both differed among readers, and deferred for a particular reader, over time. The interpretation of a novel written say, few centuries back, by a current day reader would be different from the readers in that century. There could be a different reading experience, resulting in different evaluation and appreciation of that novel now. Barthes critiques the idea of 'originality' and 'truth' that one associates with the author. It is falsely assumed that one can fully understand the author's intentions. Another wrong assumption is that there is a fixed meaning of the text that one should try to find.

As per the theory of Barthes, the author is not a divine creator who creates new text or meaning out of nothing. He is just putting together various pre-existing thoughts and ideas in a skilful way. Barthes shifts the focus from the author to the reader. There is no 'true meaning' of text, as both the reader and author bring with them their own biases, knowledge libraries, and ideas that affect their reading of the text. Hence, there could be different ways of reading and interpreting a text depending on the number of readers and their backgrounds. Barthes concludes by proclaiming the 'birth of the reader' in place of 'death of the author.' Barthes essay laid the foundation for various theories like post-modernism and reader-response theory.

The above argument is equally applicable to cultures. Since cultures have unknown or unrecorded origins, it is hard to link them with any identified person or even a particular community. The meaning and relevance of a culture many times get lost, over longer periods of time. This is due to the accumulated experiences, changed circumstances, influences of other cultures, and general living conditions of the people. Cultures, traditions, and norms are interpreted by the users of a given time. And these cultures evolve based on on-going reinterpretations and understandings of new generations. Some underlying logic and meaning of cultures will also be lost in cases where the traditions are orally transmitted over multiple generations.

Arnold Toynbee once said that 'civilizations die due to suicide and not by murder.' The same logic applies to cultures as well. They mostly die on their own, by becoming irrelevant rather than getting killed by outside forces. By allowing such cultures to vanish, societies would only be rejuvenating themselves, and marching forward by furthering the overall welfare of people.

Looking Through a Prism

Given the dynamic nature of societies, it is preferable to allow cultures to prosper on their own merits. But some of our cultural leaders think otherwise. They try to interpret the key elements and images of their cultures with the help of prisms, which can distort their meanings and understanding. The cultures get distorted, when looked at through the prisms of one's own ideologies, biases, and prejudices. Such prisms are abundant not just in different societies, but also within same societies, in the form of say, gender differences, inter-generational differences, etc., creating biases.

One major problem in a system where cultural values are predominantly validated and promoted by self-serving groups, politicians, or religious activists is that these values tend to get either fossilized or misrepresented. They lead to *'cultural fixation,'* where the past cultural or ethnical greatness, real or imaginary, are over emphasized and perpetuated. The misrepresentations and distortions in them, if any, cannot effectively be countered by uneducated masses, who are more likely to be tradition bound and easily manipulable. The better educated among them may be open to questioning long held beliefs. They are also likely to embrace liberal ideas like protection of minority rights, respect for alien cultures, and dignity of human beings irrespective of their cultural background.

Politics of Cultural Purity

Many believe culture is just a vanity. Purity of a culture cannot be easily verified. Their origins are mostly unknown. The paths they have followed so far are generally unrecorded and their future roadmaps are unpredictable. Cultural Purity is based on a multitude of factors, including the concept itself, potential contaminations, causes of pollutions identified, the purifying processes adopted, if any, etc.

Religious cultures have their own benchmarks. The mental images of human beings relating to the material world around them are seen as a kind of 'maya,' (in Sanskrit: 'magic' or 'illusion') a strong concept in Hindu Vedanta Philosophy. Maya is the powerful force that creates the cosmic illusion that the phenomenal world is real. For the *'advaita'* (nondualists) supporters, maya is the cosmic force that presents the infinite *brahman* (the supreme being) as the finite phenomenal world. Maya is experienced at the individual level by human ignorance of the real nature of self. The real self is identical with *'brahman'* or the supreme. So, the human culture, by extension, is a part of that 'maya,' and cannot be real. Therefore, the purity of the Supreme will, is always intact. The deities, derivatives of the Supreme, are also deemed 'unpollutable.'

Adhering to 'pure' traditions, mainly religious traditions, can be highly restrictive. In that sense, insistence on cultural purity can become a self-restraining chain. Crossing a sea, also known as '*Samudrolanghana*' or '*Sagarollanghana*,' was considered an offense by Hindus in ancient India. The persons who undertook such journeys were considered out-caste. As per the 'Dharma Sutra' of Baudhayana, sea voyages cause the loss of 'varna' (caste). The reasons behind this were supposed to be the inability to carry out daily rituals of traditional Hindu life and the sin of contact with the characterless, uncivilized lower-level creatures of the foreign lands. According to another belief in the pre-modern India, the '*Kala Pani*' (sea water) was inhabited by bad spirits and monsters. Thus, clinging to pure form of culture can land one in trouble or restrict him from undertaking new initiatives. For violations of such traditions, some religions also prescribe purification processes. But the vital question remains as to whether such a high level of purity is relevant at all.

In the context of a modern nation, cultural purity is a goal that can be achieved only by cutting itself off from external entities and interactions. In a connected world, such purity objectives cannot be few milestones that are fixed and dead. Instead, the cultural set of goals must aim to reach multiple destinations, as desired by different segments in a nation. Such milestones can be achieved by application of will and skill by the relevant segments and nations are expected to facilitate them.

Since these destinations keep changing, the set of goals must also be flexible. Else, in a culturally diverse world, the aim of strict adherence to preservation of cultural purity by a nation would not only be difficult, but also be a backward looking, regressive idea, leading to its cultural stagnation. It would be like stopping the flow of fresh water in a river or shutting the doors and windows of a room keeping the fresh air out.

Do nations care about purity of cultures? Many nations like India, Australia, Canada, US, UK, Indonesia, Singapore, etc., are muti-cultural. Nations like Australia, Singapore and Canada officially promote multiple cultures. Countries with relatively open systems and liberal immigration policies indirectly promote cultural diversification. Kingdoms and dictatorships which do not generally have autonomous institutions restrict freedom of expressions. They do not provide permanent citizenships to outsiders and do not care for it either. In fact, cultural exchanges are taking place world over, in the sense that different cultural bits like recipes, songs, new consumer products, etc., are all shared by people all over the world. These so-called memes do last longer and get transmitted to newer groups and generations through imitations and dispersions.

Delusion of Cultural Purity

Culture is dynamic and it is always in a flux, as changes happen in societies, with unexpected turns and twists. Cultures are conflict prone, by their very nature. In such a situation, cultural purity as an aim, could at best be an illusory one. Mega trends await most nations. Take immigration. Countries with too many immigrants like the middle east countries, cannot protect cultural purity. Countries with dwindling populations need to replace the same with inward migration. Therefore, they cannot stop a multi culture. The OECD Ministerial and Forum on Migration Report "Towards 2035 – Strategic Foresight - Making Migration and Integration Policies Future Ready" identifies three interconnected mega trends likely to impact future immigrations. They are 1. Environmental changes and extreme weather events that may lead to displacement of millions of people, 2. Geopolitical instability and conflicts, including higher levels of youth unemployment, inequality, insecurity, etc., which are the traditional drivers of out migration, and 3. Demographic shifts and related pressures.

May be the relatively well-off in the middle-income nations could be keener to preserve and even project the cultural heritage of their forefathers. One driver of such an urge could be their desire not to be labelled as 'history less' or 'rootless' people. But then, these backward-looking actions can potentially lead to unwanted societal breakdowns and conflicts. In order to prevent this from happening, there could be special social integration projects in societies. Integration of the cultures across various beliefs could be an ideal project, which can put an end to or at least reduce, the simmering cultural wars. The fuzzy logic of winning by dividing will then see its own end.

Blind followers of both religion and politics are hard walls to break. Cultural sheep in general are blind to experimentation, new learnings, and scientific ideas. They need to be tackled by way of both creation of awareness and deliberate social integration policies.

Social awareness must be built on the potential perils of unholy social alliances and imaginary fears created by them. It is possible that we may face more challenges relating to identity clashes in future. Human beings are likely to create newer mega identities in the future. These identities could be across boundaries and cultures. Such mega identities can also possibly change the course of history.

Cultural Osmosis

Culture is basically a unifying mechanism. Its walls are typically porous. So, when two or more different cultures mingle, even though they are logically separated by strong walls of beliefs, there is a high probability of a cultural osmosis. Their porous walls will allow a sort of osmosis to take place, with the weaker ones getting into the stronger ones and merging with them. In the process, the stronger ones would indeed get diluted. Thus, in a connected world, the norms and practices of various global communities get mingled and, in many cases, irreversibly integrated. There are strong forces that try to keep them separate. But such efforts are likely to fail as tactical and strategic alliances are very much a part of social life for nations, Civil societies across the globe will always need a range of intra and inter group relationships to make economic and value-driven progress.

In the cultural or spiritual world, the real liberation is not individual liberation post death, as advocated by many religions and spiritual leaders. It is the liberation of society from the clutches of unbridled urge for consumption of material luxuries, unwanted hatred, dubious practices, religious fanaticism, and other dogmas. An attitude of 'live and let live' is the best way forward for humanity.

Self-knowledge or '*atma vidya*' is supreme as per the Indian seer, Sankaracharya. Seeking knowledge continuously and practicing communal harmony are far more critical for an interdependent mankind, than sticking to the imaginary purity of one's 'own' culture.

Let the world promote the idea of cultural osmosis.

Chapter 5

<u>MYTH OF CULTURAL GARDENS</u>

The purity of culture, discussed in the earlier chapter, was all about the cultural past of humanity. This chapter is about the present and future trends of culture and its growing compartmentalization.

Cultures relating to certain nations are getting rediscovered, differentiated, rebranded, and showcased. In this process, many economic, political, spiritual, historical, and ideological differences are emerging and they are creating barriers between nations and their people. This phenomenon is driven by the fact that unlike the natural world, the human history is rich and varied with changing human behaviour, social structures, multiple civilizations, ideologies, mythologies, allegories, and traditions. Using some of these, men have created few beautiful cultural gardens around them, through which they disseminate the sensory, aesthetic and even imaginary values of their nations. Entries are conditional or restricted, to some of these gardens. But encroachments and new shoots continue to be unabated in them, despite being 'protected.' World is witnessing the paradoxical situation of attempting to replace the mysterious human 'mind effect,' and 'reasoning' power, supported by state-of-the-art technologies like artificial intelligence on one side, while digging, and analyzing the ancient cultural remnants and artefacts on the other. Ever since human beings started carving out their 'own' territories and groups, one of the anxieties they faced has been the curious case of them wanting to consider certain traditions as their 'own' unique ones.

Cultures typically flourish in nations during their economically prosperous periods. Hence, cultural gardens are also symbols of prosperity. In these gardens, the 'owners' do not want plants or flowers that are considered 'misfits.' In many societies, the decision to select a plant for the garden itself is taken by few powerful players based on their aesthetic sense and values, rather than collectively by the inhabitants. The self-styled gardeners and gate keepers of such cultural gardens thereby tend to rob the common people of their rights and invaluable experiences. As a result, the relationships between garden owners, keepers, and individual admirers have become problematical.

Prosperity Induced Retrospection

Why are people so fuzzy about their own gardens? One reason could be the fact that when people become relatively well off, they tend to go back in history to search for their rich legacies and traditions. It is perfectly fine to relive or revisit one's own traditions, real or imaginary, especially when a nation has achieved an acceptable level of economic prosperity and ensured welfare of its citizens. But taken to extremes, it can lead to a situation where a group of 'prisoners of retrospection' get created in societies. Such a strategy could be an intentional, political one, designed to polarize communities, by creating a sense of fighting old, imaginary enemies. Another reason could be that people are unwilling to create new value systems and traditions for fear of offending the existing social order. So, they revisit past glories and prefer to be eternal 'karaoke' singers. We are also witnessing emergence of repositioned societies, where traditions are being preserved and showcased using non-traditional, modern marketing techniques, commoditizing traditions. The commodities so marketed include 'imitation environments' and 'museum culture.'

There are other reasons to look back. Some of the identities of certain groups are linked to oppressions and marginalization suffered by them or their ancestors in the past. These memories still haunt them. Hence, a separate garden is created by the new generation to maintain their identity. One such oppression was prevalent among Hindus in India. The Hindu concept that all living beings are part of the same God, was not applied in the case of its old caste system, a system that used illogical moral standards, which arguably stood in the way of creating a fair and progressive India. Many believe that the denial of education to the lower, productive segments of Indian society stopped India from achieving new knowledge and improving economic productivity for centuries. This system is now being discontinued, and efforts to create an inclusive society, with full participation of all segments of community irrespective of their history, are being put in place. The next steps must include ushering in new social meanings, in line with the aspirations of a modern world, implementing real inclusiveness. Ideally in future, the inner aspirations of every individual must be in sync with the common global good.

Cultural Determinism

National cultures are determined by a host of factors including their geographic locations, economic development models, and the social, spiritual, and philosophical outlooks. It is believed that geographic factors contributed to cultural and political unification of large countries in the past, like China and India. An unmistakable geographical determinism is evident in respect of these cultures. Though national borders could be determined by geographies, the possibility of a homogeneous nationwide culture is lesser in cases where the land masses and population are very large. It would, in most cases, be an amalgamation of few cultures, given the fact that physical mobility and cultural exchanges were minimal in the earlier centuries.

A reverse phenomenon is taking place now, in the form of cultural determinism. Culture driven identities, politics, and policies along with the overt and covert, so-called cultural wars are major influencing factors in global arena now. Nations are being reimagined and repositioned as cultural entities and people within a nation are fighting for separate states based on assumed or perceived, distinct cultures within those nations. Cultures are therefore becoming determinants of geographies and nations. Fierce conflicts are taking place in many nations for separate, culturally homogeneous future nations. As per a project on 'Civil Wars, Violence, and International Responses[11]', appeared in Daedalus, a publication of the American

Academy of Arts & Sciences, there are some thirty ongoing civil wars in places like Syria, Afghanistan, and Iraq, with an average duration of continued conflict of more than twenty years.

There are of course, different views on this. In 'The End of History and The Last Man' (1989), Francis Fukuyama says that the Industrial Revolution and technologies lead to homogenization of societies regardless of their cultures. He cited the example of science, which was once associated with the West, and later became universal. However, this view is debatable and most non-western societies do not accept this logic. Societies are divided on cultural lines. Non-Western societies view Fukuyama hypothesis as one supporting cultural imperialism, which they feel, is equally dangerous as compared to political imperialism and colonisation. They believe it makes the target nations 'soulless.'

Samuel Huntington in a way, confirms the above fear. He says in 'The Clash of Civilizations,' that "the West is attempting and will continue to attempt to sustain its preeminent position and defend its interests by defining those interests as the interests of the world community." This view indicates the existence of culture wars. Some sociologists believe that humanity is culturally moving towards homogenization, whereas others feel human cultures would be more fragmented, going forward. Connecting social classes internationally is not an easy task. A case in point is that of Britain, which, despite the political hegemony it enjoyed in the 19th century, could not bring out a global cultural hegemony. As per German historian and philosopher Oswald Spengler, history is the story of various discreet civilizations. Many distinct cultures emerged, developed, flowered, and then perished. For Spengler, there can be no universal culture or civilization and no culture can be imposed upon another, peacefully or forcefully. However, the American decline or western decline as predicted by Spengler in 1918 in his work *Der Untergang des Abendlandes (The Decline of the West)* did not happen.

Conflicting Identities

Human beings are considered as social animals. Immanuel Kant referred to the same as our 'unsocial sociability.' We work with each other in order to survive and prosper. In-spite-of this inter dependency, we do not gel each other much. Most human societies are fragmented due to human egos and conflicting interests of numerous kinds, creating instability, a basic characteristic of human identities. These identities often originate from cultural issues related to the likes of languages, religions, castes, classes, economic status, nationality, and colour. The degree of instability varies. For any group, the core identities and values like nationality, religion, race, language, etc., are relatively more stable, whereas others like working environment, mobility, etc., are less stable. Changing contexts and environments make some identities and long held beliefs more flexible. Immigration, for example, is a key factor that can result in major changes in identities. Identities also get changed due to cultural shifts resulting from changes within a group, or due to demographic shifts brought about by external influences like natural calamities, wars, other conflicts, etc. Assimilation of alien cultures take place in many large societies where the dominant culture of that society or nation gets adopted by the new entrants or immigrants. In the process, the new entrants many times lose their heritage culture. In some rare cases, the migrants also pass on their traditions to the host societies.

The core identities of a group create ingroups and out groups. Groups often like to maintain prejudices against other beliefs and value systems, mainly driven by the fear of losing their own beliefs and values. But when identities become primary focus of societies, they tend to become unstable, as some members would be unable to face the challenges that come with it. Some people cannot face the dynamic changes brought about by new knowledge and technologies, as they find it difficult to adapt to the changes brought about by such knowledge and accept the game-changing innovations.

Maintaining a collective self-esteem, based on old norms, traditions and beliefs is more important in a group that has a static culture and attendant group-based nostalgia. The theory of cultural inertia states that stable groups resist change whereas groups in motion continue to change. This is akin to *Laws of Motion*. *Newton*'s third law of motion states that whenever an object exerts a force on another object, the second object exerts an equal and opposite force on the first. This is broadly applicable to stable, predominantly conservative societies. Changes that are perceived to be against existing social norms and culture can lead to violent backlashes or hostilities. Interactions between unstable identities are therefore likely to create social stress.

Cultures are unstable for a different reason as well. Culture has a range of meanings like artistic, economic, scientific, moral, religious, institutional, long held norms and beliefs, etc., that characterize a society. Culture as an art and culture as a way of life are also different. The upholding of a high culture by one dominant group more often creates friction and instability within societies. Such attempts for cultural domination or self-glorification or brand building are visible aspects of an imperial domination. While the cultural satraps' imperial impulses and ambitions drive them to hold on to power on the strength of such domination, the dominated segments feel dispossessed. That creates unstable social conditions. Cultural marginalization of minorities, aboriginals, and dispossessed can be highly disruptive.

French political scientist Dominique Moisi argues in 'The Geopolitics of Emotions' (2010), that whereas the 20th century was about ideology, the 21st century will be very much about identity, specifically about the special emotions to which identity gives rise to, like fear, humiliation, and hope. He associates these emotions with concrete behavioural patterns of certain countries. Moisi believes that in order to achieve stability, the world will have to strike a balance between the above three types of identity-based emotions.

Echo chambers in Tribal Caves

A culture is not unidimensional and its moves are neither unidirectional nor linear. Cultures may barely change during certain periods, but transform dramatically or unexpectedly during certain other periods. They always interact with, and get impacted by the society. Components of cultures can become less or more relevant over a given period as well. For example, portraiture was a highly respected art form in the ancient era. With the advancement in photography, its relevance and demand, both have significantly been lost.

Cultures evolve all the time, with the inter play of various actors and powers, based on the rules of system prevailing during a given period. Cultures also mean differently to different segments of the society and there could be changes in cultural viewpoints of same groups or individuals across different time periods.

Cultural practices cannot be confined to closed echo chambers where traditions and beliefs are reinforced by their monotonous repetitions. Such echo chambers will prevent people from listening and adapting to external ideas and movements related to political, economic, social, and even natural forces.

Cultures can be hegemonic. Another potential dominating entity in a society is a political party. When a powerful political party uses a hegemonic culture, the result is almost fatal. Recent political history of many democratic nations show that the major movers of cultural polarizations are almost always political outfits. Political parties colonize the minds of voters and polarize them, nudge them, or force them to take sides on contentious positions relating to cultures. In some cases, these positions are linked to theologies, but there could be other non-religious positions as well. People are made to believe that there are severe existential threats if they do not hold on to certain cultural positions or cling to their centuries-old dogmas. For many of them, their pre philosophic culture is the most natural one, and the only one with a potential to be a universal culture.

Polarized societies are trained to believe that in the absence of certain core beliefs, one's life becomes virtually meaningless. People are asked to elect their representatives not for taking care of their economic interests or common welfare, but for preserving their arguably illusory culture. Abstract, 'shared values' replace the more concrete, shared economic good. Consequently, polarized, divided, weak nations are created in place of stronger united nations with blended cultures and broader outlook.

The quest for self-determination and identity of a person involves finding one's place within a moral order. In this materialistic world, social contracts in many cases, are made with a view to benefit certain sections of the population, which might be detrimental to the interests of others. Powerful players in the game ensure that their interests are kept high in the order of priorities, in these social contracts. As the philosopher Martha Nussbaum states, the pursuit of 'individual ends' must "include shared ends." In such a situation, the tribal, sectarian attitudes can be counter-productive.

In developed nations, generally there are liberal institutions that strive for social cohesion. But in places where citizenships are defined in ethnocultural terms, ethnic entrepreneurs use polarization techniques for political mobilization by invoking ethnic appeals against certain identified groups like immigrants. Such efforts in turn create counter strategies by the attacked ethnic groups, thereby aggravating the social divide. Timur Kuran[12], the Turkish-American economist and political scientist, Professor of Economics and Political Science, and Gorter Family Professor of Islamic Studies at Duke University, explains this bandwagon approach and balancing act as "When members of one ethnic group start engaging in more ethnic activity, attention is drawn to society's ethnic divisions. Members of other groups are thus reminded of their outsider status vis-à-vis the group that initiated the process. In order to ensure that some group accepts them, they feel pressured to get together and make more public displays of their identity." The game goes on.

To the Labyrinth

Samuel Huntington showed how identity politics shaped global politics in the post-Cold War world. In his widely discussed 'The Clash of Civilizations and The Remaking of World Order' (1996), he wrote: "The years after the Cold War witnessed the beginning of dramatic changes in people's identities and the symbols of those identities. Global politics began to be reconfigured along cultural lines." In other words, according to Huntington, identity and culture emerged as the new fault lines in a likely clash of civilizations.

The indirect support from weak or biased state institutions can have serious impact. These institutions can be used to nudge the people on the fence to join any group, thereby increasing the conflicts. There is a strong feeling among many political parties across the globe that the idea of pleasing every segment economically in a society does not sell. This is because it is practically impossible for most nations, given the scarcity of resources at their disposal. In other words, inclusive politics does not make political sense. Identity politics that favours certain groups sells, and it does not involve much resource spending. The groups could be selected based on any common factor like a language, region, religion, class, caste, etc. Once power is achieved using polarization of voters, the game is normally continued by discriminatory resource allocation policies that favour the aligned groups, thus reinforcing the policies of division and hatred.

Identity politics is increasing worldwide. In this game, each group believes that their values and beliefs are supreme and universal. They try to silence other opposing or different identities. One up man ship is the name of the game. In order to achieve higher status and material benefits including political power, these groups go to any extent. As the American political scientist Joseph Nye said, "politics in our Information Age is not about whose military wins, but whose story wins." Most overt and covert cultural wars waged today are a result of this approach, which is more about perceived, or even illusory unique cultures and traditions. And in an increasingly politicized world, there are no easy ways to get out of this labyrinth. No thread in hand, and no Ariadne in sight.

Super Cultures in Deeper Valleys

All cultures have their own uniqueness and they all contribute to the broader human culture. Diverse lines of thinking must be encouraged by all of us, as they are critical for human progress. Samuel Huntington said that "the Western civilization is valuable not because it is universal but because it is unique. The principal responsibility of Western leaders, consequently, is not to attempt to reshape other civilizations in the image of the West, which is beyond their declining power, but to preserve, protect, and renew the unique qualities of Western civilization." This is true of each nation that pursues an identity based, nationalistic politics.

Societies with a strong set of home-grown beliefs and ultra-sensitive approach to other beliefs are clearly in a deep valley, when it comes to tackling a globalized, multi-cultural population with rising aspirations, higher levels of education, and widening outlook. Multiple camps or groups that get created in societies based on allegiance to various schools of thoughts fragment them. Such divisions will indeed have long term negative repercussions, mainly in socio-political and economic areas.

These societies can come out of these valleys only if all the sub sections of community can work together for a common good, irrespective of their individual cultural beliefs. However, some institutionalized traditions and cultures tend to be backward looking and hard to change. They are normally backed by vested interests, with strong political patronage. More so, when these are part of or linked to a non-economic interest group like religion, where the leaders try to instill the fear of contamination of their 'unique' culture.

Poisoning the well is not a solution, if you do not want others to drink from your well. Economies today can jointly prosper if they work together in solving human problems. In a scenario where the knowledge horizons keep expanding, islands of research and non-inclusive growth cannot address the human issues effectively. Therefore, the expansion in knowledge should be on global basis, benefitting maximum people. Such a strategy can improve the global social order to higher, universally acceptable, and sustainable levels. Disconnected communities and groups in a connected world can have disastrous effects. A divided society simply adds new problems with no apparent or easy solutions.

Cultural conflicts can be tackled by efficient, neutral, and inclusive institutions. The primary requirement for creation of such entities is ensuring that the so-called democracies are fair and liberal in the real sense. Many practices, including the cult of personalities, will have to be minimized in that exercise.

Many countries have restrictions on various types of human rights and freedom rendering their average citizen virtually powerless. In such cases, the imaginary protection provided by the likes of ethnicity and religion become appealing. These are masks that must be removed.

Despite having well-meaning supporters of traditions and nationalism, cultures will continue to evolve, based on differences in citizens' opinions and world views. They are always in the process of becoming rather than being. The focus of a society in a dynamic world must therefore be not on who its members currently are, but on who they might become in future. In the absence of this realization, there can be no real progress in any society.

Validity of an idea, including that of a culture or a norm, must be regularly questioned for demonstration or proof. Unchallenged dogmas that are kept alive without any logical grounds will lead to stagnant societies. All societies must therefore create a strategic forgetting plan to bury the unwanted traditions. Multi localism, which is the ability to live in more than one location as if they were one's own and get influenced by the cultures of those locations, must be encouraged. A '*diasporized*' world is a far superior one than a collection of homogeneous 'island' nations. It is even more important for people like Indians, a significant number of whom are migrants and are already living abroad.

Arguments in favour of cultural preservation sometimes turn out to be attempts at turf preservation by vested interests. For example, glorification of a mythical, unknown, or unknowable past, a trend seen in few countries, is a strategy aimed at driving the nationalistic agenda. Here the society goes down in its efforts to uplift its people. In order to reverse the trend, cultures must operate as open systems, amenable to criticism. Left to themselves, cultures will get created or transformed due to ongoing, knowledge seeking mental processes of people. There is a continuous renaissance going on naturally in each open society, which must be encouraged. By clinging on to illusory past cultures, and by fossilizing a mega or super culture, a society loses this benefit.

Destroying Gardens

There is an interesting incident in 'Ramayana,' the Great Indian Epic. Hanuman, the emissary of *Rama* goes to Ravana's Lanka in search of Sita. He finds her in the beautiful garden of 'Ravana,' the 'Ashoka Garden.' As per the epic, this garden was more beautiful than the heavenly garden maintained by 'Indra,' the Hindu God. Hanuman destroys the Garden on behalf of *Rama*, as a retaliatory measure. The destruction is seen as a perfectly justified, symbolic destruction of a devil-infected culture. Today, people destroy each other's cultural gardens, to take revenge on their enemies. In the process, the valuable traditions, accumulated knowledge, and a whole range of aesthetic experiences are lost.

The above example is from a Hindu epic. Such destructions have indeed happened in real world as well. The Islamic Golden Age from the 8th to mid-13th century is considered one of the greatest periods of human advancement in knowledge, with Baghdad as its focal point. The rulers of Baghdad had encouraged scholars from across the world to come there and contribute to knowledge. Baghdad's population had reached one million in a century, making it the world's largest, most prosperous, and celebrated city of its time. But it came to an end in 1258, with the Mongol conquest of Baghdad. The entire population there was either killed or sold as slaves. The river Tigris reportedly ran red with the blood of slaughtered men, women, and children. Every building in Baghdad was destroyed, including the world-famous 'House of Wisdom.' Hundreds of thousands of priceless manuscripts and books were dumped into the river, which became black with ink. It is argued that Mongols destroyed the cities because their priority was for land, for grazing, rather than for cities. A real cultural garden of knowledge, among others, was destroyed by those who did not understand or appreciate its value.

History is full of destruction of symbols of cultures. Many pagan structures and city temples were destroyed or changed to churches in Europe by Christian activists. In India, many temples were arguably changed to mosques by Islamic zealots or rulers. Prior to that, many Buddhist places of worship were allegedly destroyed by Hindu rulers. The destruction of the towering, 6th century statues of Buddhas of Bamiyan in Afghanistan by Taliban, happened as late as in 2001.

Mutually assured destruction is not confined to physical objects. It is equally applicable to racial and cultural sphere. The process starts with an innocuous, 'we are the best' attitude in a group. Then comes the not so innocuous shift in attitude with the brain washing of members. Rather than looking for the fundamental goodness in human beings, group members are asked to invent and preserve some special or unique goodness in groups' 'own' legacy systems. The slogan then changes to 'eliminate the aliens' mode, and it becomes dangerous. This siege mentality is possibly being advocated as a strategy for gaining and maintaining political power, in the guise of offering sustainable solutions for the complexities of modern social life.

Historically, human societies always found reasons to divide themselves. Ethnic conflicts take place regularly in all types of nations, irrespective of demographic divergence. A recent case is that of Myanmar, which had a long history of persecuting the Rohingya, a mostly Muslim community of more than a million living in western Rakhine State. In August 2017, the military, in response to an alleged attack from a faction of Rohingya, undertook violent measures against civilians which many consider as ethnic cleansing. Over six lakh Rohingya were forced to seek refuge in neighbouring

Bangladesh. Radical Buddhist leaders reportedly supported the cleansing.

Incidents like the above can happen in any multi ethnic nation like India, United States, Bulgaria, Malaysia, a member state of European Union, etc. It can happen in relatively homogeneous states like England or Germany or in majoritarian states like Egypt or Algeria. Religion was a major dividing factor in the 16th and 17th centuries. Class struggle was another divider in the 19th century. Today, in the information age, many politicians are searching for newer, more effective tools to divide the societies and reap the benefits.

Research reports and comments on ethnic conflicts advance few theories or approaches for these cultural conflicts. One of them suggests the prevalence of centuries old 'accumulated hatreds' between tribes, groups, and nations. This approach believes that the opposition and non-acceptance of other cultures goes back to our ancestors. The argument suggests that the politics of identity, with its exclusivity, and tendencies for intolerance and xenophobia are natural to human societies. Society faces serious conflicts only when sectarian and cultural identities get legitimized, and are then transformed deliberately or otherwise into political identities by vested interests.

A second theory suggests that there are perceived security concerns that create conflicts. Absence of effective mechanisms to maintain social order in a society creates a sense of anarchy. Groups then set up mechanisms to safeguard their group interests, which create insecurity for other groups. Those groups, in turn, set up their own security mechanisms to safeguard them, which threaten other groups. These mutually threatening measures form a vicious circle.

A third approach suggests that these conflicts happen in the absence of economic freedom. When there are liberal economic and democratic political institutions, they can effectively mitigate ethnic and sectarian conflict, as free markets create wealth for all irrespective of cultural affiliations. There is no need to fight for allocation of resources. Democracy permits political entities to represent all social interests including sectarian interests. The idea of territorial decentralization embedded in democracy can devolve political power to local level, which can improve both autonomy and self-determination. Hence, a liberal market coupled with appropriate decentralization of political and economic powers, can make individuals better in terms of resource sharing.

There are intentional, man-made divisions in societies. People keep creating divisions like common vs elite, majority vs minority, men vs women, our culture vs their culture, rich vs poor etc. One of the aims of this approach is to eliminate the neutral, tolerant segments of society. Ethnic machines are used by divisive politicians, to garner support in democracies, especially when the ethnic target group is in majority. If the target ethnic group is a minority, then the card of autonomy is played. These players give signals to neutral members that they must take sides or else they will suffer. Neutral members get scared by penal actions, and some of them take sides in sectarian conflicts.

Politicians who rely on sectarian support always try to mobilize support by building a myth around the glorious past of a cultural group. They create a sense of culturally linked mission for the group, sometimes even invoking divine powers. Cultural identities are then effectively transformed into political identities during this process and the aim of 'nation-building' gets transformed to 'preservation of culture.' In extreme cases, these movements lead to autonomy or even to creation of separate nations. This process of a cultural identity getting converted into a politically strong institution is primarily led by institutional disruption, and weakening of prevailing social contracts. In such a situation, the political entities try to mobilize support based on cultural appeals and even by resorting to violence.

Polarization strategies are resorted to by political parties who believe that they cannot possibly ensure economic welfare of all its members. Therefore, a better, implementable strategy would be to ensure keeping few prominent members of the population happy. Rest of the members could be kept on a steady diet of rhetoric, bordering on reinforcing hatred, using unverified information on alien cultures. When the targeted ethnic group is in majority, the incentive to make common enemies based on ethnicity for electoral support is quite high.

There is a visible paradox between centre and periphery here. Those at the centres of power, in the institutional, political, economic, or cultural sphere, freely mingle with outsiders and alien cultures. Their lives are enlightened by regular interactions with the multipolar world, global leaders and thinkers, and power centres. They attend important global conferences and seminars on all conceivable subjects, widen their knowledge horizons, and offer ideal, politically correct solutions to the world audience. Occasionally, someone in their group may knowingly or unknowingly fall off, and get replaced by a new entrant. But such occurrences are rare. Otherwise, these networks are self-perpetuating. The ordinary citizens in the periphery on the contrary, are cautioned to be vigilant towards outsiders. They, and the society at large, are kept in mental siege all the time. A reset is long overdue.

There could be unintended consequences of some well-intended decisions as well. In India the Green Revolution made the Indian State of Punjab the breadbasket of the country. This came at the cost of industrialization and it was accused by some that the central government treated Punjab in a step motherly manner, in respect of industrial development. Punjab was exploited, the argument goes, in order to ensure food security for other Indian states. This argument was also used for liberation of 'Khalistan,' as a separate state.

Weaponizing Culture

Life is a struggle against disorder. Positive and negative interventions by the cultural leaders in different communities contribute significantly to social disorders. These disorders broadly depend on the nature and intensity of interactions between the members, and the types of major differing world views in a society.

A disturbing trend emerging is the creation of disorder by weaponization of culture related aspects like history, religion, etc. Weaponization of culture is done by using the insider - outsider theme. Within religion itself, there is a weaponization of human guilt, where all human sufferings are linked to past sins of an individual, virtually delinking the welfare of people from the rulers and absolving them and the elites in power structure from their failures of commission and omission.

Modernisation does not destroy cultures. Cultures are path dependent in many countries. Therefore, the old value systems and traditions more often persist, despite modernisation. The situation becomes complex when politics and religions collude and their dangerous, stronger combination emerges. This happens mainly because political and religious powers operate in same territories with more-or-less similar objectives. Their clientele is common, and they make almost similar set of promises. They use identical set of strategies, techniques, and tactics, which they borrow from each other and mutually imitate. Creation of make belief icons, branding them effectively, packaging and marketing them to clients as demi Gods, and virtually living off these branded icons using the make belief identity, are all common in both segments.

There is also a case of over generalization. Anne Frank wrote in her diary, "What one Jew does is thrown back at all Jews." Similarly, what one person belonging to say, one religion or group does, is projected to have been done by all persons belonging to that religion or group and innocent persons in those identified groups are then attacked based on the flawed rationale.

During the Holocaust, millions of Jews were tortured or killed using this logic. The trend continues. Fundamentalists attack moderates, bisexuals attack homosexuals, and so on. Based on the imaginary myths and symbols associated with people, society many times try to stigmatise and isolate people belonging to 'other' groups. Such stigmas were attached to people belonging to certain tribes and castes in India in the past. The working class suffer various types of stigmas in their work places.

The social media that has emerged in the last decade is also promoting the weaponization of all sorts of identity linked conflicts. Using their free-for-all platforms, one can intimidate another person or a group of persons, without the support of facts or evidences. Partisan and fake news spreads faster than neutral, fact-based news. Cultural tutorials and brain washing using social media are highly powerful and effective, though dangerous for the society in the longer term.

Highbred Nations, Hybrid Cultures

The ancient cave men never believed that their land and other resources were limited. They did not crave for ownership of assets. Nor did they fight for their illusory group culture. The kings who followed them also did not focus on 'own' cultures. They did not need polarization of subjects based on any unique culture, as kings were not chosen by public. Some of them used religion as a tool to discipline the subjects. Few with aesthetic sense encouraged artists and artisans, mostly aimed at showcasing the dynasty's brand.

Modern nations are different and they are rediscovering themselves. There is an increasing focus in many nations on identifying and preserving their 'unique' legacy cultures. Post independence from USSR, Uzbekistan resurrected Tamerlane or Timur, who was a symbol of tyranny earlier, as a hero. Kyrgyzstan repositioned 'Manas,' the epic warrior.

The dilemma faced by modern states is that they have a hybrid culture, thanks to continuous migrations, colonization, media exposure, international trade, cross border investments, cultural exchanges, etc. Societies are unable to insulate themselves from outside influences. Differing and even opposing views get filtered in and cultures are forced to introspect, correct themselves, correct others, and evolve continuously. Some nations are unwilling to acknowledge this reality. They believe that their nations are different, thoroughly highbred, and far superior to others, culturally. These nations are taking their subjects back to the tribal caves, with their 'valuable' possessions, and they want to ensure that entries to the cave are limited to members of the same tribe, with secured swipe cards and digital passwords.

A basic question that could be posed at this juncture is whether concepts like 'nation' would remain important in future. An understanding of the past, and likely future, of all the humanity would indeed be more critical in a networked, connected world. The 'stories' of a particular nation's past may not necessarily be so exciting for a vast majority of population. In such a multi coloured eco system, a diversified cultural outlook is eminently preferable. A myopic view of culture will be both unhelpful and dangerous in many respects. Hence, all local traditions and beliefs will have to undergo a filtering process to understand their global utility and relevance.

Shared Gardens

A pluralistic society, that promotes the particularities of different world views and traditions, is essential in this post-modern world. Differences in world views can be catalysts for any society for accelerating its growth. Divergent views are like oxygen for a society. Instead of creating polarizations based on cultural differences, societies must encourage dissemination of scientific knowledge and non-controversial moral values of each culture. For creating an inclusive society, we need to envision and encourage intellectual, logical arguments among people.

Nations can display their unique heritage by creating electronic libraries of their valuable cultures and traditions. These libraries can showcase the nations' religious and philosophic teachings, classics, other heritages, etc. They could be made accessible to the whole world. Let the external world have a look at them, adopt the suitable ones, or ignore them. Thus, while the 'ownership' of cultures would be re-established, there would be no attempted domination. A shared garden is certainly a better approach. If all nations follow suit, we can have a set of different national treasuries showcasing their unique traditions and cultures to look at, experience, and emulate on merits.

There could also be public galleries in the internet, maintained by each nation displaying their prestigious and historical products relating to arts, languages, etc. The 3D pictures of say, illustrious buildings and plastic art products like sculptures created by past nationals could be shared for public view and information.

Symbolic Projection of Culture

Like the Maslow's hierarchy of human needs, modern, democratic nations apparently maintain an unofficial hierarchy of priorities for their nations. Such priorities must have been there in the past kingdoms as well. If we are to assume that such a set of priorities did exist during the liberal, welfare period (from end of World War II to nineteen seventies) and that they exist under the current neo liberal era (from late nineteen seventies), they would possibly be ranked in the following order:

Priorities under Liberal Economic Policies broadly would have included: 1. Social welfare. 2. Protection of democracy. 3. Economic growth. 4. Promoting globalization. 5. De-weaponization and 6. National border protection. The changed priorities under the current Neo-Liberal era would broadly include: 1. National border protection. 2. Private business growth. 3. Protection of democracy. 4. De-globalization. 5. Cultural protection (part of nationalistic agenda) and 6. Social welfare.

As per the above indicative list of priorities, border protection is emerging as a critical, though costly objective. During post World

War II, the risks related to wars got reduced mainly due to focus on de-weaponization. But this risk reemerged after the Vietnam War, and with the recent Russia-Ukraine war, many continuing civil conflicts, and the latest war between Israel and Hamas, it has increased manifold, thereby improving its rank in national priorities.

The economic growth of nations got equated with the growth of private businesses. Privatization is a key focus in the neoliberal policies, and it continues as there are arguably no better alternatives. Under that system, the national task of economic advancement has virtually been handed over to the private entrepreneurs in most nations. Nations are also willing to bear part of the costs of these businesses, by way of subsidies, tax exemptions, land allotment, etc., to help the private enterprises establish businesses. Governments are performing a business facilitation job, in the hope of generating jobs and furthering nations' economic welfare. Many governments are also keen to ensure that their domestic businesses are not adversely affected by external competition. Hence anti-globalization moves are on the rise.

Protection of democracy cannot be neglected, as the very survival of politicians depends on it. Hence, it is in the priority list. Getting elected democratically warrants a strong, solid, supporting group of voters. The think tanks in the war rooms of all political parties are therefore busy inventing, manufacturing, and warehousing newer varieties of political ammunition. They keep preparing strategies to beat their opposition.

Since the benefits of economic growth are not getting equally shared by all citizens under neo liberalism, rulers and politicians are forced to use different strategies to keep supporters united. One such strategy is to bring the cultural protection objective to the forefront. Such objectives were not in their radar earlier. Today, patriotism and culture are projected in many nations as major focus areas. They are seen as less costly, but symbolic and highly effective for political positioning and repositioning. The welfare measures are understandably very costly. They are presumably taken care of by the 'trickle down' effect of private business growth. The social welfare objectives are therefore mostly confined to rhetoric. They are not in the scheme of things of politicians when it comes to execution. People are expected to take care of themselves.

Private Gardens, Public Fragrance

National Cultures badly need a repositioning. Let the cultural gardens, across the world, be of, and for, all. In any case, it is impossible to stop the breeze of interactions that take place at the individual level or between communities or through the ever-increasing global networks. The seeds of plants are destined to travel outside the gardens and sprout. It is as natural as that.

Let us revisit the teachings of 'Doctrine of Honey,' mentioned in chapter 2. As per the doctrine, the Earth is 'Honey' for all beings and all beings are 'Honey' for this Earth. Honey, here, is the economic prosperity, social bliss, cohabitation in harmony, and ultimate joy of living. Hence, if human beings are to march forward, communities and societies must pool their resources, ideas, and leading practices of their individual members, firms, businesses, teams, and different groups, across functions. Even within a nation, ideas of various sub groups need to be aggregated.

There is no harm in celebrating the great traditions and achievements of a nation. But cultural exchanges across all locations, within a nation, and internationally, are highly desirable. Better ideas will prevail, even if they get diluted in the process. Such a process must be encouraged by all the nations at the government level, as also by NGOs at the broader, societal level. Informal interactions can be value additive, in the exercise.

The issue of narrowly conceived nationalism, which is a key part of 'own garden' concept, can be a major hindrance in the above effort. One option for tackling it is the promotion of an 'alternate' concept of patriotism, where everyone in the world must be linked to, and concerned about the welfare of all human beings in the world. Needless to mention, it goes with the concept of *'vasudaiva kudumbakam'* - world is one family - of India. A culture capable of understanding the intricacies of nature and bettering lives through scientific discoveries and innovations is always a possible, superior solution. People do not need to be prisoners of their 'own' geographies. Mankind does not progress with a backward-looking nationalism. Instead, it must aim for a forward-looking humanism.

There are superior themes and knowledge banks in many cultures and beliefs that can elevate human beings mentally and materially, irrespective of their origin of birth. The only requirement is an open mind and accessibility to newer set of ideas. Our border lines and network systems must be reasonably porous to facilitate such transmissions. Knowledge sharing warrants bridging of boundaries. The social teaming up initiatives can be hugely effective if carried out with the help of hard and soft bonding. Hard bonding could be in the form of formal, official collaborations between nations whereas the soft bonding could be in the form of personal, informal relationships that promote creative dialogue and exchange of ideas.

Let the global, cultural fragrance be shared.

Chapter 6

<u>MYTH OF SOCIAL LADDER</u>

Many anthropologists believe that human beings had a shared, more-or-less egalitarian life in the ancient past, when cooperation was the norm rather than exception. Hierarchies were rare back then. Social hierarchies reportedly came about 6,000 years ago along with the emergence of states. Otherwise, the argument goes that by the very nature, men are cooperative. Competitiveness is a 'learned' skill for them.

As we know, from hunters, men graduated as food producers during the great agricultural revolution. Once food became surplus, men developed secondary industries and ventured into other creative activities. Later, as the population increased, products and economies became diversified, and cities got developed, men started getting identified with their occupations. Traditional rural cultures and life styles gave way to urban civilizations. Social classes and structures took birth. Men began differentiating themselves, created social ranks, and boxed themselves as per social rankings.

Today, human identities are intrinsically linked to the social status of an individual. Such a status has a formal structure requiring some members to accept lower status so that others enjoy a relatively higher status. The notion of social status as a top-level goal has become a 'prime mover,' which in turn, is forcing men to indulge in unethical behaviour with resultant conflicts. Societies cannot eliminate such conflicts easily, while promoting aspirational human values.

Status preservation and status upgradation have become critical goals for the entire population. Status preservation is being pursued by individuals who are already in the top layer in societies, whereas an upward movement in social status is a coveted objective of those stuck in the bottom layers. The social ladders are visible in human relationships at community level. At the workplaces, these hierarchies are very formal and more evident.

The subjective social status (SSS), is a concept that people develop, as a sense of the perception of their own standing in a society. Among other things, SSS considers one's socioeconomic status, and the understanding of where one thinks he stands in the social hierarchy. This is determined by how a person compares his resources and ranking in relation to those around him. Achieving a college education, for example, is an event that objectively places people at higher social status. The feeling that one has higher status relative to others enhances one's mental health. People of higher status tend to have more power and resources to fall back on, when they face critical, adverse situations. On the other hand, this understanding can have a hugely negative impact in the case of members of poor families, as access to, and availability of resources, become difficult for them. In fact, the financial standing of a person at any given point of time is well captured today and made available to potential lenders for a fee. The official personal ratings of individuals primarily determine whether he or she is eligible for credit.

Imaginary Ladders

In almost all societies, imaginary social ladders are created and maintained by the social and political powers. These ladders are mainly derived from the economic or social power they possess. People are sorted and ranked in almost all walks of life, based on their wealth, current positions of authority, financial standing, educational status, location and type of residence, and other similar criteria. This social stratification process then creates both visible and invisible hierarchies in societies. And such identification of hierarchies helps the top layer, as the political masters who write the rules of the game can use the information to favour the elites, the rich, the powerful corporates, and other stronger players in the economy.

Regulations generally facilitate profit maximization. They often significantly and irreversibly change the worker-employer relationships in work places. The emerging trends in many countries show that workers are being re-grouped in their current organizations. They are increasingly getting converted as contract workers. Their job profiles remain more-or-less same, but their relationships with employers are changing. This is being done to create flexibility in some cases, and to reduce worker related longer term, post-retirement costs in others. As a result, an important safety net, hitherto available, has virtually gone out of the window. Consequently, some of the affected are forced to climb down the social ladders.

The theme running is simple. The message from the elite rich to the rest of mankind is this. Welfare measures using our resources are limited for you; but we will use your resources for unlimited gains for us. The labour class is generally lazy, and therefore deserves and gets less; the top layer represented by us deserves and gets unlimited. The interest on savers' deposits must be low or preferably negative; the equity returns for us must be unlimited. We may inflate away the interest cost, if any, in any case. Your values are invaluable and heavenly; our values are material, ordinary, measurable, and earthly. The public is dear to us; but our wealth, friends, and relatives are a lot dearer.

Mirage of Ascend

The sad part is that there is hardly any evidence of a social upward movement of members in most societies. It is often said that the new generation is better off than the earlier one, but it is unclear whether the common people in current generation across the globe, are moving up in the social hierarchies or are sliding down. Apparently, our social contracts are designed in a manner that certain privileged people only get to move up these magical, highly visible hierarchies and others are destined to be mere spectators. Social catch up is a perennially elusive myth.

As per a Report of OECD, the time taken by those born in poor, low-income families to catch up with the mean income of their respective societies / countries would vary. In Denmark, it would roughly take about two generations, whereas in India it may take about seven generations and in Columbia, about eleven generations. Such a situation has serious implications in terms of stalled social mobility across generations, with the possibility of newer generations born into these families getting trapped for life, at the bottom of the pyramid.

This phenomenon must be viewed against the fact that rich are getting richer and we get a highly distorted picture of social progress. The lack of social mobility can affect the social fiber of society, with a vast majority of people not having any meaningful opportunities of income and economic progress. The society does not get to use the talents and creative energies of those who are left out of such career options.

Who Runs the Table?

Some of the major hurdles in climbing up the societal ladder include the existing rules of the games and the playing space. These rules are arguably made by the rich, for the rich, and they play the table all the time, not allowing others to play. There is a vicious circle of inequality that feeds into further inequality. The world's poorest people bore the steepest costs of the recent Covid pandemic. Incomes in the poorest countries fell much more than incomes in rich countries. As a result, the income losses of the world's poorest were twice as high as the world's richest, and global inequality rose for the first time in decades.

The above apprehensions have been confirmed by various theories based on the factors leading to consistent, and increasing income and wealth inequality. In a symposium organized at Kansas City in 2021[13], Atif Mian, Ludwig Straub, and Amir Sufi argued that high income inequality is the cause, and not the result, of the low interest rates and high asset prices seen in recent years. According to them, as the rich get richer in terms of income, it creates a saving glut, and the saving glut then forces interest rates to fall, which makes the rich even wealthier.

Economist Simon Kuznets' much popularized hypothesize was that industrializing nations experience a rise and subsequent decline in economic inequality, following a supposedly 'bell-shaped curve.' However, inequality steadily increased, particularly post 1970s, in both newly industrialized as well as in advanced industrial societies, as shown by various data-based research studies.

Wealth by Stealth

The roots of current day inequality lie not in the institutions we have set up, but in the very consciousness of societies that is rooted in the quest and worship of money power. Powerful create laws and regulations in all nations. These laws, in turn, favour the powers that be. A major reason why the corporate houses are getting richer and more powerful is that most lenders and even central banks do not take on them due to their networking abilities. Social welfare, more specifically people centered welfare envisioned as a just and caring society, is the casualty here. The social power structures that create and govern laws and institutions are run by individuals, who in turn, are led by their support groups. Under such an environment, it is only natural that the quest for domination presides over more idealistic values.

Another significant factor identified by economists for the unhealthy rise of inequality is the way wealth is created in modern economies. The capital invested in productive and commercial activities create new wealth. That wealth is widely distributed to different groups of players in the economy, including the investors of capital, workers engaged to produce and distribute goods and services, suppliers of raw materials, as tax to Government, etc.

If the above wealth or capital is multiplied using speculative financial markets, a totally different pattern of wealth creation and distribution emerges. When market players create profits by just buying and selling financial assets, no new wealth is created and the real impact is that either there is a creation of notional wealth based on changed market value of assets, or there is a net transfer of existing wealth to those who made correct speculative market calls. It is estimated that about 85% of global financial transactions today are speculative. The speculations could be on an identified economic, financial, or commodity index, or on any economy, or on a particular sector in an economy, or on a company stock, or bond, or on a currency, or on the possible variation in interest rate, etc. Any imaginable event or trend in an economy could be speculated upon.

The emergence of electronic money, created by just recording accounting procedure by banks and financial institutions, is now providing more space for the already crowded speculative businesses.

Speculation has reached a stage where well-functioning, productive companies are bought and sold just like equity portfolios, by cash rich financial giants and conglomerates.

A classic example of how passive wealth is accumulated can be seen from the widely publicized transactions relating to the sale of one of the paintings of Leonardo da Vinci. His famous painting, *Salvatore Mundi* was sold for a mere £45 in an auction in London in 1958. The painting was, at that time, attributed not to Leonardo da Vinci, but to one of Leonardo's students. Even with this shortcoming, it was sold for US$ 10,000 in an auction in 2005. Some years later, after the painting was proven as an original one by Leonardo, it was bought by a Swiss businessman for US$ 80 million who later sold it for US$ 127.5 million to the Russian oligarch Dmitry E. Rybolovlev. The Russian's family trust then sold it for a record price of US$ 450.3 million. It could be seen that the growth in the value of the painting has been mind boggling, creating financial wealth for all those who held it at various periods of time, but with no real value addition to the object. An interesting point here is the fact that such paintings are normally kept in lockers, thereby denying the aesthetic value from being experienced or admired by those who want to or care for. Astronomical prices for unseen, unappreciated products, based on imaginary attributes!

The above-mentioned speculative investments are not limited to high net-worth individuals. Big, cash rich corporates and even countries with trade surplus like the oil rich Middle East countries, Norway, and China have earmarked funds that invest in financial instruments, hoping to multiply their wealth. Various types of global funds like pension funds, sector funds, country funds, commodity funds, hedge funds, etc., have huge investible resources that they invest in financial assets all over the globe, in order to maximise returns on behalf of their clients. These funds are likely to swell more in future, with the percentage of elderly people, who typically have larger savings, bound to increase. This is a self-feeding mechanism in the sense that with higher demand, the value of financial assets increases. At the other end of the spectrum, the 'nests' for poor and the elderly are yet to be created in most of the under developed and developing countries.

Two other important developments have aided the growth of speculative frenzy. One is the increasing level of high net-worth individual participation in these speculative investments. This phenomenon is a result of a combination of factors, including the high decibel publicity of high return stories in the stock market and active marketing of investments by wealth managers and brokers. The increased use of quantitative easing and related monetary policies followed by global central banks after the 2008 financial crisis is the second driver that helped the markets to reach higher levels. By investing public money in the financial markets, governments are indirectly aligning the interests of public with the speculative private investors. After the financial crisis of 2008, global central banks bought stocks, bonds, and other financial assets in very large quantities. Post Covid 19, they repeated it. The Swiss National Bank owned more A-Class publicly-traded shares of Facebook than Mark Zuckerberg himself, as of March 2018, as per the newspaper 'Handelszeitung.' The Bank of Japan owned about 7% of all shares listed on Tokyo Stock Exchange at one point. These speak volumes on direct government support for speculative transactions.

Globally, the financial markets have grown multi fold, after the 1970s. The increased pace of globalization and market deregulations initiated by governments from the 1980s increased stock market valuations all over the world. These were also helped by regulatory reforms like introduction of fungible securities, facility of online, anywhere trading, seamless clearing and settlement, and easier fund remittance systems. Nations indeed benefitted from market growth during this period. But the average return on capital during the same period was higher than the rate of return on labour as shown by many researchers, thereby widening the rich-poor divide.

Speculative gains make some richer at the cost of those who are unable or unwilling to participate in such transactions. The passive wealth creators reduce the purchasing power of poor by the inflationary impact they produce. For example, the wealth effect of stock markets drives up the real estate prices and make them unaffordable for majority of common people. They create higher lease rents for occupiers and higher or longer period EMIs for home buyers. The same rule is applicable to other goods, commodities, and services. Contrary to this, higher levels of inflation are considered good for businesses in general as the rising prices increase profits and the real value of debt that they have taken falls. The common man's purchasing power and savings get reduced in such a scenario. Thus, high inflation also increases the inequality.

The current drivers of inequality are attributed to factors like the technological progress, increased mechanization, globalization, outsourcing, weakened power of trade unions, regressive tax policies, access to global tax evasion mechanisms, higher savings by high income groups, etc. No meaningful interventions are planned or made by most governments to tackle these.

Social welfare has more-or-less remained a distant dream of the common man not just in autocratic states, but also in almost all democratic nations. All self-ruled societies were expected to fulfill the reasonable aspirations of its people, including social welfare and decent employment, enabling the channeling of their productive capacities. It appears however, that somewhere in the process, our social priorities have either become problematic or gone wrong somewhere. Our current list of policy priorities, globally, look clearly visionless.

Modern world is witnessing a trend where certain segments in societies are continuously on an upward curve in terms of economic progress, whereas the majority are on a steady, downward march. This trend is not just between nations. There is a segmentation taking place within the borders of each nation, where some citizens continue to dominate, while the rest are destined to just survive, get exploited and forced to obey the orders of the former.

The concept of a welfare-oriented society envisages a scenario where most of its people are meaningfully engaged and reasonably happy. This state of well-being, however, is on a relative basis. The most important hurdle that a community faces in ensuring such a state of well-being is the existence of social stratification or prevalence of hierarchical structures in those societies, represented by both visible and invisible social ladders.

Human lives are highly complex, and so are human beings themselves. Interactions between human beings cannot therefore be anything but complex. Social hierarchies that arise out of these interactions are naturally not easy to fathom. These hierarchies exist in various forms and types relating to jobs, ethnicity, religion, skin colour, nationalism, power, money, gender, skillsets, academic degrees, etc.

Entrenched Ends of Elites

It would be worthwhile to ponder over the efficacy of certain laws that have been enacted by various governments. In many places, there are more laws to restrict the freedom of an average citizen than there are laws to protect him. There are more laws to protect the interests of rich and powerful corporations and multinationals, than the interests of lower-level workers, small suppliers, and other stake holders like ordinary consumers. There are laws to protect, some may argue, the unreasonable interests of politicians. For example, there is a hundred percent tax exemption for political parties in many countries on their income. Their sources of income need not be disclosed compulsorily, and there are no mandatory audits of the accounts of political parties in certain countries. Another debatable point is the question of whether state law enforcement mechanisms, including the police and army, are used more to suppress the basic rights and liberties of people than to protect these rights and liberties.

When the rules of the socioeconomic game favour the powerful, the chances that the least advantaged will rise to the top are dim. According to Hayek, equality of wealth can be achieved only at the expense of liberty. Continuous games are going on, all the time, and in all markets. The market order is a constellation of games, played using sophisticated networking platforms run by smart entrepreneurs. This is certainly not a game recommended for the uninitiated or not-so-brave. There are no permanent winners or losers in these games. However, there are actual markets out there, where the regulations and referees favour big, rich, established businesses over their smaller competitors. This bias is quite evident as large corporate houses receive government bailouts during financial downturns. The richer, powerful segments get tax breaks for starting new ventures. Biggies also succeed in getting regulations passed that make it harder for other businesses to compete.

Almost all market societies are forms of political capitalism, which are unique systems where the rules are created and interpreted in such a way that elites win at the expense of rest of the society.

Political systems give huge powers to those at the top, and they use that power to limit the extent of redistribution as also to shape the outcomes of games in favor of some. Rules of the game are formed in a manner that enhance the prospects of winning for selected people.

There are various research reports that suggest that well-designed welfare policies by states can increase overall economic performance. A lot of empirical evidence show that societies that are more egalitarian or equal, perform better, both in terms of higher growth and more stability. One of the ways to improve welfare in a society is to meaningfully connect people in various fields. Here again, the focus of certain groups through covert and overt associations of various sorts, is to regiment people and allow them to be captives of theologies, ideologies, and doctrines. As a result, people, instead of getting connected to the whole world, remain in the loops of small segments of societies. In the process, their interactions get limited to notions and doctrines related to a particular religion or narrowly defined nationalism, bypassing many times, other important aspects of life like human economic welfare, arts, sports, literature, cultural programmes, etc. The opening up of communication channels can lead to more innovative societies as individuals would then be willing and ready to take higher risks.

Human history talks about huge inequality that existed from time immemorial. The ancient civilizations like the Sumerians, Egyptians, Harappans and other early human societies operated in a complex, class-based system, propagated through generations. As per Scientific American[14], in ancient Rome, the wealthy patricians ran the empire. The second-class people worked in farms and elsewhere. The rest of the workforce, which formed about a third of the population, were slaves. Today, only the powerfully organized groups can enforce their rights and demands. Only they get recognized and rewarded. What is done in the name of 'social justice,' is arguably unjust and highly unsocial. Those actions mostly benefit the entrenched interests.

Myth of Kali Yuga

As per the Hindu epics, the human history keeps getting deteriorated, morally, over the 'yugas.' According to these epics, there are four yugas in a cycle of universes. All four yugas combine to form a 'Mahayuga' or Great Epoch. These four yugas get repeated in same order perpetually. In the first, 'Krita' or 'Satya' yuga, only truth prevails and all people in the world would be highly moral during its period. In the second yuga, 'Treta,' about 25% of truth would be lost. In the third or 'Dwapara' yuga, half of truth would be lost. Things would deteriorate further and in the last yuga, 'Kali,' which is the yuga that we are currently in, only 25% of truth would remain in the world. So, as per the Hindu epics, we are witnessing a loss of morality now, with few unethical, powerful people subjugating rest of the population with unfair means.

The 'Mahabharata,' a Hindu epic, also tells the story of 'Pandavas,' the rightful rulers of a country, who were forced to go to live in forest ('vanvas') for 12 years and then live an additional year in disguise. If we borrow this story of 'vanvas' and spin it a bit, then we can see that the common people of most countries in the world, who should have been the real rulers (Pandavas), are today forced to live in forests and in unrecognizable identities, while the usurpers (Kauravas) of these nations are ruling their lands. Epics are no more unreal.

The current ruling classes also have, apparently, close similarities with the literal meanings of the characters belonging to the clan of 'Kauravas,' in the above-mentioned epic, Mahabharata. They include characters like *Dhritrashtra* (one who clings to the state power), *Duryodhana* (one who misuses financial resources), *Dussasana* (one who gives wrong orders), etc.

In order to clean itself, societies need to collect data on the percentage of population within them that are value conscious, in terms of say, inclusiveness, tolerant to other world views, etc. To improve this percentage, divisive forces must be identified, counted, and tracked. Data in respect of those who maltreat others, exploit the marginalized, and prosper at the cost of others using unfair means, must be recorded, maintained, and published regularly. Efforts must be made by each nation to reduce the share of negative forces in a society, as a percentage of population. It must be possible for us to rewrite the epic by transforming 'Kali' yuga into a 'Krita' yuga.

Values of social justice today include equality as well as inclusivity, diversity, and multiculturalism. It has become difficult in democracies to constrain strong, vested interest groups from obtaining special privileges offered by governments. This puts strain on other varied array of public services. As per Hayek, many calls for reform in the name of social justice have simply led to special interests seeking more privileges from governments, often to keep their own current social positions rather than to help the least advantaged. He argues that government should instead stick to universal, generalizable rules (such as the freedom to pursue one's own goals and interests) that apply to everyone.

Universal Declaration of Human Rights

The Universal Declaration of Human Rights (UDHR) was created by the United Nations in 1948 as a global expression of rights to which all human beings are entitled. Consisting of 30 articles, the declaration is the most frequently translated document in the world. In 1966, two covenants were added by the U.N. General Assembly, namely the International Covenant on Civil and Political Rights, and the International Covenant on Economic, Cultural, and Social Rights. According to the U.N., this is the first global expression of rights to which all people are inherently entitled. Some examples of these rights include right to education, rights without distinctions like race, colour, sex, language, religion, political opinion, national or social origin, property, or place of birth, right to marry with free will, right to life, liberty, and personal security, protection from torture and from degrading treatment or punishment, etc. When the Universal Declaration of Human Rights was adopted in 1948, none of the signatory countries were willing to accord the UDHR the status of law or grant powers to enforce it. Yet these values constitute the very foundation of the Sustainable Development Goals (SDGs) adopted by 193 nations in 2015 with a commitment to achieve the targets latest by 2030.

The 17 SDGs address the full range of human needs including the abolition of poverty, hunger, provision of clean water and housing, enabling gender equality, safeguarding the environment from pollution etc. However, a large portion of people do live in dangerous and polluted environments in many countries even today. Efforts must be taken by the so-called enlightened nations and activists to ensure that these pathetic conditions are improved at the earliest.

Amnesty International and War Resisters International have advocated 'The Right to Refuse to Kill.' Various declarations of human rights are essentially targeting recognition of equal social status for all individuals based on common values. These concepts act as guide maps for general freedom and fair treatment of people, that are critical for any human society. As per Pitchford (2009), 'freedom allows people the ability to see the choices they have and to decide how to act on those choices and potentially transform their lives'. Such a freedom has also to be used purposefully. It warrants deeper, critical analysis of any given situation, testing the underlying assumptions and arriving at logical solutions. While doing so, the inherited or received wisdom and social hierarchies that are not logical must be questioned. Critical thinking should help the society question blind following of legacy norms. A set of values that uphold human dignity of each member of humanity can be beneficial for the mankind, in an interdependent world. The perpetual domination of certain segments is not tenable in any society, in a globally integrated world where the finer expressions of human beings such as respect, love, empathy, etc., are more critical.

Flattening the Ladders

In the prevailing unfair and unfriendly environment, people are clueless. It is extremely difficult for the laggards in a society to achieve even an incremental 'catching up,' in economic terms. In many nations, the social ladder is not in the vicinity of the marginalized. Governments can and must help the weaker sections get easy access to these ladders and facilitate their ascend. This will require approaches different from the ones hitherto followed. Some of the initiatives could be planned in a manner so that they make the ladders flatter, easily accessible, 'climbable' even for the weaker, and more importantly, worthy of climbing. In the process, their vertical distances from the base level should also be made shorter, reducing the inequalities. The social differentiation factor would then be greatly diminished.

Many believe that an inclusive society is just a myth, a dream, and an unachievable goal. It may not be a proper assessment. We can have growth oriented economic policies that are pro-employee, pro-consumer, and pro-business, all at the same time. The policies can leverage on the achievements of science and technology, which could, in turn, be inclusive in the sense that they are aimed at encouraging a spectrum of entrepreneurs ranging from small scale to large ticket innovations.

How do we specifically flatten the social order or ladder? It would depend, to a great extent, on the special social characteristics of a particular nation. However, there could be few common approaches and solutions as well. Some of the possibilities that could be explored, can include the following:

Defocus Material Comforts

Material comforts, beyond a certain limit, are just for ego satisfaction. Instead of chasing these unending lists of good-to-have facilities, a society could focus more on other community related issues. This would render descending or ascending of social ladders irrelevant. For example, if the philanthropic efforts are considered superior to wealth generation, and if people involved in it are recognized socially and politically above the celebrated rich club, there could be a social image make-over.

Any service that promotes humanism must be considered the supreme form of service. There could be a variety of social programmes, where many can contribute. Some of the participants in these programmes would admittedly be just spectators, which must be acceptable. But many others can organize them in their own unique ways, depending on their interests.

These programmes can start with common events and festivals and then get upgraded by including the likes of creation of community help groups, skill development fora, non-profit cooperative ventures, etc. Well-constructed policies targeted at social uplift, through government and private institutions can help achieve these goals. These must also include events aimed at integrating different religions and other social classes. The more decentralized and localized these events are, the flatter the ladders would be.

While focus is on social cohesion, care must be taken to see that poor are helped to move upwards economically. Equality of opportunity is critical for any citizen to come up in social ladder and the people at the starting point cannot be neglected. In a world where a vast number of people are born homeless and landless, grown education-less and live job-less, there must be a recognition of certain basic rights of all citizens, irrespective of their identities. These include rights to healthcare, basic education, fair treatment at work, unemployment insurance, etc.

Social justice is about the fair distribution of power and wealth in society. Social discriminations based on race, etc., have relatively declined in recent decades. But issues related to inequality and social standing are apparently without any sustainable solutions. Inequalities are mainly arising from the actions of powerful hierarchies, market participants and even government agencies.

Get Out of Boxes

The question as to whether a non-hierarchical structure is possible in human society remains. Alternate power structures and social contracts must be possible which can focus on human welfare without any formal hierarchies. We must reimagine a new world, where man is not caged in any boxes. Conflicts including civil conflicts originating from these 'boxed' societies must be minimized, if not fully eliminated. May be, going forward, we need to end the concepts of man-made nations and borders as well, that lead to wars and conflicts in the first place.

Two major factors that aggravated the creation of a steeper social ladder in India, are the caste-based system and the 'Adivasis' (tribal men) system. These sub systems are still realities in India as they form the basis of the nation's reservation (affirmative action) policy. A policy shift in favour of say, a National Universal Basic Income, can reduce the need for such reservation. The policy paradigm change can, over a period of say, one or two generations, eliminate the caste and 'Adivasi' systems as well, thereby making the social ladders much flatter.

Elevate by Educating

One major leveler of inequality is a good education. An educated person gets superior opportunities in the job market and he would be able to position himself better in society. Education also induces confidence in one, and prepares him to take logical decisions for himself and for society. Therefore, all governments must endeavour to impart high quality education to its people, preferably for free or at subsidized cost. That can flatten the ladders on a sustainable basis, as compared to quick fix methods and elevate the overall quality of the society itself.

Shorten Shelf Life for Power Positions

Inequality is continuing unabated, world over. It has become extremely difficult to remove or replace power centres, given the social, legal contracts that are existing and evolving. The situation warrants few drastic measures like limiting the office holding period of a person, which could be an effective tool to limit the power of a person.

The United States of America does not allow a President to continue in that position for more than two terms. Many other nations legally restrict the tenures of Presidents, Vice Presidents, and Prime Ministers to few terms of four or five years. Similar rules could be made across nations, at least in democracies, limiting the period of appointments to powerful posts of Presidents, Prime Ministers, Chief Ministers, other Ministers, etc. Such a restriction could lead to reduction in inequality both directly and indirectly. Similar restrictions can also be imposed on religious leaders (at appropriate regional / organizational levels), business leaders, and institutional and corporate heads as well. In effect, there should not be any 'permanent throne.'

Some of the key advantages of above measure would include 1. Removal of the myth that formal positions are required for serving people, 2. Bringing in the notion that the concept of retirement is applicable to all including those at the very top, thereby stopping the practice of creating and maintaining pocket army of followers, 3. Forcing top leaders to perform within a prefixed, limited period, 4. Allowing fearless decisions by administrators and lower level cadres, 5. Giving chance to more number of people to come up the ladder, and 6. Giving a clear signal that no one is indispensable.

Tame the Towering Titans

In order to bring down economic inequality, the above restrictions should also be extended to corporates, which is a tough call. The corporate culture has deep roots and it is well entrenched in almost all societies. A corporation is an ideal vehicle for raising large amounts of capital for commercial investment. They are legal entities and can generate *unlimited amount of profits, but have limited liability.* Thus, the shareholders can get unlimited returns, but their losses are limited, a principle that is asymmetrical in terms of risk-reward. There are incidents of rampant accounting and other manipulations, insider trading and various types of unfair practices, that lead to astronomical and unjustified share prices that inflate the wealth of shareholders. The wealth of corporates can be for indefinite duration and its shareholders can pass on such wealth to their heirs and nominees.

The modern business corporations have become too powerful and they control a huge amount of wealth. As per a 2018 report of Global Justice Now, 157 of top 200 economic entities by revenue in the world were corporations and not countries. And they continue to build on it. Some of them accrue more wealth than even middle income / rich countries. Their principal aim is to maximise profits and many governments help them achieve it by allowing lenient tax structures, human rights violations, subsidies, incentives, land, trade deals etc. There are laws to prevent monopolies, restrictive and unfair trade practices, etc. Some laws also provide for breaking up of ultra powerful corporates. But these are hardly effective. Part of the reason is that political and business interests are more aligned today. Therefore, laws and regulations get created and modified jointly by these two classes, obviously ensuring their mutual benefits. Large business firms are arguably more innovative and productive. But these come at the cost of impoverishing many smaller entities. In addition, big institutions and businesses, many times create huge, global level financial crises.

In order to control these behemoths, we need to look at some hard options that must be implemented simultaneously by all major nations. These options could include the following.

1. **Removal of '*limited liability*'**: Once a company, including its subsidiaries, exceeds a market capitalization of say, USD 50 billion, its limited liability condition must get removed. After exceeding such a limit, all shareholders must have unlimited liability. The position can be reversed only after a steep

subsequent correction of say, 50% from this limit. To begin with, this limit could be higher.

2. **Abolishing Tax havens and Special Economic Zones (SEZ)**: All tax havens must be abolished. SEZs may be allowed to be set up in a nation for promoting smaller firms only.

3. **Phasing out all existing shell companies**: This could be implemented in a phased manner, without disrupting markets much, and not allowing creation of any new ones.

4. **No inorganic growth**: Private, for profit, commercial entities with a net worth of over say, USD 75 billion should not be allowed to acquire other companies. Such large corporations must grow only organically.

5. **Banning sovereign funds from speculating:** Government money should not, under any circumstances, be used for purchase of private company equity shares from the secondary market.

6. **Natural resources**: Private companies that have long term rights to exploit natural resources like mines, oil fields, etc., must share wind fall gains with their governments, over and above normal taxes. There must be an assumed private public partnership when such situations arise.

The above measures must be implemented by all major nations together, in order to eliminate possible regulatory arbitrages.

Back to Square One

These are difficult times that are reminiscent of Hindu concept of 'yuga' cycles. As per Hindu cosmology, all living beings are reborn again and again, endlessly. Hindu epics say that the roles of all living beings, including those of the reincarnations of Gods and Goddesses, get repeated in each '*Mahayuga*.' Each '*Mahayuga*' or Yuga Cycle or '*chatur-yuga*' (four yugas) lasts for 4,320,000 years and then gets repeated. Thus the cycle of four yugas with Krita (Satya) Yuga, Treta Yuga, Dvapara Yuga, and Kali Yuga gets repeated with same incarnations of Gods and others in these yugas. Thus, there is an 'eternal return' for all living beings.

If that is the case, a philosophical question that arises is as to what is the great point in climbing up the social ladder, which would in any case remain elusive for certain people perpetually.

Let us create dignified lives for all human beings.

Chapter 7

MYTH OF SOCIAL WELFARE

Social welfare broadly includes certain fundamental human rights like access to basic needs, freedom of expression, non-discrimination, equity including equal opportunity, policies promoting quality of human lives, human capacity development, social peace, etc. The concept of quality of life in a welfare society in turn, includes not just the material well-being or standard of living of a person, but also his sense of social belonging and achievement of spiritual needs as well. Social integration must be added as a major welfare objective now, given the increasing racial and civil conflicts in various countries.

Different nations approach the issue of welfare differently and adopt methods and policies deemed suitable to tackle it. The polices they follow would primarily consider the resources available, prevailing social support systems including the formal and informal welfare facilities available, family bonding, coverage of insurance benefits, expected or desired inter-generational and intra generational distributional patterns, and the like.

A welfare-oriented nation acknowledges that the basic human needs are critical for each citizen, and that it is fundamentally the duty of the government to ensure access to these. Admittedly, there are many hurdles on its way. For example, it is extremely difficult to accurately measure the actual income of citizens, especially in large countries where the number of informal workers and self-employed in unorganized sector is too high. One of the basic objectives of a welfare society is equal opportunity, mainly in terms of education and healthcare, especially for the children in their initial years. The governing entities must always endeavour to facilitate meaningful jobs to all its people who are able and willing to work.

Welfare states are aimed at not just creating a better, just society. It is more about creation of a society where people are sensitive to other living beings, and more specifically to their fellow human beings. Members of a welfare state must trust other fellow human beings, demonstrate that they are compassionate, and develop a social conscience that cares for all. They must display a sense of solidarity with their fellow citizens. Social welfare objectives also cannot be limited to activities that contribute positively to a society. It is equally important to eliminate or minimise the impacts of negative contributors in a society. The negative contributors are not limited to just frauds and crimes. They include the likes of business practices that encourage consumption of unhealthy foods, drugs, and other spurious products, etc. An effective regulatory oversight in such cases is a critical part of social welfare.

The Genesis

We live in a society that is commercialized to the core. A welfare society is not a guaranteed one in most nations, but one that is envisioned by many. Economic welfare itself is understood differently by different sections of people. As per Adam Smith "every man is rich or poor according to the degree in which he can afford to enjoy the necessaries, conveniences, and amusements of human life."

The concept of welfare state arguably entered literature, with the Beveridge Report, created in 1942, though as per some historians, the origin of welfare states dates to 1601, when Poor Laws were put in force in UK. This law was passed to provide social security to protect the old, sick, and wounded people in the society. Many consider that the social welfare began when Germany became the first nation in the world to adopt an old-age social insurance program in 1889, designed by Germany's Chancellor, Otto von Bismarck. Welfare states, based on that argument, emerged first in Germany and then in Western Europe, North America, and Australia. The common feature of these welfare states was that they all had industrialization with developed market economies and democratic systems.

South Korea and Japan, Hong Kong, Singapore, and Taiwan, all went through industrialization process, and all accepted the concept of welfare states in the 1970s. Soviet Union made efforts to become a welfare state after the Bolshevik Revolution in 1917. China, Cuba, and Eastern Europe all declared their intentions to join the category, but the results are not comparable due to lack of accurate information and freedom of choice.

The concept of modern welfare state emerged mainly in 1930s and 1940s. The 1929 economic crisis and the two world wars in the first half of twentieth century, in a way, propelled the idea of social welfare. The economic policies that led to the concept of welfare states, often referred to as 'post war consensus,' came into prominence post World War II, and gave birth to a sense of social solidarity. The idea was to consider a country as a large single family, where members take care of each other. The objective was to give some level of societal protection to all members of the community.

In contrast to the policies adopted during World War II aimed at allocating more funds for fighting wars efficiently, welfare states aimed at promoting social policies like health care and education. The Keynesian approach supported it. It was strongly argued that more inclusive, 'welfare states' were the need of the day. What then followed, mainly in developed countries, was more-or-less in line with this vision. The time period between 1950 and 1973, a period of rapid economic development in both United States of America and Europe, is often referred to as the 'Golden Age of Welfare States.' More importantly, this was a period of shared prosperity, as most segments of societies grew economically, and those at the very bottom of the society saw their incomes grow faster than those at the top. As a result, the income inequality dropped during that period.

Off the Cliff

After the passage of few decades of its introduction, the sense of shared prosperity ushered in by social welfare policies and social solidarity started disappearing. The capital class was virtually kept under check after the post-war consensus. With the introduction of neoliberalism, they got new ammunition.

The change in focus is attributed to a set of crises that got developed in the 1970s, which increased national social expenditures. The extra burden forced many states to increase taxes and reduce their social responsibilities. The crises arguably developed due to large scale state interventions with huge financial outlays, which allegedly damaged economic and social balances. The conclusion was that unmanageable social expenditures were hurting nations' economic growth. As a reaction to the above, new sets of policies were made by the major nations, which came to be known as neo liberalism or new order of liberalism.

Under the neo liberal policies, businesses were deregulated and free trades, privatizations, etc., were promoted. Markets were expected to regulate businesses. Social rights like healthcare got restricted, and welfare responsibilities were transferred to non-profit organizations, and private sector. Social policies were broadly left to the discretion of civil societies, NGOs, international agencies, and supranational organizations instead of sovereign governments. On the other hand, liberal tax breaks and other benefits like free or subsidized land, etc., were offered to large corporates in the hope of creating faster economic growth and employment.

This collapse of social welfare, which started from late 1970s, referred to as 'Welfare State Crisis', continues even today. The situation is arguably worsening. One of the primary reasons for such a worsening condition is the fact that it has become extremely difficult to arrive at a national consensus on welfare policies itself. There is a view that human welfare comes naturally with economic growth. But many do not agree. They feel that when the growth is at a broader level, it does not lead to social welfare, as its 'trickle-down' effect is a slow and painful process. At the same time, the idea of free money to poor is resisted by the so called 'productive' segments in a society. Their argument is that a welfare state ends up creating and supporting lazy sections in society, at the cost of hard-working people. Based on this logic, welfare states are accused of promoting a culture of dependency on state. Social solidarity, according to many, is just a myth and an unsustainable exercise. Instead, they suggest a free and fair, market determined welfare and support to drive societies, an approach described as neoliberal.

There are strong opposite voices as well. The neo liberal policies are accused of working for the benefit of private sector. The opposing groups point out the fact that though public sector is always criticized for poor performances and inefficiencies, it is this very sector that typically bails out failing private sector businesses. The major argument of the neoliberals was minimal intervention of government in businesses. However, when the private enterprises fail, the cost of such failures were mostly transferred to public entities and funds across various nations. Thus, the heads were won by private sector and tails were lost by public sector.

Some of the welfare measures were arguably not properly structured or well executed. For example, pension is a part of social welfare. However, unfunded pension schemes were creating huge future liabilities for many governments and corporates. The deteriorating economic situation prompted many nations to stop welfare measures altogether or reduce them considerably. Though targetted welfare measures were expected to replace them, it was at best half-hearted in most nations.

To be fair, it must be admitted that neoliberalism did not come into play as a result of any major failure of the welfare state. There were a multitude of factors that paved the way for the unhindered growth of neoliberalism and its popularity. To begin with, the United States faced high inflation in the late sixties, mainly due to its war with Vietnam. This situation was further aggravated by the oil price shocks in the seventies, which led to higher inflation, recessions, and stagflation in many places, especially in countries that were highly dependent on oil imports. These problems were not primarily caused by the welfare measures of the concerned states. But they provided an opportunity to the opponents of welfare states to push for a different model, which appeared to promise a faster growth. This new model did increase growth, although a skewed one. It resulted in relatively higher growth for the richer segments and corporates as compared to the lower, poorer segments. As a result, the welfare measures became less efficient. Arguments hovering around neoliberalism, its blind focus on corporate profits, and its indifference to the dire needs of communities, are doing rounds once again now.

One of the reasons generally attributed to failure of liberalism is the wrong understanding and application of 'free' will. What we call 'free' will is not actually free many times as it gets impacted not just by government regulations, but also by factors like one's identity, ethnicity, religion, genetics, financial and social status, political affiliations, etc. The distorted understanding and application of 'free will' often create undesirable end-results in the economies of nations. These results continue to be irreversible and unpredictable, given the fact that human beings are always in the process of constructing and reconstructing their 'free' wills.

Many governments toyed with the idea of a system of direct cash support to its people, in the form of a fixed income, based on a pre-defined set of criteria. Direct cash support, it was argued, could be a much-needed basic resource the poor can be sure of, and which can help them tide over their survival needs. Another option considered was provision for certain identified, segmental support. For example, segments like social security and healthcare could be chosen as areas where governments could offer financial assistance. The vulnerable citizens in these segments could be spotted and direct transfers could be made to them or to the service providers like hospitals. The primary objective of all these measures was to ensure that a livable income support is provided and that the basic dignity of a citizen is upheld.

Currently, governments face many challenges while pursuing welfare state policies. A case in point is the level of borrowings by government. Most governments in the world are currently highly indebted. Economies driven by such huge levels of debt cannot last forever, as the unborn children will neither be able nor willing to pay them back. The higher levels of debt also means that the countries' future resources have been significantly pre committed. Therefore, many governments have become unresponsive to the welfare needs of the people. Private help is indeed available in various forms in some of these countries, but a structured, government sponsored care is considered a political responsibility and a cherished right in many societies. The trickled down effect of charity from private, wealthy individuals and corporates is too insignificant and unreliable for the vast number of extremely poor.

Poor human conditions are not entirely due to market failures. They can result from a variety of factors including the poor initiatives of individuals themselves, or from natural calamities or due to poor policies, or their faulty implementations by the administration. It is true that welfare societies cannot address all social evils and crisis situations. But they can certainly address a major part of them successfully and make a huge, meaningful difference in a society by way of appropriate interventions. For example, generation of jobs is primarily the duty of governments, who can facilitate creation of jobs by providing a suitable set of incentives, regulatory support, and enabling infrastructure to entrepreneurs.

Right, Left, and a Third Way

Welfare policies are globally split, though vaguely, on political lines. The rightists argue that the welfare states can overcome the crisis only by shifting to neoliberal policies. According to them, the social policies need to be developed and implemented by the supranational organizations, private entities, and NGOs. The new economic model, which is also referred to as the free-market economy, has a central idea underlying it. It is the idea of Adam Smith, that claims that individuals in the pursuit of their own self-interests, would promote the overall well-being of society. While the free-market approach did result in improving the economic welfare of some sections of society, it is showing signs of depriving most of the other sections, who form the majority in almost all nations. It is still being debated whether the policies helped create over all social welfare or not.

As per the leftists, welfare states can adapt themselves to changing conditions, and overcome the crisis through reforms and restructuring. It is suggested that the neo-Keynesian approaches should be adopted instead of the neoliberal approach in the reform process. Economists who support the idea of welfare states believe that markets are vulnerable to manipulation and are not efficient. Neoliberalism, according to them, has made corporates and individuals more selfish and profit seeking, to the detriment of common man. Supporters of welfare states argue that challenges like these must be taken care of by the states themselves by way of appropriate policies and methods of redistribution, as they are part of basic human rights.

The major risks faced by the people in any country are the likes of unemployment, illness, and post-retirement care. Access to these minimum necessities was declared a basic human right under the UN's 1948 Universal Declaration of Human Rights. Large scale deprivations in these areas lead to stresses in societies. Such inhuman situations are not acceptable in a modern society. In many communities, voluntary help is indeed available, as a part of philanthropy and some states give irregular, event-based dole outs. Both are neither reliable nor sustainable and they do not recognize the basic right of a citizen to a longer-term, life supporting benefit. Many believe that a right for a universal basic income from the government is warranted to make the lives of the poorest slightly better.

The neoliberals and conservatives in the developed countries have started new initiatives under the name of 'New Right,' It has conservative activists who oppose a variety of issues like affirmative action and other forms of taxation. The 'New Left' criticizes the state's role as being too weak compared to the markets, and suggests a reformulation of the state's role in societal development. It is supported by few left-wing activist movements that arose in western Europe and North America in the late 1950s and early '60s. Social liberals have their model of initiatives called 'The Third Way.' This is an alternative to the left-wing and right-wing. At the end of the 20th century, it acquired a different meaning with the British sociologist Anthony Giddens using it as an alternative to neoliberalism and social democracy The term now describes a centre-left policy programme.

Creation of a welfare-oriented society does warrant a positive economic growth rate. The average annual national growth rate of the Gross Domestic Product (GDP) must be more than the rate of population growth, in order to improve the per capita income of the nation. These averages, however, can be misleading as highly unequal incomes could be smartly hidden in blind application of averages. Hence, a relatively high per capita GDP is not a sufficient condition for prosperity. It may not indicate a fair distribution of income, which is critical, as in its absence, incomes could be highly skewed in favour of the already rich, thereby widening the inequalities.

Vanishing Social Progress

There is a strong argument that social welfare programs lead to weakening of work culture. Subsidies, direct transfer of money, and other freebies are, as per this argument, factors that create idleness and a permanent culture of state dependency, leading to a socially undesirable and unsustainable concept of 'salvation by society.'

Policy makers who adhere to this argument normally tend to reduce fund allocations for social welfare programmes. However, there are recent research reports that suggest that these conclusions are not correct. Some of these findings suggest that when families receive predictable financial support for longer periods, they do much better.

There is a strong argument that meritocracy is a better system in any society. It is certainly a better system as compared to other systems. However, it has few dark areas. The sorting done based on university degrees or formal researches carried out successfully by a few in a service dominated society cannot be the only differentiating factor deciding productive and not so productive citizens. Nor can it be based on technological advancements. The competitive few, selected based on academic success or state of the art innovations, need not be the only acknowledged and respected elites in a society. The only prevailing voices of the society need not be of these conventionally meritorious individuals. Human and civic values are also critical.

Discardable Population

Theories and policies come and go. Labour theory of value is now getting replaced by knowledge theory of value. The basic understanding and focus of job-related knowledge are changing. In the agricultural era, the job knowledge revolved around past patterns of climate, its impact on plant lives, fertility predictions based on natural phenomena, etc. In the industrial area, the focus shifted to mass production aided by technology. In the current knowledge-based economy, the focus is more on the future needs of consuming class.

The marginalized segments of population are getting larger in many societies. The rich class are getting richer and poor are getting poorer, despite all social welfare measures. The trend is visible in job markets as well. There could be many reasons for the same. The most obvious reason often alluded to is the stagnation, and in some cases, the decline in the inflation adjusted real wages of workers. There has also been a huge rise globally, in the number of temporary workers, with attendant loss of related employee benefits. The relatively recent phenomenon of platform workers is resulting in loss of welfare benefits hitherto made available to organized sector workers. The much debated fourth economic order, which is the gradual replacement of the workforce by cyborgs and implementation of advanced Artificial Intelligence on a global scale, is set to make workers' future even more uncertain. These workers are in a manner of speaking, used and discarded.

There are other drivers as well, for the marginalization of workers. Historically, the educated have been getting a wage premium over the uneducated. However, there have always been misfits in the job market where in a job situation, employees' talents are not optimally used due to multiple reasons. Things are worsening now. While the mechanizations in the industrial era were mainly targetted at increasing productivity, the current automation drive is eliminating not just manual repetitive jobs, but logic-based computations, and logarithm-based outputs. This trend virtually replaces a whole lot of jobs performed by educated workers so far, by smart machines. Lack of upskilling and reskilling is rendering these workers less productive and less commercially useful. Many low-end jobs today call for just the physical presence of a person, with no real or identifiable personal contribution to productivity. In the increasingly mechanized information age, talent is not only sub optimally used, but also increasingly wasted in dead end occupations.

There are invisible job losses as well, of people clinging to their traditional turf. In the villages of Kerala, a southern state in India, there are talented artists who specialize in '*kalam pattu,*' which involves drawing, rendering religious hymns, dancing, etc. But they do not get engaged throughout the year. Many of them spend their time waiting for the next engagement, without trying to learn a new skill or engage in any other productive manner. The 'lose-lose' situation is costly for both the individual and society. A similar fate awaits a whole lot of current day educated employees who do not plan to reskill or upskill themselves.

These developments create highly lopsided societies. On the one side, wealth creation is unbridled and continuous. So are business innovations. But dispossession is also happening faster. Secure, well-paying, life-long jobs are getting vanished. Many who lack digital skills are left out of job market. The cumulative impact is aggravation of inequality.

We are going through a period of unprecedented economic growth for few, with a dim future for the vast number of income earners. The decision takers, policy makers, and the politicians who chart out strategies for the poor, are hardly held accountable for such a situation in any nation, be it a democracy or an autocracy. Welfare states are getting confined to grand policy announcements, unverifiable resource commitments, impressive documents, and catchy slogans. The ground realities suggest that societies are becoming choiceless and citizens voiceless.

There are more players and onlookers in the game. When economies are driven by personal greed, and enhancing personal entitlement becomes a culture itself, it is difficult to inculcate a sense of social welfare. Public goods become commodified, and society becomes fragmented with many sub groups, each having their own special agenda and welfare objectives. Democracy then gets weakened by the increasing bargaining power of these influential groups. In such a situation and in the absence of proper, institutionalized, and efficient welfare programmes, the under privileged segments of the population become 'discardable.'

With the formal sectors of the economy becoming less and less labour intensive due to automation, the objective of creating a self-reliant society becomes virtually impossible which can potentially result in social disintegration in the long run. Participation in nation building by common people in a way, then becomes part of the problem in societies, instead of becoming part of the solution. Such a situation warrants investments not just in raw materials, tangible assets, and innovative technologies, but also in human development in terms of education, skill upgradation, etc. This function cannot be abdicated by any state.

Neo Regulations Needed

Given this difficult and turbulent scenario, can governments ensure social welfare? Should they reconceptualize the welfare policies? There are different welfare models that could be looked at. Bhutan and New Zealand have happiness indices as welfare measures. New models based on asceticism that promote simple living, and defocus on excessive consumption can be thought of.

Calmness Index

It is important to promote internal peace, as a core welfare indicator, in nations. To measure it, a social *'Calmness Index,'* built on society's ability to control their internal and external conflicts, could be developed. This could be implemented in places where people would prefer to just enjoy say, common celebrations and nature, and preserve their humanity. For this, people need to get rid of their obsession with getting rich, or turning too religious or too political. Instead, social harmony and human welfare should be their main objectives.

In the case of material welfare, however, these options would not work. When some segments of the population in a nation lead a luxurious life, it is hard to suggest a simple living for the rest. If the finances of a state are comfortable, the logical policy should be extension of a helping hand to the people who are economically weak. This could be in the form of social safety nets like subsidies, direct cash transfers etc., wherever required.

Regulation for Welfare

A system akin to universal basic income can be introduced for the benefit of those who are left behind, to ensure some level of comfort for them. Since the resources at the disposal of most nations are limited, it is important to prioritize welfare measures. Welfare programmes will have to be redesigned to make them both targetted and sustainable.

Goal focused, knowledge seeking people are a necessity for on-going human welfare. This yields best results when pursued as a collective effort. However, rulers, law enforcing agencies, and people in general have viewed and treated laws differently. Martin Luther King, Jr., distinguished just law from unjust law as, "Any law that uplifts human personality is just; Any law that degrades human personality is unjust" (King, 1963). An opposite view came from Adolf Hitler in Germany, where it was illegal to provide resources or comfort to a Jew, a standpoint that his courts considered 'legal.'

The first and foremost action plan for a state is to ensure that the laws created are fair to all its subjects, carefully designed, and oriented towards upliftment of human welfare with dignity. Welfare objectives must be driven by logic-based principles backed by clearly defined parameters. In order to ensure deserving targets, their identification is extremely critical. The set of conditions under which a person struggles to survive and prosper are different in different nations and even within a community itself. Various factors including chance affect these conditions.

One clear welfare target could be ensuring that at least one member of each family below a social floor, is employed or income earning. In order to achieve this objective, in some cases, the merit-based employment criteria may have to be tweaked. There could be other flexible models as well. Realising that a total dependency on state is an undesirable and unsustainable welfare model, the United States of America introduced a program styled, *Temporary Assistance for Needy Families* (TANF), which positions the programme as one for a limited period, a model worth looking at. India has its own MNREGA (Mahatma Gandhi National Rural Employment Guarantee Act, 2005), which ensures a minimum number of job days for the unemployed poor, in a financial year.

In any society, in order to improve welfare, people must be connected physically as well. In the absence of adequate and affordable transport systems, unemployment levels can rise. One of the problems identified for lower participation of women in Indian labour market is believed to be the lack of convenient physical connectivity between rural and semi urban areas where they mostly live, and the work places, which are typically in urban locations. When unemployment levels go higher, they put downward pressure on wages, creating further inequality.

In the final analysis, the critical aspect is the viability of a welfare system. Welfare measures and projects could be divided into two basic categories. While one could focus on creation of policies to reduce inequality, the other could include programmes to directly support the weaker sections. We need neo regulations to address the inequalities.

Strings for Speculators

In the earlier chapter 'Myth of Social Ladder,' we saw how speculators are getting richer, without creating any real value additions. Look at another set of regulations, in respect of income from bank deposits, which distort the incomes. The interest rates on these deposits are directly or indirectly controlled by central banks of nations. While savers were getting near zero interest on their deposits in many nations, there was no cap on the equity returns. It is granted that equity investors do take higher risks. However, the debt investors are also taking interest rate risks and credit risks. Equity investors are leveraging cheap debt to magnify their investment returns.

There is an incentive to speculate using third party, cheap money. When money could be borrowed at near zero percent interest rate, investments in riskier projects, programmes, and complex instruments tend to increase. One way to curb this is to cap the returns on equity. Any returns on equity or equity linked instruments for any time period, above a cap of say 4 or 5 times the ten-year government bond rate in that country, could be forcibly transferred to a Universal Basic Income Fund or so. This could disincentivize market manipulations and speculations to a great extent. Similar rule could be made applicable to investors speculating in commodities, without real need for owning them or hedging.

In the neo liberal era, it is difficult to stop flight of capital, as money could be transferred from one place to another in nano seconds. Private capital flies to places where they grow faster. Hence policies like the ones mentioned above cannot be considered by individual nations in isolation. They must be taken jointly by major economic nations. Big nations can effectively deny access to defaulting corporates and institutions to their financial and securities markets.

In the second category of welfare measures, two schemes that could be considered include: 1. Creation of a Social Protection Floor, and 2. National Level Basic Income.

Social Protection Floor

One possible, workable solution that has been suggested by the United Nations, is the creation of a social protection floor. This could consist of two main elements that can arguably protect the basic human rights.

1. *Essential Services*: ensuring the availability, continuity, and access to public services (such as water and sanitation, health, education, and family-focused social work support).

2. *Social Transfers*: comprising a basic set of essential social transfers, in cash and in kind, paid to the poor and vulnerable to

enhance their food security and nutrition needs. It should ensure a minimum income security and access to essential services including education and health care. An unemployment insurance scheme could also be considered as a good social safety net.

The United Nations agencies believe that in countries that currently lack strong social security and income support programmes, a social protection floor is a must. This can consist of a basic package of social transfers, combined with actions to guarantee that the poor and vulnerable have access to adequate and affordable sources of nutrition. Social and health services, critical for mitigating the poverty and welfare fall-out of various crisis, could be add-ons, which would also provide a significant stimulus to the economy.

Countries can grow with equity, i.e., providing some form of social protection from the early stages of their economic development. There are now evidences to show that economic growth that does not include a concern for equity and equality is not sustainable in the long run. A social protection is critical, given the fact that presently about 80 per cent of the global population has less than adequate social protection coverage.

Calculations by various UN agencies including ILO, UNAIDS, UNICEF and WHO indicate that a basic floor of social transfers is globally affordable, even if the funding is not yet available everywhere. The ILO estimates that a set of minimum transfers is not costly in per capita terms, although it will possibly require external support for certain nations. An ILO costing study of 12 low-income developing countries showed that the initial gross annual cost of the overall basic social transfer package (excluding access to basic health care that to some extent was financed already) was projected to be in the range of 2.3 to 5.5 per cent of GDP in 2010. The individual elements in these calculations appeared even more affordable. The annual cost of providing universal basic old age and disability pensions was estimated in 2010 at between 0.6 and 1.5 per cent of GDP in the countries considered.

A social protection floor, as per the United Nation Agencies, would indeed have a major impact on poverty, access, and use of key resources, on services including those for AIDS, tuberculosis, and malaria, on child labour and on child trafficking. When properly implemented, already existing cash transfer and basic health systems in many developing countries would have further positive impacts on poverty, child labour, health and nutrition, education, social status of recipients, economic activity, etc., without having negative effects on adult labour market participation.

A Harvard Kennedy School project undertook by Rema Hanna found that the welfare measures can have real and tangible implications for the poor and the protections they need. They observed that when the provision of government assistance is for over an extended period, it could yield high social and economic returns. In order to determine whether social programs lead to dependency or independence, Rema and her co-authors studied the effects of Indonesia's cash-transfer scheme, Program Keluarga Harapan (PKH) ('Hopeful Family Program'), a programme the Government of Indonesia launched with the help of the World Bank, as a policy experiment in 2008. 14,000 households were surveyed to assess the program's outcomes.

The program was implemented in 180 randomly selected sub-districts, which were compared to a control group of 180 sub-districts that did not have the program. PKH provided quarterly cash transfers to the country's poorest households, for those within the bottom 7% of the income distribution. Payments constituted 7 to14% of a recipient's income, which did not cover all the household's needs. The program was directed at families, which were encouraged to use the benefits to invest in their children. Only households with children or a pregnant woman could enrol, and a portion of the stipend was made conditional on fulfilling various health- and education-related obligations, such as basic immunization and the completion of at least nine years of school.

One important feature of PKH was that it did not merely provide a few weeks or months of assistance between jobs or during a financial shock. It focused on the very poor, and was administered for a minimum period of six years, with the assumption that climbing out of poverty takes time and requires consistent support and stability. In 2011, a study of PKH's initial effects showed that it had a positive impact on short-term indicators of health and educational outcomes after about two years. As per the findings, the program did lead to increased recipients' visits to post-natal care facilities, as well as increased enrolment of their children in elementary and middle school.

Given this initial success, the Indonesian government expanded the program widely over the next few years. By 2013, it was aiding about 2.3 million households in 3,400 sub-districts across the country. Now the government was targeting specific districts, rather than following the previous random-selection process. As a result, many of the sub-districts in the initial control group were left out, and they did not receive the program benefits. This offered an opportunity to understand as to what happens when poor households receive continued assistance beyond the scope of their immediate needs. Upon re-surveying the 14,000 households in the original treatment and control groups, the following key outcomes were observed.

1. The first observation was about stunting, or impaired growth, which is one of the most serious child health problems in Indonesia. Children grow slower when they are malnourished and a child's height relative to the age can therefore serve as a proxy measure of nutrition. Research has shown a correlation between stunting, lower IQs, and poorer socioeconomic outcomes later in life. At the two-year mark, PKH had no impact on child stunting. Height is a measure that expresses itself cumulatively over time. Hence it was assumed that stunting would get reversed only after continued assistance from the program. And that was what happened. At the six-year mark, children whose families had regularly received extra assistance from PKH were 23-27% less likely than those in the control group to experience stunting.

2. It was found that there were similar effects with respect to education. At the two-year mark, PKH had increased school enrolment for children aged 7-15, but not for those aged 15-17. It was argued that older children, who had dropped out prior to the program would not be able to return to school, as compared to their younger counterparts, even if their family resources had improved in the meantime. It was suspected that if families could benefit from sustained access to the program, their kids would not drop out at an earlier age, with enrolment among those in the 15-17 age bracket improving over time. Again, this turned out to be the case. At the six-year mark, children whose families started receiving PKH benefits when they were around 9-11 years old (meaning they were now 15-17 years old) were about 16% more likely to be enrolled in school.

The importance of these improvements in health and education are extremely significant. These investments in low-income households were expected to translate into longer term economic benefits, including increased labour-market participation and productivity. That, in turn, could lead to reduced participation in social programs themselves. Indonesia's cash-transfer program yielded significant improvements in some of the most problematic areas of public health and education. These gains were made possible by a cumulative investment in children over a period of six years. Most likely, these results would not have been achieved under a program providing temporary benefits.

There is an argument that if recipients expect losing eligibility for benefits on their earning more, they may abstain from work. This is a moral hazard that arguably leads people to remain poor and rely on welfare indefinitely. But evidence, as per findings, does not support this theory. In a study by same authors, they re-analysed data from seven different experimental trials of government cash-transfer programs in developing nations, covering Philippines to Morocco to Mexico. They found that in most cases, men who received benefits were working already, but there was no evidence that systematic income support reduced work. In another study, Sarah Jane Baird, David J. McKenzie, and Berk Ozler of the World Bank undertook a review of literature on this topic and came to a similar conclusion.

Researches point out that there are benefits in following welfare policies like creation of openness. With social protection, individuals become more willing to accept change and openness. A welfare state is more than just a matter of social justice.

National Level Basic Income.
World is currently saddled with highly indebted economies. The trends projected suggest prolonged, secular stagnation in many nations, threatening people's incomes. The concern is driving a growing demand for a Universal Basic Income (UBI). UBI or National Basic Income (NBI) is a socially transformational concept. It is a policy where a nation makes regular cash payments to virtually every citizen, unconditionally and regardless of their other resources. There could be some exclusions like children, richer segments, and non-citizens.

Universal basic income has 3 critical words. It is universal, in the sense that every citizen in a nation gets it, it is basic, because it is just enough to live, and it is an income. When introduced, UBI becomes the right of a citizen. Hence it has significant longer term economic implications for introducing nations.

UBI has many opponents. It has been criticized mainly on the grounds that (1.) It does not target the support at those who really need it most, (2.) It involves a huge cost, forcing diversion of national resources from other critical investments, expenditures and uses, and (3.) It is unconditional. Hence there is a high probability that it will reduce the incentive to work. Most politicians prefer occasional dole outs as they make the people dependent on them. Therefore, they tend to exaggerate the negatives of UBI. As per World Bank, the concerns over the negative effects of a UBI on labor markets might be overstated.

There is currently no formal UBI in place in any country, though there are targetted subsidies and assistances of various kinds in areas like food supply, healthcare, etc., in many countries. Some nations are seriously examining the economic and political repercussions of implementing such an idea. An experiment on Basic Income was conducted in Finland in 2017–2018 in which a total of 2,000 unemployed persons between 25 and 58 years of age received a monthly payment of €560, unconditionally. The major findings from the evaluation were that there were positive employment effects, and better perceived economic security and mental wellbeing, for the basic income recipients, as compared to the 'control group' who received ordinary unemployment benefits. Experiments in Netherlands also indicated a positive effect on recipients, with less educated people benefitting more.

Since 1982, the US state of Alaska is paying every citizen an unconditional dividend, largely out of revenues from the state's oil industry. The scheme did not have a significant employment effect. The Alaskan experiment has existed for 40 years. But Alaska can afford it due to its huge income from oil.

There were discussions on UBI in India as well. The Economic Survey of India for 2016-17 (Chapter 9) argues that serious consideration be given to the idea of a universal basic income as an effective way of achieving the objectives of the 'father of the nation,' Mahatma Gandhi, of "wiping every tear from every eye." It details the pros and cons of the idea. On the cost front, the survey said that the Indian central government ran about 950 central and centrally sponsored welfare schemes then. The financial burden on these existing welfare schemes aggregated to about 5 percent of nation's then GDP. The survey concludes with a positive remark "but on balance, he (Mahatma Gandhi) may have given the go-ahead to the UBI." However, no binding, final decisions have been taken so far on the proposal.

Financing Basic Income

Finding resources to fund a welfare measure like UBI has been a major problem with sovereign governments, mainly in developing and under developed countries.

UBI requires significant increases in taxation of the affluent segment or corporates. But there could be ways and means to raise the resources. In order to start the project, the government must estimate the likely annual expenditure first. It could be, say, five percent of national GDP [though the ILO study shows it to be between 2.3 to 5.5 percent]. The government can then create a budget and plan its allocation. The collection of revenues could be in various ways. A potential set of income sources could include the following:

1. A dedicated Tax or Cess could be levied on the super-rich towards their social responsibility. The identified segments could be from 1. Most profitable corporates working in the country, 2. All multinational firms that have a minimum predetermined number of customers in the country, and 3. High net-worth individuals (HNIs) in the country, with a wealth of more than a pre fixed level.

2. Part of inward remittances for charity / NGO funding could be targetted. Most developing and under developed nations get global donations from various individuals, charity organizations and corporates. A percentage of the same could be collected by the Central ministry towards UBI.

3. UBI can collect a share of profit after tax from all corporates and businesses who are making a profit of more than say, double of a benchmark rate. The benchmark could be the interest rate on a Government Bond for say, 10 years.

4. The governments can also stop almost all the existing welfare schemes and allocate the funds to UBI. This could possibly meet a major part of the expenditure envisaged.
5. Most critically, the governments must reduce their overall size and expenditure, by improving efficiencies and using state of the art technologies like artificial intelligence.
6. *Nations can and must reduce their defense expenses significantly by having better relations with other nations and by forging defense affiliations and peace agreements with neighbouring nations. A coordination council of nations must be formed by nations, with all their neighbouring states and with special invitees from United Nations. Such councils must identify, take up, and solve potential conflicts before they materialize and ensure peaceful co-existence of nations.* This strategy / policy shift can save a significant amount of expenses for a nation, which could be diverted to UBI.

Let us feed the needy, and bridle the greedy.

Chapter 8

MYTH OF MAHABALI

Mahabali, as per Hindu epics, was an 'asura' (devil) king. However, under Mahabali's rule, the epic says, his subjects lived in a state of perfect happiness. All the subjects of his kingdom were treated equally. The entire kingdom was peaceful and in complete communal harmony. People felt secure, and did not face any form of crime or physical violence. They cared for each other, and were free from all basic wants. They were even free from envy. The regime was so fair and just, that it was a sort of heaven on Earth. No king in the planet was able to rise to his level. This was made possible because Mahabali ruled his country in the fairest manner, which was a role model. The mythical story says that even the Gods were envious of his rule and wanted to eliminate him as they feared that people may not care for Gods, given their happy state of existence. Mahabali was finally eliminated by God himself, as per the epic, as he arguably had megalomaniac tendencies.

May be, the above epic story simply reflects a fundamental human desire to be happy. For achieving that, equality is the key, as one of the major reasons for unhappiness in any society is the natural human urge to compare oneself with others. The perception of a relatively lower, unequal status for self, is the major cause for human unhappiness. Absence of inequality creates the sense of a perfect society, a sense that is broadly agreed upon by all sections of people. In today's consumption-oriented world, where display of wealth, physical comforts, and material prosperity are seen as major drivers and determinants of a person's core identity, an equitable society looks like an unachievable, utopian dream.

The concept of a perfect society has become highly vague and uncertain for various reasons. What is considered good for a section of community, is not ideal for another as their value systems and benchmarks would be different. Their expectations from society in general and from other fellow human beings would be different. A magical, social reconstruction is warranted for a near-perfect society.

Far Away Rainbow

Equal economic opportunities and benefits have long been a dream of humanity since the dawn of civilization. But it has remained a hope, a wishful thinking, a far-away rainbow. Societies continue to be unequal in many spheres including political, economic, and social sectors. In the ancient era, inequality was not a disturbing social issue. With civilization, men became more aware of their social standing, and rights. Consequently, inequality started getting projected as a serious situation that distorts and destroys the social fabric. In the late 18th century Europe, socialist philosophers and communists envisioned models of a classless society, with assured education and employment. But equality of power, privilege and wealth remained far from ideal. Communities were expected to be empowered more, with States taking a back seat. But instead of weakening, the modern States have become all-powerful.

Human history does not show, at any point in the past, a high degree of equality. The very idea of equality is often described as meaningless. Recorded history tells the story of individuals and groups who benefitted by their place of birth or family of birth or simply from the location of, and timing of birth. Male members all over the world, were comparatively more privileged, for most part of human history, and even today. The common people who lived in the fifth century B.C. Athens, arguably had better freedom and few democratic rights. Slavery affected significant part of the world, and all those who were born slaves suffered, for no fault of theirs. Even today, those who are born into wealthy families and who inherit ancestral wealth, have better access to education, career opportunities and they enjoy relatively higher life expectancy. They wield more political and economic power than the rest of the population.

Inequality has many drivers. The non-material culture is lagging the material culture in almost all countries. In the material world, the increasing levels of inequality demand a fairer redistribution of income. An ageing population calls for higher spending for healthcare. Knowledge is the fulcrum on which the modern societies are revolving. Such a knowledge-based economy demands higher allocation for schools, colleges, and skill development. In a market driven economy, employment is the most critical element for economic freedom. And political freedom without economic freedom is in a way, useless. A moral sensibility must therefore drive governance, to make it humane, just, and sustainable.

Human needs are expansionary. They are neither constant nor limited. And our resources are, in comparison, limited. Thus, there is an imbalance inbuilt in meeting the human needs. Increasing productivity through technologies do meet a part of this additional requirement. We do not know how Mahabali maintained a welfare state. In the real world in which we live, smart politicians keep promising even highly unachievable goals. Hopes are generated just to win elections and grab power. Post elections, these unfulfilled promises become propaganda tools in the hands of opportunistic politicians on the opposite side. And the cycle of games goes on. Sometimes, the failures to achieve targets are converted into new opportunities by the ruling politicians. The unfulfilled employment targets are attributed to the presence of alien citizens in nations, and slogans are raised against all types of migrants. A cultural war starts. Marketed properly, these unjustified and immoral strategies many times pay off, as evidenced in many nations.

Economic inequality in the world has serious moral issues. It has been associated with a higher crime rate, lower overall economic growth, and a tendency of the market to go "from bubble to bubble." A recent study found that economic inequality also leads to higher unrest and even terrorism. In a world that is relentless, unsentimental, and highly competitive, bottom-of-the-pyramid citizens certainly deserve a protective government. Else, most nations will become unlivable for most of the population, in a set of challenging conditions with disorder becoming the order.

Inequalities in societies could be related to the inequalities in income distribution, or to political participation or to the sharing of other seats of authority. These broadly show distributive inequality, a situation where social goods and services are unequally distributed. Another form of inequality is the social inequality, where say, one is forced to get out of someone else's way merely because he or she belongs to a particular group or when a person is not allowed to draw drinking water from a common well. Social inequality keeps people in different classes, with groups divided based on their racial rankings, social status, and order of certain hierarchies finalized typically by the tribal heads or similar authorities. The persons perceived to be in the lower segment as per this categorization tend to lose their self-respect in the process. The Indian caste system was one such ghastly, in many ways cruel, system based on racial hierarchies, decided by birth. The slavery system that prevailed earlier, in old western world, was another.

A good or equal society may not necessarily mean that all persons get to buy the latest available set of gadgets or are able to travel to most exotic places. In any case, it is difficult to empirically prove that the needs of all men are similar. That could include factors and determinants like one's ethical and social values, need for individual autonomy, allocation of time for family, conformity to social norms, creation of more public space, etc. This could, however, possibly be achieved by man's greatest weapon of all times, reason. And this purification of mind and taming of ego by reason is a mental revolution in a way. It arguably leads one to the ascetic path where all are indeed equal.

In contrast to the ascetic world, the real, material society, with its changing politics and economic dynamics is always under disequilibrium. Inequality is a reality there. At a global level, in the 1960s and 70s, the developed countries were reportedly trending towards egalitarianism. But now the trend is clearly getting reversed and inequality is on the rise. One of the reasons identified is the spread of colonization of all public spaces by private entrepreneurs. Individuals are left to take care of themselves. People are at the mercy of profit maximizing private businessmen. Apparently, there is no faith in the collective human capacity for furthering common good and nation building.

There are other views on this as well. In 'The Myth of American Inequality' by Phil Gramm, Robert Ekelund and John Early, the authors observe that the current understanding of income inequality in USA is not correct, as the official statistics overstate inequality. They believe that income inequality is lower now than at any time in post - WWII USA.

Rich Growing Richer: By Design

Human history is full of incidents where a few appropriated the benefits of a change in society. All major revolutions like the agricultural, Industrial, informational, digital, etc., have benefitted a few disproportionately. Even the political revolutions have economically helped only a few, and have virtually bypassed most of the common people in most nations. The same trend is expected to continue in future as well, unless we take some bold initiatives.

Poverty, in many nations, is mainly due to structural issues rather than due to lack of individual efforts. As per the World Bank Report, 'Poverty and Shared Prosperity 2022: Correcting Course', the world's poorest people bore the steepest costs of the Covid-19 pandemic. Incomes in the poorest countries fell much more than incomes in rich countries during that period. The income losses of the world's poorest were twice as high as the world's richest, and global inequality rose for the first time in decades. The year 2020 marked a historic turning point in the sense that an era of global income convergence gave way to global income divergence. The poorest also suffered disproportionately in areas like health and education, with serious consequences. The economic recovery from the COVID-19 pandemic has been uneven. The richest economies recovered from the pandemic faster than low - and middle-income economies. By the end of 2022, as many as 685 million people were still living in extreme poverty. This makes 2022 the second-worst year (after 2020) for poverty reduction in the past two decades.

The World Economic Forum's (WEF) annual meeting in Davos is many times referred to as the conference of super rich. The billionaires of the world control nearly 14 per cent of the global gross domestic product (GDP) as per some reports, and have been prolific wealth creators. According to Oxfam International, the international non-profit organization, the top 10 richest persons in the world have more wealth than that of 3.1 billion people combined, or the total income of the bottom 40 per cent of humanity. Oxfam says that based on the analysis of wealth creation in the last two pandemic period years, it was found that every crisis that has struck this planet has hugely profited certain people, while hitting harder the already poor and pushing those in the margins to poverty trap. Gabriela Bucher, Executive Director of Oxfam International, said that the billionaires in fact convened in Davos to "celebrate an incredible surge in their fortunes." As per her, the pandemic and the steep increases in food and energy prices have been a bonanza for them. She was referring to the data from 'Profiting from Pain' report. In 24 months since the pandemic struck in 2020, the wealth of the world's billionaires increased more than the combined growth of nearly two preceding years. Some 573 new billionaires have been added in the last two years. Corporations in the energy, food and pharmaceutical sectors, the key sectors in which the world faced crises, recorded the maximum profits in their lifetimes. For the billionaires in the food and energy sectors, the two years, 2020 and 2021, have been great with a wealth increase of $1 billion every two days. The top five energy companies, BP, Shell, Total Energies, Exxon, and Chevron, made a profit of $2,600 every second as the world remained under lockdowns and extreme economic stress.

The pandemic also created many new 'pharma' billionaires. "Pharmaceutical corporations like Moderna and Pfizer were making $1,000 profit every second just from their monopoly control of the COVID-19 vaccine," said the report. At the same time, high food prices, health cost, loss of livelihood and the overall dip in earnings arguably pushed at least 263 million into poverty in 2022, "at a rate of a million people every 33 hours." Wages in the three sectors that profited the most did not increase. The burden of the crisis was felt by the poor. And, the billionaires' fortunes did not increase because they were more efficient or were working harder. The super-rich had apparently manipulated the system to reap the benefits. Inequality increased by design.

In another study, economists from the IMF and other institutions analysed 12 years of tax records from Norway, offering an understanding of how wealth evolves over time. Norway has a wealth tax system that requires assets to be reported to third parties to prevent errors. The data is made public and researchers were able to analyse them from 2004 to 2015. The data showed that the rich really did get richer, and it was mainly because they got higher returns on their investments. Norway is one of the richest countries in the world. Norway is also one of the most progressive countries in the world, with regards to taxation. The country even levies a 0.85% net wealth tax on a person's global wealth. The tax is levied on net wealth over a pre-fixed level. In-spite-of this wealth tax, the rich got richer. So, while the people generally were financially well-off, the data showed that most of the rich people tended to be richer down the line. If a person in the poorest 25% slab of the spectrum would have invested $1 in 2004, that investment would have grown, on an average, to $1.5 by 2015, giving a return of 50%. However, the same investment by someone in the top 0.1% would have grown to $2.4, thereby giving a far superior return of 140%.

There were other important findings as well. The people in the top of the wealth scale are not apparently dropping from the list of toppers. In other words, the top layer is in some manner economically protected and it is a sort of an elite club, membership of which is almost stable. It is difficult to get into it if one is starting as a laggard. The distance to be covered for an upwardly mobile person remains more-or-less same or it increases. Another interesting finding was that the wealthy status appeared to be persistent across generations. While the children of rich people continued to stay rich, they did not generally have as high a return on their money as their parents did. The conclusion drawn was that wealth is inheritable, but skill to build it are partly acquired. Property inheritance is still a reality, though arguably an unfair one.

These findings render the concepts like economic equality just a dream. Why does such difference in earnings happen? One argument advanced was that richer people can and do take additional risks on which they make higher returns. This argument does not have a universal acceptance. However, it is a fact that the rich and powerful have better access to both capital and technologies. They can buy up innovations. Another argument is that the top layer of society in all nations, including the wealthy business men, are always networked better and wider.

There are multi-layered political, financial, and cultural networks in societies. Most of them work together and some even work with their opponents in same segment. They also tend to select their networking members based on similar socio economic back ground, akin to the practice of 'arranged marriages' prevalent in India, where the caste and status conscious parents select partners for their children from similar social background. As a result, the power structure in society keeps the members of the network always insulated against possible risks while ensuring that their exclusive club members have access to key developments and policy decisions.

Researchers are proposing another reason as well. They believe that richer people are normally privy to special, high return ventures like private equity, or other private investment opportunities. Many of them can also use wealth managers like portfolio managers or family office advisors. Financial literacy, access to non-public information, critical business relationships, etc., are all significant factors where the high net-worth individuals and businesses have an edge. That is what tilts the table in their favour. The study also showed another surprising result, which was in line with what economists claimed. It proved that a wealth tax system may not stop the rich from getting richer, but they would increase their wealth at a slower pace. Thus, the taxation system appeared to be reducing the extreme levels of economic inequality.

Like richness, poverty is also an inherited trend. One born in a poor household would most probably end up being poor for a long period. Economist Lucas Chancel, lead author of the World Inequality Report 2022, spotted the inequality gap driver, by saying "50 per cent of the world's population does not have any assets to build up". The rich use the existing base of wealth, and the government policies support them in ensuring their access to businesses and profits. Most economic policies are focused on generating wealth irrespective of any distribution concern.

Inequality, in many ways is unexplainable and it tends to deepen during crises. The poor will hardly ever get the yearly earnings of the rich in their lifetime. Oxfam's calculation showed that it would take 112 years for a worker in the bottom 50 per cent to "earn what a person in the top 1 per cent gets in a single year". The wealth accretion and social inequalities arising out of it, are mostly determined by design.

What the Shadow Told

What did the shadow tell you? It must be something like "I do not take any orders from you." A critical question that arises is whether people can create their own future by hard work or using their imagination. This is like creating one's own shadow. It is yours, but its creation, shape and direction are all decided by external factors. Similarly, one's future is decided by many external factors including the 'unearned' privileges or disadvantages handed down by heritage. In such a scenario, societies have the responsibility to take care of those born under challenging conditions, for no fault of theirs. It is unfair to assume that they are destined to struggle themselves.

These concerns are even more serious when we consider the fact that the commercial rights on natural, national resources like minerals, coal, oil, etc., in many nations are not with their current or future generations. They have already been sold off to rich private entities by past governments at prices considered good by them then. The nation's future generations will have no rights on them. The playing level is highly unequal, to begin with.

Self-care is not without merits. But structural injustices based on flawed policies ruin the economies and lives of many. Modern societies that benefit from new inventions and technologies have common goals that can be achieved by working together and supporting each other, sharing knowledge, experiences, and skill sets. This is no more an option for humanity, but a dire necessity in an exploitative world. If all the nations retreat into the comfort of their own islands, it could be relatively less complex, but awfully sub optimal for the common prosperity of communities. Self-love does not take us too far. It may be remembered here that human progress made by us so far is due to the collective work of ethical and unethical groups and persons. The same is equally true in respect of man-made miseries. Societies must therefore try to have a relatively larger number of good people rather than bad ones, so that the Gresham's law (of bad coins driving out the good ones) does not get activated.

The median age of population in developing and underdeveloped countries are also rising. Some of them will become grey, with most of their population not even in middle-income category. So, the question of equality will remain out of their reach. Such higher levels of inequality, with no hopes to escape, can have serious political and social consequences that may undermine the social harmony on which the societies of these nations rest.

Killing the Joy of Living

Nations can learn few social lessons from countries where inequality is less. Inequality is generally less in those places mainly due to the absence of crony capitalism, limited interventions by non-value-additive middlemen, and minimal worker exploitation. The high levels of farmer and producer exploitation by middlemen and traders is one of the long-standing hurdles in reducing economic inequalities. Many believe that the growing inequality is primarily fueled by the twin factors of globalization and information revolution, developments that have divided the world's rich from the poor over the last few decades. In the past few centuries, there have been tremendous improvements in healthcare, education, communication, technology, etc. These benefits have, however, not reached all segments of societies due to a variety of reasons.

Human development in an ideal, fair society, would be a function of its values, attitudes, and the personality traits of its members. A fair society must have few common values, a sense of human dignity, a collective identity, and a shared understanding of cultural belonging. It should also ensure that the ownership of assets, including knowledge-based assets is not confined to a few elites. Here, it is debatable whether the extreme form of capitalism will lead to more equality or will create a socialistic society. Capitalism with large enough number of market players can eliminate monopolies, reducing the scope for abnormal profits for corporates. Thus, lesser consumer exploitation can be a possible, paradoxical future end-result of capitalism. But in the real world, smart businessmen ensure that such free competition does not take place in their segments.

The joy of living is constrained by increased fear, social conflicts, desperation, and uncertainty. Respect for other human beings is vanishing, while violence and inequality are increasing. Living with prosperity and dignity is becoming extremely difficult.

This is a post capitalist, post-communist society. The major and critical means of production today is neither capital nor labour. It is knowledge. Wealth is being created by innovations, driven by knowledge. Focus is on productivity of knowledge. The future social challenges, therefore, must include protection of the dignity of those who are less educated and less skilled.

Socialism with a human face is a favourite agenda, but these ideas are considered by many as unworkable. We need economically viable, implementable ideas that promote equality and social welfare. We must modify the attitudes and approaches of individuals and corporates as well, with the objective of creating better welfare societies.

Modern Mahabalis

Mahabali, the above-mentioned king, was liked by all his subjects and he had an open 'Darbar' or court. Politicians in modern democracies use social media platforms in place of 'Darbars' to maintain a symbolic presence in the lives of their constituents, equaling that achieved by autocratic rulers. Many times, there is a power gap between rulers and power-subjects.

The Greek historians describe the reign of King Deiokes (Deioces), who established the Median Empire in modern-day Iran in the eighth century B.C. After his coronation, Deiokes instituted a court ceremonial that created a distance. Except his closest confidants, no one was allowed to enter the king's throne room. State affairs were handled by messengers, and Deiokes himself disappeared completely from public view. The argument for isolation was that subjects would regard and revere a king as a special creature, if they did not see him. The court ceremonial was used by the king for self-presentation as a superhuman. The ruled had no opportunity to perceive him as a flesh-and-blood person with ailments, signs of aging, lack of knowledge, physical inadequacies, etc. They had only a remote, faceless abstract image, on which to project their own hopes, desires, and ideals.

Leaders in some countries tend to replicate this model even today, by keeping away from the public or by not exposing themselves to closer scrutiny by media and public. Equality among subjects is just not an issue with such 'kingly' leaders. It may be remembered here that the stories narrated to common men in the ancient days were of powerful kings and their victories. Gods often sided with these kings in those stories.

Rulers use another type of strategy to maintain inequality among subjects. This is primarily aimed at preserving and enhancing the image of a charismatic ruler. The tool used for the purpose is illiteracy, forced or otherwise, of major sections of society. This was arguably used by South African leaders during the apartheid regime. Taliban in Afghanistan is not allowing women to get educated. In ancient India, for a very long time, lower castes were denied education.

The themes running are similar and the signals are clear. Common people do not matter. The hidden agenda is to keep people away from information and knowledge that can help them understand the power structure which may then lead someone someday to question the rights of hierarchy. Many leaders deliberately brand themselves as 'Semi-Gods' and promote the culture of hero worship. The followers are expected to bask in the reflected glory of their unfailing leader.

Subjects' attention can also be diverted from the core issue of equality by other means. One such strategy is indoctrination of the subjects using the culture of remembrance. History is never a settled place. It is always disputed, and continues to be re-written by those who are victorious and continue to be in power. Therefore, the history of a nation remains unfinished always, and is under potential reconstruction by those in power at any given point of time. Objective history does not exist and the concept itself is a misnomer. History gets newer narratives and interpretations all the time. Anyone in power with the authority to interpret the past of a nation can narrate it the way it suits his agenda. He can create imaginary heroes, or enemies, or events, with a view to further his political ideas. The unsuspecting, illiterate masses could be effectively mobilized using the new narratives and stories. A ruler can also lead his masses to a war based on the newly created narratives.

Diversionary tactics can be successful if the whole nation is driven to collective memories. It is tough to build or maintain a culture of remembrance in nations that are collections of strangers. An average Indian, for instance, may not know more than a thousand other Indians close enough, in a country of 1,420 million population. The situation would not be different in other nation states. However, the political narratives can incorporate the history of a whole nation, to create a common set of images. Such histories of the communities can then be conveyed to living members through various historic documents relating to past wars, freedom struggles, national heroes, literature, art, philosophies, etc., and using objects like ancient buildings, sculptures, and architecture. It allows the community to be conceived as an ongoing project uniting generations and centuries, whose values and traditions are transferred to the present living members.

An illusory equality is sometimes created by smart politicians by invoking common heritages like 'nationalism.' Collective memory can be directed at reinforcing nationalism, by continuous interpretations of past testimonies, and cultural traditions. These will remind the current generation of their moral obligations to the ancestors, of historical guilts, of past achievements, and generally regenerate nationalistic feelings. When nationalism becomes the only or main organizing principle of a nation, it can lead to increased violence. Charles Tilly and Michael Mann offer a systematic account of the role of war in creation of modern nation states[15]. Both wars and states are mutually re-enforcing, according to Tilly. His dictum is "war made states and states made war." As per historians, the concept of a state focussed on territorial consolidation and related obsession with nationalism led to many wars in Europe prior to World War 1. It is believed that more people died in the first half of 20th century due to wars induced by nationalism.

In order to recreate a kingdom today, somewhat comparable to Mahabali's, a nation must be clear about the notion of who its stakeholders are, what their genuine needs are, and what kind of valid expectations are there, from a welfare state that is being planned.

The state's governing policies cannot be focussed on welfare of a few chosen segments of the society or on political score settling. Nor should they be used for brand building of rulers or brand demolition of opponents. In order to replicate a kingdom of Mahabali, a society needs to be progressive in terms of its approach to human dignity. It must ensure that economic systems are embedded in society in such a manner that it improves the quality of life of all its members. Using the past to glorify the present can be a regressive practice. Instead, the lessons from past can be used to guide present generations and to illuminate the dark areas.

In this globalized world, nations must ensure that their governance structures and rules are fair to all players. An awareness of human rights in the process may drive up labor cost, which must be accepted as a sign of social progress. Multinationals cannot as a rule, get away with relaxed norms in terms of applicability of income tax, labour regulations, etc. Financial activities that do not contribute much to real economic activity must be controlled. Hugely speculative financial transactions must be discouraged by way of higher taxes. Offshore tax centres must be removed altogether or brought under taxable regulations so that more money flows to regulated, real economic activities.

Back to 'Chathur Varna' (Four Castes)

During the Vedic Period (c. 1500-1000 BCE) Indian citizens were categorized according to their 'varna' or caste. 'Varna' was strictly based on the hereditary roots of a new born. There were four principal castes. They were Brahmins (priests, gurus, etc.), Kshatriyas (warriors, kings, administrators, etc.), Vaishyas (agriculturalists, traders, etc.), and Shudras (labourers). Each caste had specific rights attached to it and specific duties and functions. As a result, the social order remained highly predictable for many centuries. One's status in community, culture, job opportunities, likely future, all were decided by a single factor of his or her birth. Under that system, symbolically speaking, a person was not allowed to sing even with best of talents. The Varna system has been detailed in '*Manu Smriti*' (an ancient legal text from the Vedic Period), and other '*Dharma Shastras.*'

The caste system was arguably created to preserve the purity of each caste, and establish a social order. A Brahmin was highest in the social hierarchy, followed by Kshatriya, then Vaishya, with Shudra at the lowest level. The system allocated specific tasks to all designated 'varna' categories. There were some later day reinterpretations and clarifications that put conditionalities of proper deed instead of birth for inclusion in these categorisations as 'add-ons.' However, in real situations, most people were boxed in separate caste brackets based on their birth. Shudras were at the lowest level in society socially, economically, and politically. They were in a way, the most physically hard working, and productive people. The idea propagated behind the caste system was that such an orderly system in a society would lead to all round happiness, appropriate levels of freedom, peaceful co-existence, adherence to law, etc. It was also emphasised that adhering to Varna duties or performing one's '*karma*' would lead to the attainment of 'Moksha' (salvation). As per the '*Vedas*,' only the ones who follow their duties as per their varna could get freedom from rebirths and deaths. Performing inappropriate life responsibilities by any varna would invite the wrath of Gods. Thus, the caste system, with the help of religion, created divine incentives and penalties to keep it firmly in place.

The current world is apparently recreating a global caste system, in economic and social terms. We have four different categories of people in almost all countries, who are performing duties that are more-or-less stratified. We have the 'Kshatriyas' or Kings or Rulers in various designations (form of government does not matter) at the top, followed by 'Brahmins' or Priests or Religious Heads who play critical advisory role in many countries. Then comes the 'Vaishyas' or business men, who are rich and highly powerful, and at the very bottom, the largest number of 'Shudras' or people who are labourers and ordinary workers, who get least respect in society.

Varna Based Taxes

One more application of the principles of 'Chathur Varna' is visible in the global tax collection method. An efficient tax collection system, presupposes elimination of, or effective control on, tax evasion. Such a system is critical for reduction in inequality. But there is a serious issue with the system now. It is widely known that huge multinational corporates typically pay very low tax on their global income. An average billionaire also pays tax at lower rates, while for the common man, the rates are much higher. Addressing tax evasion is a difficult task, as there is a virtual competition to facilitate and even promote tax evasion in various places globally, using structures that legally allow tax avoidance by individuals and multinational corporates. This is done by creating and maintaining shell companies in so called tax havens. Some countries also allow dual citizenships which make tracking of an individual's income almost impossible, thereby indirectly helping avoid payment of due taxes.

Countries that lose tax incomes in the process have not been able to stop this phenomenon. There is no global agreement on how to address this. Governments across the globe lose billions of dollars of tax revenue every year due to these smart financial structures set up by large corporates and ultra-high net worth individuals in tax havens. Most governments are reluctant to formally publish the information on corporates using tax havens.

There is an argument that the jurisdictions with lower income tax rates cannot increase their tax rates as their very economic survival depends on large number of these entities operating out of their locations. But such locations or territories cannot be allowed prosper by unethical means and at the cost of other nations. In a technologically enabled world, tracking and tackling big corporate tax evaders should not be a serious problem, if major nations are willing. In the recent past, governments got reasonable success in tracking terrorism funding. So, tracking tax haven related transactions may not be too difficult, if countries have a common objective and they sincerely, collectively go for it.

Here we revisit 'Chathur Varna' system. There were well planned and recorded economic concepts and doctrines in ancient India. The Hindu *Vedas, Upanishads, Dharma Shastras, Neeti Shastras, Smrities, Epics* and similar books have glimpses of socio-economic policies. The most celebrated and arguably the first systematic set of economic policies written in the 4th century BC, is in Kautilya's *'Arthsasthra.'* Kautilya, also known as Chanakya, was the minister of Chandra Gupta Maurya. *'Arthsasthra'* was written for streamlining economic and financial administration of Chandra Gupta Maurya (Maurya Dynasty).

In the document, Kautilya advised that those who perform sacrifices, the spiritual masters, priests, and others well - versed in Vedas shall be granted lands, yielding sufficient produce. They were then considered productive on account of their land ownership, and it was suggested that as productive people, they should be exempted from taxation and fines. This is exactly what is happening now. In the name of productivity, business firms are protected, they are given land either free or at subsidized price, and their incomes are either not taxed at all or taxed less.

The rich and powerful do not and need not pay tax, again. We are going back to the millennia old 'Chathur Varna,' globally.

Mahabalis Do Not Speculate

Governments are fully aware that speculative transactions are not productive for the real economy. They help in creating liquidity for sure. Some transactions are also used for hedging. Generally, they are not very helpful for a nation or its people. But, these transactions, supported by 'noise,' multiply and magnify the wealth of speculators.

Speculations as above are mostly based on fear and greed. Governments should not encourage them. Instead, they must have policies in place that promote real investments. Unfortunately, many governments themselves are players in the speculative markets today.

One policy which many governments had earlier, was the concept of investment allowance or tax deductions for investments made in real economy. Such policies can be brought back. Again, like in the case of tax havens, these policies must be coordinated between major countries. Else, capital can fly to least regulated, unknown regions and multiply with minimal taxes.

Let there be many, benevolent Mahabalis.

Chapter 9

<u>MYTH OF SELF RULE</u>

As per Margaret Thatcher, the former British Prime Minister, there is no such thing as a society. Only individual matters. The ascetic Indian religious teacher, Siddartha Gautama, known as 'Buddha,' born around two thousand five hundred years ago (567 BCE?), thought otherwise. He was probably the first thinker to stress on community living, based on his *'sangham saranam gachhami* (group, the protector) philosophy. He believed that community's problems can be solved only by the reasoning ability of related groups. Self-correcting groups are the best options for a society. Add to that the concept of critical scientific thought and you get a society that can take on the world more efficiently.

Democracy, in a way, could be considered as a system based on a logical extension or formalization of the self-managing, self-correcting groups as above, on a national basis. But over a period, it is observed that democracy or self-rule has become a myth, created by and for the rulers, in different forms and formats. Democratic governments are legally engaged in self-rule, but many have become too powerful, with citizens being rendered helpless and powerless. In few countries, the fear today is not only of big businesses, but also of insensitive, powerful governments who try to control people. Governments can, and many do, track actions, movements and associations of its subjects using state of the art technologies. The image of a modern government is becoming one of an 'octopus,' with its tenacles reaching out to unsuspecting citizens.

Some elected governments believe that they must use force to effectively rule. According to them, it is impossible to rule without creating fear or using lethal weapons, or without a big army or a massive police force. Governments are therefore continuously upgrading their security and policing services with latest ammunitions, to address potential external and internal aggressions. This is in addition to the enforcement of newer, stronger laws and tighter controls on the population.

Delusion of Self-Rule

Democracy exists at two basic levels. One is the political reality of what exists, and the other, at the aspirational level, where the people want it to be at. The second level keeps changing, with changes in possibilities and expectations. Major gaps in these two levels can result in what could be called a crisis of legitimacy or a delusion of self-rule. Such a situation was anticipated by the English Philosopher Thomas Hobbes (1588-1679). His main concern was as to how human beings can live together in peace and avoid the danger and fear of civil conflicts. The alternative is to accept an unaccountable sovereign power, in the form of a person or group empowered to decide on every social and political issue. In the absence of such a 'compromise,' we are all in for civil wars. This idea was later developed by John Locke, David Hume, and Immanuel Kant.

Democracy is all about self-rule. But we have a complex, opaque, and interpretive world, and we interpret events and ideas with partial or no understanding of relevant or underlying factors. Good governance is when the ruled have the power to challenge elites and authorities, using independent institutions, without any fear. Question is whether the modern self-rule systems allow such effective interventions.

The efficacy of democracy is different across nations. According to The Economist Intelligence Unit (EIU), democracy is at its lowest position in 2023, since the Democracy Index's inception in 2006. As per EIU's annual survey on democracy in 167 countries based on five criteria - electoral processes and pluralism, government functioning, political participation, democratic political culture, and civil liberties, more than a third of the world's population is subject to authoritarian rule, while only 6.4% enjoy full democracy.

Self-rule becomes a selfish rule, when there are special interest groups, especially majoritarian ones. Members of these groups often vote keeping in mind the groups' vested interests, which in turn could be based on their religion, race, or culture. When such groups become successful, there is a virtual 'race to the bottom' by all shades of political parties. These trends are indeed against the common good. Nations deserve a neutral rule.

Added to these is the sad fact that a vast majority of voters do not understand or discuss critical issues or social priorities. In many situations, truth is mostly hidden from public. For example, underfunding of social security systems including pensions, and their likely longer-term repercussions are hardly discussed openly by politicians, in order not to create panic or unrest among people. Political class is, in any case, unaccountable, even with their misplaced priorities. Depending on the commonly perceived trends and narratives, the social pendulum in a nation keeps swinging and it is never resting.

Chaotic Societies

Political systems are generally not just imperfect, but hugely chaotic. All members of a society, as citizen stake holders, get affected by the uncertain and many times unreliable words and actions of politicians. Political power under a democracy is expected to be used to achieve certain social and economic goals that are beneficial to the society. It is however, difficult to discern political facts from political fictions. Hardly does the common man understand the nature and intricacies of political games. In such an environment, the transition from tribal chiefs to modern day politicians would not have been an easy one. The structure of societies into governable models must have been achieved by trial and error with the use of might, right, invocation of divine powers, etc. The space is unsettled, and the process in still on.

Self-Rule under democracy is a process involving large segments of population with unpredictable behaviour, and relational dynamics. Societies, made up of different classes of people, have conflicting interests, moral positions, and beliefs, including social, personal, commercial, financial, political, and religious interests, to name a few. Societies are also being pulled in different directions by different players including but not limited to politicians, corporates, workers, unions, media, power brokers, activists, spiritual leaders, speculators, special interest groups, etc. Many of these groups simply try to prosper at the cost of others.

Political institutions are required to take care of the interests of different individuals and groups while taking decisions that affect the entire society. They have a tough job of balancing the interests of these conflicting classes, while ensuring an overall fairness in governance, which in turn must be value-based, and reflected in their policy priorities. At the same time, party politics many times include leaders who consider power and prestige as values that are to be merely enjoyed, for its own stake. This phenomenon creates a breed of political activists who are in the field just to enjoy these values, at the cost of broader society, rendering good governance even tougher.

A perfect democracy needs certain basic requirements like a functioning multiparty political system, a competitive environment, free and fair elections, an open state that respects the laws, peaceful power transfers, autonomous media, respect for civil liberties, and political rights for every citizen. These rights and privileges must be available to all citizens regardless of his or her status as a member of any majority or a minority segment.

The ground reports on democracy are not very promising. Apparently, voters have become disinterested in election participation. As per Pew Research centre, 57% of independent countries were democratic in 2017. But political participation is getting weakened in these nations. The Institute for Democracy and Electoral Assistance (IDEA) reports that voter turnout has been declining from 1990s. Despite the increase in both global voter population and the number of countries that hold elections, the global average voter turnout has decreased significantly since the early 1990s, as per IDEA. The global voter turnout was relatively stable between the 1940s and the 1980s, falling from 78 per cent to 76 per cent over the period. Thereafter it fell sharply in the 1990s to 70 per cent, and then to 66 per cent in the period of 2011–15. Clearly there is a voter fatigue.

One major factor responsible for this situation is the below par economic growth. Many democracies are facing the wrath of people whose economic conditions are worsening. The ordinary voter is rendered powerless in policy domain, and is treated as a weak and ignorant person to tackle his or her problems. Politicians create fear in them and then fear-sanitize them by rhetoric and occasional handouts.

Another disturbing issue is that of minorities and aboriginals. The identity of a person in nations, particularly in nations with long histories, is traditionally ascribed by the social class to which he or she belonged. Though this structural identity is getting changed, the pace is painfully slow. A case in point is the 'lost' space for aboriginals, which is an issue in nations like Canada, New Zealand, Australia, India, etc. According to the 2011 census, tribals or 'Adivasis' constituted 8.6 per cent (about 104 million) of India's total population. They predominantly live in or around forests and the concepts of modern societies like neo-liberalism, globalization, private property rights, etc., are alien to them. Their identity is linked to their habitat, traditions, culture, and ethos. The Adivasi community is casteless and classless. This is a marginalized class, and they remain way behind the main stream in terms of economic growth, educational levels and health care spend. Adivasis have constitutional, legal, and traditional rights, including the right for self-determination. But millions of them have been displaced due to modern development projects.

There were attempts by all major religious groups and reformers to 'civilize' the tribes in India, by assimilating them into their respective religions. Some of them even provided financial support for the purpose of assimilating the tribesmen into their community, which was described by others as forced conversion. The situation continues to be sensitive.

Trust Deficit

Democracy is a system that must be used for solving the human, collective, national, and global level problems. It is expected to focus on institutions that ensure rights like freedom of choice, expression, etc. But there are many doubts on the efficacy and utility of democracy as a system, world over. The trust in democratic institutions and national governments is decreasing, in line with the reduced level of commitments to these institutions. Though more than half of world has embraced democracy, there is a democratic 'frustration' in a way. The democratic meaning itself, and its' very objectives are being questioned in some cases. Many doubt whether, over the years, the nations' democratic values got strengthened or became weaker.

Some societies have become virtually ungovernable with ever expanding list of aspirations of the citizens on the one hand and the burgeoning debt of governments on the other hand. The proliferation of civil society with non-governmental organizations, sometimes called as the 'third sector' (after the Government and Market Sectors) are creating more hurdles in nations' natural progress. And there is a strong argument supporting public sector, based on the widely held expectation that it fulfils a whole host of societal aspirations that only government agencies can fulfil. These relate to areas where private market is unwilling to enter in any meaningful manner.

There are serious democratic gaps in nations and some of the major ones include the following:

Divergent Systems: Democratic processes, globally, use different election systems. There are majoritarian, proportional, mixed, and multi-tier electoral systems, to name a few. In addition, there are single-member district plurality (SMDP) systems, single transferable vote (STV) systems, single nontransferable voting (SNTV) systems, block votes (BV), limited votes (LV), etc. Some of these have further sub variations. Under majoritarian system, for example, the candidates or parties that receive the most votes win. However, a winning candidate is required to obtain an absolute majority of votes in some of its variations, whereas other variations require the candidate or party to win more votes than anyone else. The rationale of Proportional Representative system is to reduce the disparity between a party's share of the national vote and its share of the parliamentary seats. Single Transferable Vote, where voters rank-order candidates in multi-member districts, is a popular proportional system.

Under mixed systems, voters elect representatives through two different systems, one majoritarian and one proportional. There is a party block vote (PBV) system where a party with the most votes wins all the district seats (winner takes all). Under the absolute majority systems, the alternative vote (AV) is a preferential voting system. Two round systems (TRS), are where candidates or parties get elected in the first round if they obtain a specified level of votes, like an absolute majority. If no one obtains this level of votes, then a second round of elections takes place. In a majority-runoff TRS, the top two vote winners go through to the second round, where whoever wins the most votes is elected. In a majority-plurality TRS, all candidates who over-come some preordained threshold go through to the second round, where whoever wins the most votes, irrespective of absolute majority, is elected.

In addition to these variations, there are presidential (American) systems and parliament (British) systems of democracy. The tenures of elected representatives also differ in different systems. It is debatable whether the once-in-few-years franchise is appropriate. A permanent monitoring of politicians' performance is desired by many, along with a right to recall.

While all these systems have their merits and demerits, the diversity confirms a lack of consensus on the very approach to elections. It displays absence of agreement or acceptability of logics applied on various processes, thereby questioning the concept itself, in a way.

Hybrid or Flawed Democracies: Once in power, some elected governments use the mandate to suppress people. Political voice is a right for all adults in democracies, but many nations have curtailed civil liberties and have turned self-righteous, authoritarian regimes. These nations are called 'hybrid' democracies, where electoral frauds regularly happen, preventing free and fair elections. They have power centres that oppress differing voices and political opponents. They weaken the independence of media and judiciaries. They promote non-transparency in critical government policy decisions affecting common man. Hybrid democracies combine autocratic and democratic features and are not open societies.

Democratic nations also get converted to hybrid democracies or autocracies when they are taken over by extreme elements and rebels, including military leaders, via coups, with or without the help of foreign powers.

Unfair Processes: Many election processes, globally, are manipulated. Rigging of elections, exclusion of eligible voters from lists, booth capturing, etc., happen regularly in certain democracies. In the modern age, technology aided manipulations relating to elections are also increasing. In addition, there are alleged external influences in the election processes of weaker democracies, where the foreign forces are accused of trying to install puppet governments.

One of the primary requirements for the functioning of democracy in a nation is the exercise of well informed, rational decisions by enlightened citizens. Many politicians try to influence voters by way of misinformation using media, especially social media. Another, common unfair practice is promising monetary rewards, loan waivers, etc. just prior to elections, to influence voters.

Majority Domination: There are interested groups in any society. One of the reasons why democratic fatigue is increasing in some nations, is the prevalence and continuation of identity-based politics. These could be personality based or group based. Religion based, race based or caste-based politics is quite common in democracies. These elements try to capture power using the sheer strength of their number, in order to promote their group welfare, at the cost of others. This trend is also considered as a form of tribalism, where the interests of groups identified based on identities like languages, religion, race, ethnicity, etc., are foremost in the minds of politicians.

These political mobilizations are detrimental to the society in general and can lead to two major uneasy situations. One situation is where a particular group becomes too dominant. Minorities are then at the mercy of brutal majority, which is not a desirable situation. The second scenario is the mushrooming of too many groups based on any conceivable identities like language, race, caste, ethnicity, etc. Such warring groups can create perpetual conflicts in a nation. Their democratic rights can become too hot for any government to handle. Or it can lead to clientelism, where the party in power cares more for the groups affiliated with it. In all cases, the pressures exerted by different interest groups can weaken the core principles of democracy. They can also put hurdles on policy initiatives targetted to benefit the entire population.

Corporate Funding: Big corporates have a decisive say in policies and programmes in most nations. The unholy nexus between businesses and politicians in democracies is well documented. The role of money in elections has become too overwhelming. Unlike kings or autocrats, the politicians under democracies need to win elections, which warrants huge spending of money. Funding, especially from corporates, is therefore critical for current day political parties and it is natural to expect a quid pro quo arrangement between the winners and funders, post elections.

Corporates get awarded major government contracts, mining rights, access to other natural resources, etc., involving negotiations that are many times not very transparent. No government is fully transparent or autonomous in the policy sphere, as there are pressures from corporates both within and outside the country. In addition, there are geopolitical pressures, and influences from international affiliations, military pacts, strategic tie ups, cultural-religious groups, etc., which dilute the power of rulers.

One of the ways to deal with such a situation is to open-up the governance system more, for ideas from public, including critical ones. In such an environment, abuse of power would be limited, for fear of public criticism. More and relevant disclosures on donations and donors must be made mandatory. The disclosures must cover details like the corporates' names, business segments, names of promoters, their relations with elected representatives, etc. And these disclosures must be on an on-going basis in the sense that whenever a new government project is awarded to them, the details thereof must be disclosed within a stipulated time.

Domination of Markets: Markets are the most dominant part of human lives today, with neoliberalism and globalization driving new relationships and forms of control. The market domination as opposed to public or social partnerships, and its focus on profitability as opposed to social welfare, etc., are major dividers in societies. The development of market economy contributed to the spread of democracy in the earlier decades. But politics has become very much a part of this domination and it has started affecting democratic processes adversely. Individualism, an offshoot of market domination, is increasing and people in general, are moving away from collective welfare to personal or related group welfare. This increased focus on market makes politicians thrive for individual power and personal wealth, and in the process, the national welfare takes a back seat.

The corporate media houses have their own domination. Big media players like news channels, and even social media players are major political players in a way, in democracies. They interpret events, guide, and many times misguide the viewers and readers. They directly or indirectly help create politically sensitive, biased news. Unbiased public discussions on policies are vanishing. Most discussions in the media are biased, depending on the affiliations of the corporates who run the media. The discussions, in any case, are ending up as blame games. Constructive dialogues are rarely seen in national or social media. The signals are clear. Media is targeting the 'faceless' people, whose views simply do not matter. Add to that the level of political illiteracy of common man in a nation, and we have a recipe for social disaster.

Global Institutions: Supra national institutions have significant influences on domestic democratic institutions. International entities typically partner with domestic NGOs, CSOs (Civil Society Organizations) and other firms, who in turn influence elections. Some nations use the concept of hyper sovereignty to stop NGOs from receiving donations. Such a policy has both advantages and disadvantages. On the negative side, foreign entities and institutions can interfere in the internal affairs of a nation and promote change regimes, leading to creation of puppet governments. This can also lead to resource extractions by their affiliated foreign business entities in some cases. On the other hand, denial of help from benevolent foreign entities can dry up the much-needed humanitarian help in weaker nations. In rare cases, such benevolent institutions and entities can also be instrumental in removing highly authoritarian rulers, a positive, though controversial, outcome.

Dataveillance: An efficient, state-of-the-art tool used by modern governments is the surveillance technology, for tracking, collecting, and analyzing relevant information about individuals and organizations. In domestic areas, surveillance technology, in the words of the sociologist James B. Rule, acts as a "means of knowing when rules are obeyed, when they are broken and most importantly, who is responsible for which."

These tools can support a nation's key strategic and tactical actions to safeguard its security. At the same time, with the increasing integration of societies into social networks, these technologies can also help political leadership to control the unsuspecting masses. Data colonization, especially the legally enabled and authorized data collection by sovereign governments, allows the power centres to access personal and confidential data of citizens without their knowledge, and control them or scare them in many ways. This is called 'dataveillance,' which essentially involves the storage, algorithm-based analysis, and use of digitized data. This is an area of great concern in a democracy, as the practice can potentially cover members of opposition parties, critics, judiciary, media etc., and can therefore be a highly regressive social development. It can lead to totalitarian approaches by the ruling elites, with tracking and brain washing of innocent people. Self-rule can be a real myth under such conditions.

Many believe that this development is the beginning of a new era of government surveillance on its subjects, in countries including the democratic ones. Today, most governments use big data analytics as a strategic tool not just to address their external threats, but also to target internal dissidents and political opponents.

Others: There are a whole lot of other irritants as well in democracies, including immigration, politicians forming strange and unworkable coalitions leading to policy paralysis, etc. Dynasty rule and identity politics have become significant components of the democratic processes in many nations. Nationalism, associated with a nation's imaginary or real unique set of history, heroes, cultures, etc., is another game politicians have started playing now.

All About Power

Nations are being governed by power-based, rather than responsibility-based governments. Since politicians are in an advantageous position to allocate resources and even dictate social values, this is a dangerous trend. Misallocations and leakages can create wealth loss for societies and nations. The political decisions are typically back tested after generations by when many factors would have changed. Hence, fixing responsibility for a bad political decision is virtually impossible.

Power is not easily amenable to a proper definition and therefore there are no agreed upon definitions for the same. Max Weber (1864

- 1920), in his posthumously published standard work *Economy and Society*, classified power[16] as 'sociologically amorphous', i.e., without any shape, structure or form. Power is a social status and one of its characteristics is that in human hands, it tends to expand all the time and in all directions. Power enjoyed by a ruler is sometimes perceived to be proportional to the degree of brutality that is applied by the ruler on his subjects. Based on such perception, it is often believed that softer forms of leadership are neither respected, nor feared by the subjects.

Aristotle felt that democracy is the degenerate form of republican government, in which the numerical majority's unfettered power breaks down the limits imposed by constitutional government (The Politics, Book V). The probability of misuse of power by a government is directly proportionate to the degree of power that government exercises. There are non-material powers as well. Moral power is one of them.

An expanding power structure tends to become stronger and stronger, impacting freedom and vice versa. A power wielding person nearby is a potential threat to one's freedom. In an economic sense, one of the ways to measure the degree of power of a government is to measure its spending ability. Spending, as a percentage of GDP, is the proxy applied for it. Another measure of economic power is the level of government ownership in assets and businesses. In the words of Max Weber, "power is the probability that one actor within a social relationship will be in a position to carry out his own will despite resistance, regardless of the basis upon which this probability rests." This shows the likely power relation between a ruler and the power-object.

Weberian model suggests both the possibility of resistance and the over ruling of such resistance by an adamant ruler. Power, as per Foucault, is everywhere, "not because it has the privilege of consolidating everything under its invincible unity, but because it is produced from one moment to the next, at every point, or rather in every relation from one point to another. Power is everywhere; not because it embraces everything, but because it comes from everywhere."

The real freedom people have, depends on the degree and level of non-interferences by the powerful on issues that are considered more valuable, material, and critical. The materiality of the issue is a highly debatable one, though. Power distribution in a society is critical. Changes in these distributions must be oriented towards lower level of inequality, increased levels of liberty and overall betterment of maximum number of people in the society. Cultural and social elements belonging to the majority groups can otherwise silence the marginalized minority. Citizenry, as responsible social players, must not only respect the democratic norms and the institutional framework, but also be active players in the processes that make them work. This should be achieved by ensuring social harmony, and without falling prey to the tyranny of any class of majority, be it in terms of gender, language, caste, or religion. People need to be careful in selecting social movements as well. Only those movements should be pursued which do not disturb the peaceful community development.

How do we bridle the misuse of political power? Democracies are based on efficient working of certain critical institutions. These institutions are expected to work fairly and ethically. Such functioning of the institutions would exercise control over unwarranted interferences by powers that be and thereby create confidence in the democratic processes. If any of these processes in the chain go weak or if any of the players in the process become untrustworthy, such trust can get shattered totally or get diminished to an unacceptable level.

The society must also have a good set of values as a decline in values can generate mistrust. If people are less committed in their relationships and jobs, or if politicians are less committed to voters or society in general, we have a serious problem.

Political Mobilizations

An important political power enhancing mechanism is related to the political opportunity theory. Political opportunity structure theory analyzes the causes of political effectiveness of protests. The central theme of the theory is about the vulnerability of political systems to mobilizations. 'Contentious politics' is the name of the game and as per Tilly and Tarrow [2006], contentious politics becomes a social movement only in the presence of six indicators. They are 1. A plurality of independent political centres. 2. An open political system for new entrants. 3. Unstable alliances. 4. Availability of support for claims originating outside the system. 5. A level of repression that is not too high, and 6. Decisive changes provoked by earlier cycles of mobilization.

The above indicators are present in most of the modern democratic nations, thereby inviting political mobilizations of all sorts. And, these social movements impact political structures and social welfare in all such nations. However, in countries with higher levels of uneducated poor, the ordinary people really may not know what their social roles and responsibilities are, and what policy options are collectively best for them. Therefore, the social movements in those places could be driven by interested groups including business lobbying groups, religious activists, caste-based groups, protagonists of a particular language or unique culture, etc., among others. Most of these groups also use such movements to exert pressure on power centres so that government resources are allocated to areas of their preference. Some of these groups later get formally or informally co-opted to the political system and they share political power. Over the years, we have ended up in a sad situation as Thucydides said (*The Melian Dialogue),* "The strong do what they have the power to do and the weak accept what they have to accept." Are we moving collectively towards accepting the idea of fatalism?

The relationship between social movements and the state not only alters the structure of political opportunities, but also affects many other related areas as well. For example, in the Nineteenth and the Twentieth centuries, the common relationship among individuals was primarily organized around the state and capital.

With democratic set ups, awareness and growth of citizen rights, growth of political parties, and institutionalization of social conflicts, social movements have become essential part of politics. The boundaries between institutionalized and non-institutionalized politics have become permeable. The national political players, with collective interests and network, are the most critical determinants in this whole game.

There is a sort of Pygmalion effect (or the Rosenthal effect) in national politics, which supports the political opportunity theory. Politicians have typically under delivered on their promises in most democratic countries where they are answerable to voters. Due to this, people have lost faith in proclamations and promises of politicians.

Many nations are considered choiceless with political parties turning out to be less committed to people and their welfare. But these low levels of trust and expectations created by the rhetoric-focussed politicians, are happy hunting grounds for new social movements. Mirages are created and allowed to fail in succession. Activists turned politicians are reinforcing the doomsday predictors, elections after elections.

Democracy is all about choice. But when change in rulers do not result in desired policy shifts or plan priorities, citizens become choiceless. The situation can be partly rectified by way of swing voters, who are expected to vote based on performance, rather than blindly voting for parties irrespective of their demonstrated performances. However, it is a complicated situation as in this post-modern era, economic, political, and cultural values are all increasingly inter connected and overlapping.

Tainted Information

In every society there would be people who tend to seek and accumulate knowledge of various sorts. They typically improve upon the received wisdom, record their findings, and preserve them for the future generations as their contribution to human kind. These trends are now changing. They are conspicuously absent in the economic fields in most nations. This hoarding of information and knowledge has contributed to significant levels of degeneration in certain social contracts, across nations. One of the reasons attributed to such a situation is the increasing 'monetization' of knowledge, including verifiable information, euphemistically called 'applied knowledge' in business.

In the socio-political segment, information in the public domain is mostly considered free. But their reliability has, of late, become highly doubtful. There is an alarming use of fake news, extreme views, etc., especially in the social media. The Cambridge Analytical scandal has shown that data misuse, and attacks on privacy can take serious turns in a democratic set up. Profit seeking private firms can today gather and use personal data of billions of people to help politicians manipulate elections. Many companies collect and sell personal data to whoever wants it, for a price, The data governance model is a hegemonic one, in which the data collecting agent owns the data, controls it, and uses it commercially. The data is hardly used for public good. The much needed, meaningful sharing of data is just not happening.

Designer Kings, Powerless Pawns

Chess has historically been a game between kings. Today, the theme has resurfaced with a bang in politics, as evidenced by the strategic moves of political parties. Politics is an on-going series of chess games in many nations. The objective of each political entity is limited to its own king winning by checkmating its opponent. In the process, the subjects get relegated to levels of pawns, rooks, knights, etc., and get killed, which is acceptable. Such killings are called tactical 'sacrifices' in chess and as 'martyrdom' in conflicts and wars. Like in chess, there are 'sham' sacrifices of 'pieces' as well, which are just optical and meant to deceive the opponents. All strategies are aimed at ensuring the survival and victory of King. The nations themselves are chess boards designed to stage fight after fight, with no end in sight.

In chess, a pawn can also become a king. But it is a rare possibility. Same with current day democracies. Technically, anyone can make it to the top layer of power. But most of the lower strata candidates are unable to climb the political ladder beyond a low level. They are unable to get past the well-entrenched leaders from the elite class of old rulers, dynasties, businessmen, and celebrities. The system is made up, and maintained by a sort of permanent top tier comprising of the elite and rich. Whenever a lower-level candidate tries to make it to the top, the networked system gets activated and applies strings. The initiatives, struggles and uprising of the marginalized are quietly put to rest and their efforts are immobilized. The 'system' is the ultimate winner.

In a complex world with diversified people, it is impossible to use just one governing model. Varied models are required to suit the needs of economies, individuals, groups, and communities coming from differing backgrounds. This is critical, as the welfare of nations broadly depend on the progress made by all, in areas ranging from spirituality to science and technology. In order to maintain the progresses in all these areas, a nation or a community must be bound together by common values. The forces of regionalism and globalization should be integrated with these values. At the same time, special attention must be given to create and develop the innate capabilities of nation's citizens, like judgement, creativity, empathy etc., across all segments.

Democracy in the AI Age

Given the situation, can the democratic governance be improved? Can a 'hybrid' democracy be converted into a near perfect one? There are no 'scientific' procedures to rule a nation. But changeability is the hallmark of human history. A curtain of uncertainty will always keep us away from guessing the future ahead, making us unprepared to face them. At the same time, a constantly changing environment also brings with it new sets of challenges and opportunities, which the societies must collectively face and take advantage of.

The action plan for the societies need not be reactionary. Given the stage of civilization that we are in, it should be possible for us to anticipate some of the future threats and opportunities better.

Self-Goals

Some of the problems of democratic governance are in the form of self-goals repeatedly scored by citizens. The phenomenon of 'Public Choice Theory,' discussed in detail in the next chapter, where voters in general are indifferent to political decision making and costly resource allocation, is a major self-goal. Some of the other self-goals include non-participation in the election process itself, and selection of unfit leaders, especially those who change loyalties post-election. Not raising right noises at appropriate time and fora, and helping create vested interests and sub groups, are other major self-goals. The game of minority vs majority, is yet another self-damage inflicted by voters.

In large federal set ups like the US and India, there is also the danger of big states dominating and controlling central power using the sheer number of elected representatives they send to the central governing body. This is a policy driven self-goal of sort. Another self-goal is the mouse trap of dole outs, or temporary monetary gains.

Voters get enthused with the liberal dole outs timed to influence elections. Or there could be promises of immediate monetary gains to some or all sections of the people, if voted to power. Needless to mention, the ultimate losers in these games are the common men.

Rule by Rules, Away from Rulers

A close look at the prevailing democratic systems suggest that unlimited power created and maintained by any ruling class is possibly the major reason for deterioration of democratic institutions and loss of civil liberties. Such powers must be used as tools to facilitate ruling, and not for suppressing fellow human beings or for amassment of wealth by its holders or their associates. The very idea of creating state institutions is to ensure that governing powers are misused minimum. By restricting these powers, a nation can potentially recreate a society where the subjects not only co-operate with each other, but also co-determine their common fate.

It is often argued that the best way to achieve social welfare and cohesion is to keep the political ideologies at a distance, while drafting or defining common interests. It should instead be through open discussions. The genesis of social movement is intrinsically linked to this principle. Regulations are applicable to those in power and those who are ruled. Too much power for the rulers, or too liberal laws for the ruled, both are not conducive for smooth functioning of a nation. There must be a balancing of political power and societal power. The extreme cases of misuse of state power as also the lawlessness of people can both be bridled with the help of neutral and effective institutional mechanisms.

There is an interesting form of non-interference espoused by Lao Tzu. He argues in his collection of sayings: "Throw away profit and greed, and there won't be any thieves." The virtuous ruler should ideally be less active, to increase his chances of success. The keyword of Chinese philosophy, Laoism, is 'wu wei,' which means "doing nothing." Avoid ambitions and the ruler can be a role model for his subjects.

Confucius also advises against ruling by decrees and punishments, arguing that the people affected inevitably become disaffected or even lose their conscience. Conversely, if one directs by essential power and observes morality in doing so, the people have a sense of right and wrong and achieve goodness. We need to create a group of honest people with highest levels of integrity and shun unreliable and selfish people. However, the current set of politicians are mostly not in line with these ideals. Honesty is a vanishing trait generally among politicians.

In order to correct some of these aberrations, political parties can place before voters a scenario. Such a *scenario thinking* could involve imagining a future society, with tangible achievements, that could be made a reality if the party is voted to power. These '*stories*' could be the official targets of the parties, and they could include unknown and uncertain targets as well, which could be projected as probabilities. The critical requirement is that once parties get power, they must formulate their policies to ensure achievement of these 'stories.' Voters must be informed of the rationale of decisions that go with them.

To the extent possible, the above articulations must be based on verifiable data and explicit, reasonable assumptions. In order to offer varied opportunities, parties must consider a broader canvass and create a multi domain matrix of possibilities, using inputs covering economic, social, political, technological, and environmental aspects, to name a few. They should be different from the current set of manifestos in the sense that they must not be limited to old practices and promises like dole outs or favours to few selected, or all sections of society. Instead, they should aim to increase general productivity of the economy, its overall income levels, social order, foreign relations, general tax rates, etc., impacting all citizens. These projections and promises must not be difficult to measure, or unclear or vague. Most of them must also be achievable in a short to mid-term, pre-defined time horizon. There could be more than one scenario including an optimistic scenario, a pessimistic scenario, and a base level one, like the ones in business projects.

There are few major advantages in this scenario planning. Firstly, it will force the political leadership to develop a scenario mindset. The ritualistic, opposition bashing process hitherto followed will be replaced by idea generations for a better society. Another aim is the possibility of creation of a willingness to explore new alternatives and enter uncharted territories by the whole governing system, with the proclaimed support of masses. The third major objective is to move voters away from base instincts like hatred, rumour mongering and similar other negative behavioural patterns, that are deeply embedded in the societies. Embracing the unknown cannot be limited to businesses or arts. It can be rewarding for governance as well.

Networked Model

A government that governs least is the best. For a system where the major objective is welfare of the people, the power of central or top tier must not be overwhelming. A better governance model is a *networked* one. Under this model, power would be diffused, and more effective. The governing systems should allow only small and medium sized decisions, in terms of outlay, to be taken by the top tier in their central legislative body. For decisions involving larger outlays, there must be a mandatory involvement of the whole *network of legislators,* including state legislatures. These allocations would exclude the pre committed, routine expenses. An illustrative list could be as under:

1. There must be hard limits to borrow and print currency of the government. To breach them, a super majority of over say, 80% in central legislative bodies, or alternatively, a simple majority from centre and all state legislatives can be obtained.
2. In federal set ups, the same logic can be made applicable to each state in a nation.
3. All elected members of the parliament or legislative bodies must be allowed to vote as per their personal logic, irrespective of party stand on any issue.
4. All details regarding defence purchases above a floor, must be made public. There should not be any secret deals.
5. There should be an annual hard limit for the sale of national assets, and allocation of natural resources as well. Such deals must be approved by super majority as mentioned above, or with approvals from centre and concerned state governments.

To make the above system more efficient, it should be combined with a leaner government, with less bureaucrats and less ministers.

Auto Pilots

Another option to break undesired nexus is by redesigning the systems and procedures of governance using emerging technologies. One obvious choice is to have auto pilots for encouraging unbiased governance. The programmed auto pilots can take decisions based on pre fixed parameters, thereby limiting subjectivity in decisions. Parameter driven decisions do not need approvals by elected politicians. Filling a constitutional post, for example, need not be through nominations. A governor of a state in India can be appointed under such a system, by a default choice of say, the in-service, seniormost Justice in the relevant state High Court. Similar method can be adopted for appointment of professional positions in government entities. The parliament or concerned state assemblies can decide on the selection criteria. Auto pilots would reduce the work pressure on politicians and minimize misuse of their power.

The concepts of centralization of power, controlling citizens and conformity with standard, outdated regulations would need to be reworked and some abandoned. Governing structures must be based on higher levels of decentralization, using available and applicable technologies. Villages in vast countries like India were earlier less sophisticated and less networked. But the scenario is changing fast. Networked platforms are available in even remote villages, which can be used to connect them globally, so that we can create a decentralized political environment with meaningful power sharing.

While decentralization is a must for future governance, hierarchies must be reduced, and their discretionary powers curtailed. The key decisions affecting society must be made more on a collective basis. Under such a model, smaller, self-governing smart towns and villages could be formed. These could replace the unwieldy, insensitive centralized models of governance. These smart villages and towns must have more powers in terms of spending, subject to conditions and budget allocations. They can govern themselves with targets of their own. Central authorities can offer population-based or need-based resource support to each of them. Since these towns and villages would be focussing more on execution and less on planning strategies, most of their functions could easily be put on auto pilots. Here again, part of the political and bureaucratic powers could be transferred to auto pilots, in the form of logic and rule-based software, to reduce both the scope for mis appropriation and delays in delivery of services.

Under the proposed system, the central authorities would become leaner. They will get more time to analyze economic and social data, based on which they can discuss key issues with appropriate stakeholders in society, before arriving at decisions. They can focus on strategies, planning, goal setting and performance monitoring. Smaller power centres could be part of nations' shared values.

Use of artificial intelligence for governance is critical. Data-based, transparent decisions would also prevent judgmental errors. A nation's welfare institutions, for example, should not be loaded with too many people, with attendant high costs. Most of the welfare measures could be serviced using intelligent machines and customized applications.

Bottom-up Policy

The current governance style in democracies is a top-down one, where maximum powers are concentrated centrally. This is more visible in federal systems. This has resulted in a nexus between large businesses and political leaders, mainly at the central level. The elections expenses are skyrocketing, which in turn creates corporate funding a critical element in elections. This is unavoidable, as the number of electorates are increasing. In India, the average voters per Lok-Sabha seat in 2019 was more than 1.6 million. Reaching such large number of voters is not easy for a candidate. Even at the state level, the number of voters per constituency is too large and a huge amount is spent on elections, thereby promoting the above nexus. One of the ways to radically change the above unholy alliance is to have a bottom-up procedure for election of representatives. This model is worth experimenting.

Under this model, all basic political elections would take place at local level. In the case of India, it would be at the village or *Panchayat* level. The members who get elected at the local level would then elect the district level representatives, who in turn, would elect the state and national level representatives. Such a policy change, if implemented, can reduce both the cost of elections and influence of big businesses in elections. The grassroot level representatives cannot directly take major national policy decisions. Nor can they announce dole outs and freebees to influence voters, just prior to elections.

The above changes must also be accompanied by higher powers to local bodies, as mentioned earlier. There should be strict prohibition for change of political allegiance by an elected party affiliated representative, post-election. If any such representative changes his / her party post-election, it must result in his / her losing the elected position and he or she should not be eligible for any government post, for a minimum period of say 5 years. These rules must be made applicable to winning independents as well.

Empower People; Not Few Positions

In order to reduce mis appropriation of resources, there must be a realignment of power centres. Some of the measures discussed above are intended to ensure this. In the process, the job of few top politicians may become less attractive, which should be acceptable. Political power can also be diluted by replacing some of them with technical and scientific experts, higher levels of delegation, participation of subject experts, larger levels of privatization, less regulatory interventions in markets etc. In the case of free markets, there are concerns of state entirely withdrawing from socio economic sectors, with potentially serious attendant issues relating to equality and exploitation of marginalized sections. This could be addressed by a balanced approach, ensuring adequate competition by a mix of private and public participation.

There are stringent disclosure requirements in the corporate world in respect of related party transactions. These are, however, not generally made applicable to politicians in or out of power. The wealth accumulation of each politician in power, and his / her relatives, must be disclosed on a periodical basis, with valid explanation for abnormal increases. Banks must be asked to disclose funding of any sort, to corporates where a politician in power is associated in any manner.

A related question is on the number of elected representatives. It is debatable whether nations require large number of members in their law-making institutions like Parliaments or Legislative Assemblies. The same is applicable to number of ministers. The stage is apparently over-crowded. There is a strong case for downsizing most governments, as their work would not get adversely affected, if most of the decision-making functions are transferred to artificial intelligence-based computer networks.

Let the nations be ruled by their grass root leaders.

Chapter 10

MYTH OF POLITICAL SERVICE

Aristotle famously said: "Man is by nature a political animal." Human beings, by instinct, live in the company of other human beings. Historically they have lived as members of identifiable groups and their basic needs and aspirations are built around communal ties. People continue to face many known and unknown challenges in life in terms of lack of safe shelters, diseases, shortage of food, attacks by other living beings, etc. Ancient men were less prepared to meet such life-threatening situations, and an effective way to counter them was by forming groups. Cooperation with other human beings, and ability to work as a team for a common purpose were critical for their very survival. Over many millennia, different human groups got formed, which created classes of strangers and attendant new forms of threats, both real and imaginary. These developments led to the formation of group identities, based on which cooperation was selectively extended by one group member to another. Most of the groups had their formal or informal heads to guide and lead them in this process. This concept of identity created walls between social segments and, over a longer period, some identities got entrenched in societies. Ideas of 'own' society, religion, nation state, tradition, culture, values, etc., cemented the same. A society-less individual became unthinkable.

To achieve liberation from this societal bonding, one had to elevate himself spiritually by abandonment of desire and selfish thoughts, with the help of tools like meditation. As advocated by Buddha, once you achieve 'nirvana' or a spiritual state of emptiness, the societal or group power becomes irrelevant. The equivalent of the same in Hinduism is achievement of 'moksha' or salvation.

Political Leadership

Human history tells us about the leaderless wanderings of people to habitable landmasses in small groups in ancient times. Invention of spoken language helped them communicate among themselves, which led to creation of cumulative group memories and traditions. Based on reported evidences, it is now believed that the 'Red Lady of Paviland' who lived around 29,000–26,000 years ago, was a tribal chief[17]. May be that was the origin of politics. Over time, as societies became more stratified, tribal chiefs became more powerful. City states and kingdoms were formed. Some of the kingdoms grew into empires and later, disintegrated.

Today, there are mainly monarchies, autocracies, dictatorships, and democracies. Kings were unproductive members of a society, in an economic sense. They were mostly spenders and many of them did not even fight personally. Obviously, the ancient leaders must have had their risk management lessons well learnt. The confidential, repeatedly re-written social contracts regulating present day rulers are also highly ruler-friendly.

The concept of people who belong to an identified group electing some among them to lead and guide them in a structured manner, is a relatively new idea. The objective is to position them as public servants, capable of charting out prosperous paths for a group or a nation. The modern-day voter elects his leader with a set of objectives, based on his or her welfare expectations, spiritual outlook, work life, social affiliations, etc. Meeting all these objectives is not an easy task, given the fact that a human being is a combination of various traits, some of which contradict each other. A homogeneous social behaviour in this area is therefore always absent and even unattainable.

There is a greater realization today that there is no evidence of a special 'royal' gene in any man or woman. So, in current day democracies, one needs to be elected by subjects, to be a ruler. And winning is not easy. It requires generation of hope values in the voters. That, in turn, warrants attractive, corporate type strategies to build a leader's own individual brand and party images. In many cases, it requires demolition of the images of opponents.

An election process involves various tactics and cogent rhetoric as it deals with unpredictable behavioural patterns of large number of uninformed, or misinformed, complex human beings. Such tactics include polarizing people based on identities like religion, language, etc., as well.

Political leadership is an art. A politician is generally not required to have any basic qualification to lead a team, unlike say, an accountant, who must understand the basics of accounting. Many political players do not even have clear economic or political ideologies. Still, many of them survive and prosper as people do not generally want to understand or adhere to big, complex ideas. They simply want to believe in something, and belong somewhere. Political parties are aware of these affiliations and contradictions, and they increasingly use new logics and tools for achieving and maintaining power.

Unclear Goals

What kind of a society and governance do we want our grandchildren to inherit? The relationship between a government and its society must ideally be one of a partnership. However, the trend today shows that it is one of master and servants, in many ways. In order to reverse this trend, the governments need to become smaller, and societies need to become much stronger, in terms of powers exercised by them. This is not easy as most politicians, bureaucrats, and unions, by their very nature, want their own teams or departments to get even bigger and more powerful.

In the ancient times, the kings' major focus, other than territorial expansion, was on collecting revenues, and constructing memorials. Accordingly, they identified their people in one of the three categories of soldiers, tax payers, and servants. Artisans and architects were also in high demand. For collecting revenues, they typically appointed lower-level officials and allotted them territories. The practice of dividing a large empire into smaller provinces was prevalent in India since the time of Maurya dynasty (322 BC to 185 BC). Mauryan rulers made '*ksatrapas*' and '*mahaksatrapas*' in charge of such territorial divisions. It is a different story that many of those local authorities went on to become kings themselves, later.

What about the rights of subjects? As per '*Raja Dharma*,' the constitutional law of ancient India, all individuals had the right to be happy and the ruler had the duty to protect that right. *Adarvaveda*, one of the Hindu Vedas, says that all subjects have equal rights for food and water. As per *Samajnana Sukta*, "The yake of the chariot of life is placed equally on the shoulders of all. All should live together with harmony supporting one another like the spokes of a wheel of a chariot connecting its rim and hub."

How many modern-day rulers undertake above mentioned *Raja Dharma*? There are many nagging questions. Are these rulers just copies of their own past rulers or are they different, with new sets of ideologies and preferences? Are they governed by the interests of the future generations? Is it an arrangement where people from different political ideologies compete, and the winners govern the state as per promises made? Or is it an arrangement where elections are just procedures to be completed and those who get elected, irrespective of political affiliations then form a sort of make shift, convenient frame work of alliances to control and allocate resources, driven mainly by their self-interests? If yes, is it not anti-democratic? Why do the democratic institutions fail so miserably in so many countries to address and reverse the non-distributive trends in economies? Is there a continuous and deliberate mission creep in democratic values which dilutes the social transformation that it aims to achieve? All these questions need clarity, before we can confirm that we are in a democratic state.

Under the system of Kingdoms, people were not allowed to question the throne. Current day democracies do allow such questioning. And there are quite a few such questions. Will the elected leaders make better rulers with their priorities in line with the common good? Will they ensure an optimal distribution of nation's scares resources? Will they take care of the weaker sections in societies or will they favour the elite class? Or, will they be primarily focussed on keeping themselves in power by any means? Will these elected governments resort to institutionalized suppression of the rights and freedom of masses? Will they encourage free thought? Will they try to prevent inequality in the society?

On the value front, will the central function of politics be an authoritative allocation or imposition of social values, as suggested by David Easton? Will the priority of rulers be on economic growth, or on promotion of ancient, nationalistic cultures, or on modern scientific education? Will the cultural dynamics dominate the economic growth prospects of the country? Most of these questions elude answers.

An important question that arises is as to who ultimately should be the most influential, dominating source of power in a society or nation. Should it be the constitutions and related laws? Or should it be the political class that govern? Are people themselves expected to dominate each other and rule themselves effectively? Or is the control resting with the ever increasing, market forces? Who should optimally run a country? Should it ideally be run by full time politicians or by intellectuals, or by thinkers or by humanists? Should celebrities like film personalities or sportsmen govern us? Or should we be governed by self-styled spiritual, religious, or cultural leaders? Should the rule be by workers, or producers? Or should the nation be ruled by economists or businessmen or by ethical, professional managers? Should the rule be by legal experts or activists? Should we go back to kings or military rule? Or should the governance be by a combination of all these players?

These questions are still seeking satisfactory answers. It is indeed difficult to explain how any of these leaders can navigate a chaotic, roller coaster world. There are doubts about the governing style as well. For example, should the rulers try to create social 'harmony' or social 'order'? Should rulers follow an economy first or society first approach or should they please a particular group or few groups, with whom they identify? Is it desirable for the rulers or authorities to be canons or reference points or demi Gods, as projected in certain societies? It is also debatable whether an individual today can or should be classless and apolitical. Do we care whether our political system is an open one or a closed one? Or is it an 'in between'? Are social movement theories working in nations? On top of all these, we are unsure as to whether the rights and privileges of a human being are arising out of his being a citizen, or whether a citizen gets his rights and privileges from the fact that he is a human being. Given all these complexities in societies, many feel that human beings require new political theories that could refine and change the current citizen - state equations and relationships.

Political decisions cannot normally be made against public opinion, ignoring the fears and concerns of the masses. The principle of democratic popular sovereignty gives all citizens a high-level choice and freedom to determine what in his or her opinion is the common good. The elected representatives in a democracy are expected to function as trustees working on behalf of, and for the benefit of, people. Any failing in this would render the political governing system a technocratic one, that virtually believes in its deep, authentic, and unquestionable understanding of the social needs, expectations, aspirations, concerns, etc., and in their capability to offer the best set of possible solutions to address them. These assumptions can be illusory that may often lead to public disenchantment and loss of confidence in rulers. When that happens, the principle of *contra elites* can take place, under which some hitherto unknown members of society may challenge the ruling class and take them over.

Ethical Correctness.

Politics is being accused of becoming more and more populist and opportunistic. Political aspirants often masquerade as social activists, like the religious propagandists, who cleverly project themselves as sociologists. Both groups try to create an impression that they work for the welfare of people. Their ethical standing in many cases is, however, suspect. Truth is a casualty in many situations or it remains a myth. People in power want others to believe that their side of the story is the truth and that they are ethical. This version of truth is mostly the one that allows them to strengthen their position in society or one that promotes the interests of groups aligned with them. There is also the increasing notion of salvation by faith or salvation by society in many nations.

Niccolo Machiavelli (1469–1527), the Italian statesman and political philosopher, put forward few controversial ideas in his most famous work, 'The Prince,' (1532). He advocated that a successful ruler would sometimes have to commit immoral acts, such as deception or ruthless killing, in order to maintain his rule and the stability of his kingdom. Machiavelli criticizes the moralistic view of authority. As per him, there is no moral basis on which one can judge the difference between legitimate and illegitimate uses of power. Whoever has power has the right to command. A good person has no more authority by virtue of being good, and the only real concern of the political ruler is the acquisition and maintenance of power.

Goodness and right are not sufficient to win and maintain political office. Only by means of the proper application of power, Machiavelli believes, can individuals be brought to obey and only then will the ruler be able to maintain the state in safety and security. These views are considered highly anti-people by many.

Public Choice Theory

There is an interesting aspect about democratic rule. It relates to the 'Public Choice Theory' developed from the study of taxation and public spending. The theory analyses people's behaviour in the markets and applies them to their actions in collective decision making. Public choice economists point out that there are 'government failures,' just like 'market failures.' In such instances, government interventions do not achieve the desired effects. There is a lack of incentive for voters to monitor governments effectively. Voters are largely ignorant of political issues and such an ignorance is rational. An individual voter has virtually no ability to determine the outcome of an election. So, spending time on key issues is not personally useful for the voter. In addition, many voters also do not understand the ideologies of major political parties or the people behind them. They typically do not care for it.

The above choice to remain ignorant is not visible in people's personal affairs. A person who buys a house, for example, would normally take efforts to be well informed about the house he selects. The choice is important for him or her as he or she would be affected by the decision personally. A voter does not face such a dilemma. Therefore, most voters are indifferent to policies and their impact on citizens. Except for a few highly publicized narratives or issues, they do not pay attention to what legislators do. Similarly, since people hardly analyze good governance, the incentives for good management in the public interest are also weak.

People in general prefer experts in most critical areas of their lives. They do not take the risk of using unskilled persons when it comes to their personal welfare or safety. We need experts to drive our cars, and qualified doctors to treat our diseases. But we seem to be fine with the notion that a country of many uncertainties and complexities can be run by anyone including uneducated persons.

This is not a rational assumption. Many politicians are just representatives of certain collective faiths, which are themselves not founded on any convincing logic. Such leaders cannot be expected to be capable or willing to work for the benefit of a common good.

Legislators can tax and extract resources by force. Since the voters do not monitor the resource allocations effectively, as per Public Choice Theory, legislators tend to behave in ways that are costly to society. Many regulatory agencies appear to be in the hands of vested interest groups, who reap favours and benefits from governmental actions. In return, they provide politicians with funds and campaign workers. Bureaucrats do not normally have achievable targets and they are therefore generally indifferent to the idea of any form of accountability or formal goal setting. It is a dichotomy of sorts in the sense that while national resources can be appropriated by the political leadership, welfare activities like poverty reduction are not considered as their responsibility.

The concept of 'social choice' traces its roots to early work by Nobel Prize-winning economist Kenneth Arrow. Arrow's 1951 book, *'Social Choice and Individual Values,'* attempted to figure out through logic whether people who have different goals can use voting to make collective decisions that please everyone. He concluded that they cannot, and thus his argument is called the 'impossibility theorem.'

Buchanan and Tullock, in their book 'The Calculus of Consent: Logical Foundations of Constitutional Democracy,' has a view that a collective decision that is truly just or a decision in the public interest, would be one that all voters would support unanimously. While unanimity is largely unworkable in practice, the book challenges the widespread assumption that majority decisions are inherently fair. This approach has led to a further subdiscipline of public choice, 'constitutional economics,' which focuses exclusively on the rules that precede parliamentary or legislative decision making and its impacts on the domain of government.

Political Juggernaut

There is a critical argument around the question of whether the governments should ensure or at least focus on the well-being of all its citizens, irrespective of their contribution to the society. The pro argument goes like this. The governments must provide the basic level infrastructure, education, and healthcare facilities to all. They should also ensure that there is a level playing field in terms of equal opportunities for all. Special care must be provided to physically or mentally challenged citizens. Able bodied citizens must be encouraged to play an active part in building the society and work for own welfare. That, according to them, is the only sustainable economic model for a country. Many do not agree. They believe the welfare policies that try to provide salvation by state or society, is a kind of utopian social escalator for the poor, which is not sustainable, given the limited resources at the disposal of governments. Many politicians think an alternate model, salvation by faith, is convincing, based on a person's religious beliefs. Such a model indeed relieves the politicians from ensuring welfare for the voters. In any case, there is hardly any mandatory accountability for the promises made by politicians, in any part of the world.

Political ethics and logic, in a well-conducted and contested democracy demands certain critical pre requisites that are to be practiced by way of self-discipline by political parties. These relate to unwritten, but implicit values and practices. They include truthfulness, trustworthiness, and an orientation for greater common good, which are to be adhered to, by all players in the system, always. An equally important related requirement is that the political declarations and follow up actions of political leaders and organizations must coincide. The political statements from leaders must be based on certain unambiguous principles, and they must be relatively stable and credible. Mobilizing people and forging alliances without any basic agreement or common programme or commitments is neither desirable nor sustainable over a longer period.

These are ideal situations. In real world however, there are very few leaders in current day politics, who have unwavering focus on people's welfare in their radar. Most politicians do not have a strategic plan or achievable targets for their people. Some try to improve the acceptance level of their parties with the help of rhetoric and brand building. Some use the nationalistic card. Vast majority of them are just swimming with the tide, hoping for a better career for themselves. Many players need enemies to excite and energize them.

For active politicians, this is critical, in many ways. Therefore, politicians who are focussed on tactics and strategies, try to spot, target, and attack political enemies. In the process, they even invent enemies.

There are political turncoats as well. Sleeping with the enemies is a common practice in politics where different political parties work together based on a consensus-based agenda, keeping aside their political and ideological differences. Coalitions are a necessity of sorts in many nations. However, changing political affiliations after getting elected using a different party ticket, is a horrible anti-democratic action. Changing ideologies just to grab power, without a convincing reason is untrustworthy. Coalitions also lead to what is called 'Vetocracy' where small groups can veto major decisions and create hurdles in a nation's progress.

In a multiple option society, it is difficult for people to get united socially and politically. In highly controlled societies, where those at power centres are too dominating, and freedom of expression is severely limited, the thinkers and intellectuals display a sort of 'withdrawal syndrome.' They keep away from expressing displeasure over social unethical behaviour, as a dialogue is either not possible or is perceived to be useless. Add to this the fact that what constitutes the well-being of a community can only be established ex post in view of the interpretive nature of public interests. These factors reduce the pressure on politicians to perform. In order to achieve their personal objectives, the most important skill set required by a politician is the ability to excel in manipulating political power equations and maintaining the hope values of voters. The nation's welfare agenda including the target of providing equal opportunity to all, gets hijacked in the process.

Have the politicians been transforming societies? Peter Drucker, in his 'The Age of Social Transformation'[18] says that the century that went by shows the futility of politics. As per him, the most important social transformations that we witnessed in the past centuries were not due to political events. Societies moved from agricultural to Industrial world and then to knowledge-based economy, not primarily propelled by politics, but driven by scientific and technological innovations.

'Taj Mahal' Syndrome

Taj Mahal is a highly acclaimed, iconic mausoleum in Agra, India, built about 400 years ago (between 1631 and 1648) by the Mughal emperor Shah Jahan in memory of his wife, Mumtaz Mahal. Ustad-Ahmad Lahori was the main architect of Taj Mahal and it is believed to be the greatest architectural achievement of the Indo-Islamic architecture. Taj Mahal was designated as a UNESCO World Heritage Site in 1983 for being "the jewel of Muslim art in India and one of the universally admired masterpieces of the world's heritage". It is also considered a symbol of India's rich history. In 2007, it was declared a winner of the New 7 Wonders of the World (2000–2007) initiative.

Taj Mahal was indeed Shah Jahan's signature project. But it might not have been envisaged as a branding tool by him as he was an emperor, needing no branding. Curent day politicians face multi-level competitions and they badly need 'Taj Mahal' type of branding. The major difference is that Taj Mahal is a concrete, beautiful structure whereas modern day politicians keep creating for themselves intangible, imaginary structures with mostly non-existing attributes. And for that, many in power use public resources. These whimsically created events and monuments are expected to build and nurture leaders' personal and political brands. They create monuments to commemorate their founders or 'legendary' past leaders. Large sums of public resources are spent on advertising their 'dubious' achievements. Giving advertisements to media houses also aim to reduce public criticism of governmental actions and policies, and increase the chances of 'favourable' media comments. Huge resources are spent for promoting leaders' personal or party lines and images across all imaginable platforms, including print, electronic, and social media. The road sides and public places along the breadth and width of certain democratic countries are typically flooded with such brand building advertisements, in the form of imposing kiosks, hoardings, bill boards, etc. Some of these are arguably funded by 'friendly' corporates, and the public is generally unaware of the possible quid-pro-quo arrangements. Most of these expenses are borne by governments either directly or through affiliated outfits. Modern-day emperors do not, in most cases, have any public scrutiny or accountability. The current day politicians beat Shah Jahan in image building, for sure. In countries with relatively fewer literate citizens, these strategies pay off handsomely.

Why do politicians focus on building own images and demolishing opponents' images? As Milan Kundera said in 'Immortality,' in the last few decades, 'imagology has gained a historical victory over ideology in politics.' A significant number of political parties across the globe are positioning themselves as dynasties. They promote not just the brand image of the founder of the party, but also the next generation (mostly male) members of his / her family. In the modern era, these well-designed activities have become not just institutionalized, but also hugely deceptive, tech-driven, strongly networked, and virtually unstoppable. Psychological indoctrinations continue relentlessly in the social media as well, to promote these goals.

Fishing in Muddy Waters

In the ancient era, kings built their brands by circulating coins with their images. Today, brand building and brand demolition exercises are increasingly techno driven. There are wide spread cyber-attacks now, that are called by terms like 'social bot' or 'fake news.' Social bots are programmed in such a way that they are seen as autonomously acting programs on the internet, disguising their real identity. They are created by software robots using specially created net-based accounts or other social media platforms. Using these accounts, political narratives, biased opinions, fake news, stories or 'alternative facts,' etc., are sent out in social networks. They even appear in comment columns of media pages, and are meant to build someone's image or to demolish another's. The bots can independently regenerate the information themselves, adapt it to current events, or even communicate to human users in real-time chats. The social environment is cleverly made muddy first, in order to reap the benefits.

Unsuspecting people fall prey to these artificial profiles. Politicians themselves can be misled by this practice. In 2015, a botnet of the Ukrainian paramilitary network Pravyj Sector (Right Sector) spread the false news that Russia-led separatists were targeting Kiev with missiles. This technology is ever getting innovated, with newer and smarter forms of deception.

The digital technologies undoubtedly enable the state and its investigation agencies to identify potential crimes in advance and avoid them, based on a person's criminal background. But this facility can also be misused by state political authorities to demolish the image of opposition and target those criticizing the government. The chat history of an activist can be tracked and he could be jailed on charges of suspected treason.

Another technological tool in the hands of a brand building politician is big data analytics. Here, political leadership uses the combination of data driven dialogue and psychometrics. Psychometrics is a scientific method for measuring the psyche of a person and messaging according to his personality dimensions like aspirations, fears and hopes. This is aided by the fact that information about each subject is permanently recorded in the internet and it can be analyzed with the help of computers. In politics, data-based communication and 'attention harvesting' are standard norms now. Data mining and data targeting is very much a part of election campaigning.

Today, it is possible to understand the political bias of a person and his or her probable voting decision. Pressure groups can be identified, and voters can be divided into supporters, opponents, and undecideds, using big data. Customized communications can then be sent to each target group. In addition to the traditional social tools, mass media, information networks, big data analytics, business management principles, and technologically advanced tools like surveillance mechanisms are used by politicians to build own brands and demolish brands of opponents. The traditional media including television, newspapers and radio have virtually lost their political gatekeeping function. The opinion battlefields of the future apparently lie in the digital space.

Techniques mentioned in 'Art of war' by Sun Tzu are being deployed relentlessly. As a result of these trends, confidence levels in politicians and democracy in general, are getting eroded. Under the circumstances, autocracy is a possible future scenario. There is an increasing feeling in many democracies that political power is not being obtained or used legitimately. In many cases, the rules applicable to politicians are different and opaque as compared to the rules applicable to ordinary citizens.

Mousetrap of Nationalism

Nationalism is a political idea that sells. It is not ideology dependent, as even a communist China is promoting Nationalism. It works because politics is more about feelings and emotions, and not much about rational thinking. Nationalistic politics is defined by enemies, both real and imaginary, and both internal and external. So, its strategic focus is on building better mousetraps that revolve around divisive instincts, looking for adversaries.

Today, individuals in nations have been converted into citizens, with duties expected of them. Citizens are legally required to protect the nation, further its interests as defined and articulated by the ruling politicians, respect and safeguard its borders, as also behave in a manner that does not inflict pains on its other citizens and institutions. Appropriateness or otherwise of such behaviour on the part of a citizen would be decided by the rulers themselves. So much for the personal liberty. Kierkegaard once said that individual life, as a spirit, does not see the citizen in the society. The spirit also does not want to obey any man-made law, or social values, or beliefs, or rewards and punishments. But things are quite different in real societies, with so called democratic rights.

In a public talk at New York, on 17th April 1984, J. Krishnamurti, the Indian thinker, and religious teacher opined that nationalism is just glorified tribalism, with various opposing races, religions, divisions of classes, castes and so on. There are ideas against ideas, ideologies opposing ideologies, and traditions against traditions. One of the reasons for this game could be the fact that prejudices and hatred, based on one's group values or cultures are deeply rooted in human psychology and societies. People tend to firmly believe that their roots are unique and important, but forget that other people also have similar roots. The Greeks famously called anyone who did not speak their language as barbarians. Most European intellectuals considered these barbarians as primitive people 'without history.' There are different stories as well. Marco Polo, the Venetian merchant, and writer, described the customs of

Chinese with a lot of respect. Medieval European Christian theologists translated many writings of Arabic philosophers, doctors, and astrologers.

The feelings of hatred are possibly promoted by shrewd politicians who want to polarise people, for their personal, electoral gains. Success by these political parties who indulge in sectarian, identity politics encourage mushrooming of such tactics and parties, especially in nations with multiple ethnic groups. World is witnessing such a scenario now. These political parties are trying to take the population back to the tribal days, and converting their masses tribalistic. Our society is made of a variety of sub groups. They include not just religion, caste, work, and language-based groups, but also various minorities, indigenous and ab-original people, tribals, immigrants, gays, lesbians, feminists, activists, greens, etc. Recognition of their differences based on identities by the wider society itself is a big socio-political challenge.

In the nationalistic model, voters are being led to consider themselves as belonging to certain classes based on their mother tongue, religion practiced, traditions followed, etc., all of which have associations with the nation or its identity. Those who lead them want to ensure that they vote for them and elect them based on such nationalistic identification. Selling difficult and complex economic ideas and realities to a voter is tough, whereas playing on the cultural anxieties of voters is a time-tested, winnable strategy. While the economic anxieties are real and justifiable, the cultural anxieties are mostly imaginary and cannot, in most cases, be considered as legitimate. The self-styled leaders position themselves as saviours of the groups' cultural interests. Such a masking hides the obvious fact that there are multiple identities for any given voter, as he or she is simultaneously a worker, a member of a religion, an activist, etc.

When identities are used to paint one group or class as common enemies, the society develops cracks. Politicians as opinion makers, play this card all the time, ignoring its longer-term negative impact on societies. Common men hardly realize that these opinions are the lowest forms of their 'knowledge' and that these are just brain washing tactics. Nationalism is all about loving one's country men and not about hating foreigners. A nationalist must really focus more on ensuring that he or she loves his countrymen and pays his or her taxes to government correctly and on time.

All political leaders or interest groups do not always uphold the interests of the public. They may use convincing, politically correct arguments in a tactical way to express themselves. But the core objective would, in many cases, be the protection of their own self-interests. On the economic front, it is observed that collective value creation is getting eroded in many nations. Governments and public servants are ignoring potential changes in societies. The innovation centres and value creation units have migrated to tax havens and the brains behind them are floating in unknown territories. Politicians simply do not seem to do anything about it.

Practical Logic; Political Magic

Reasoning and arguing are critical ingredients of political positioning. Let us therefore try to reason as to why a political leader should spend his time on public service? What motivates him or her to come forward and take the trouble of serving a nation? Is it for fame? In the earlier era, kings were particularly interested in expanding territories, amassing wealth by plundering from newly acquired territories, and showing it off by building huge palaces, and enjoying a lavish life. In order to achieve these, most kings had alliances with local chiefs and religious leaders. Some epic wars were fought for women as well. In today's situation, where nations are in huge debt, and empire-building is off the table, what are the motivating factors behind the leadership race? Is it for promoting the self?

What is the historic objective of a democracy? The political modernism theory suggests that the political focus, or the major objective of a democracy, must always be on social integration, necessitated due to social frictions, which in turn, arise out of continuing social differentiations of various sorts. It promotes the idea that social evolution in a society is a continuous process of social differentiation. People go up or down the ladders in a society, thereby creating differences in their social status. It can also happen when people shift from one society to another by way of migrations, transfers, change of jobs, etc. This differentiation creates social conflicts. Social evolution therefore, by default, is a destabilising factor in any society. This is an area where the cultural and political leaderships must pay a lot of attention, as these can potentially create long lasting turmoil in any nation. Are our politicians focused on this objective?

Three in One

All countries have their own historical and sociological baggage and they are destined to live with them. Political movements and power evolve from these history-linked factors. They get molded by cross cultural linkages that are generated by migrations, wars, change in rulers, etc. Today, players in three key segments of society, the religion, economics, and politics, are all investing in each other making the power play a hugely complex one. The stakeholders have become common. In the past, players in these segments were competing each other for a share of power. Situation has greatly changed in democracies. Strategies invented, formulated, and applied for achieving and maintaining power in each of these areas are now converging. There is an increasing realization in the political world that in order to achieve and maintain power, the social structures including the cultural and business segments must work together.

Practical Logic

Politicians work under resource constraints, which is well documented. So are individual citizens. But political power is a socially accepted and legitimate structure that enable those in power to exercise control over both government and private resources. This control many times also gets extended to control over future income flows of a nation. When a government borrows money or sells its natural resources like say, a coal mine to a private corporate, it is essentially reducing its future income, which logically belongs to future generations. *Politicians opt for a practical logic here.*

There is a feeling that politicians, once in power, care more about their own interests. They would also normally resist changes in an electoral system, that helped them get elected in the first place. Hence, even if a system is flawed, they would continue the status quo. *That is another practical logic.*

Political morality, respect for laws and respect for people are all critical for any politician. But the value system of an average politician is more often flexible and sometimes even distorted. One such distorted value is the assumption that it is perfectly fine to use public money and public institutions to build own or party image. The practice does not get opposed by other politicians, as all are the same boat. *The practical logic is a shared one.*

Business men, across the globe do manage, and will continue to manage, politicians. They will excel in this effort in future as well and would not be deterred by local, cultural, or national issues, which are concerns of ordinary voters. Business and money power are beyond national borders and sentiments. Many corporates help politicians win elections in their local places. Such support might not be limited to finance in future, and could spread to areas like technology, psycho analysis and even to brain washing. The use of big data analytics, with remote networks and artificial intelligence in elections in the not-so-distant past, is a harbinger of sort. In turn, these corporates are expected to exploit the political systems that they help to get power, for their own advantage. Politicians are acutely aware of this situation and they also know that the interests of businessmen are mostly diametrically opposite to those of common men. But they help create 'donor friendly' economic policies, *supported by their practical logic.*

Politics is generally a zero-sum game. For every winner, there is a loser. Therefore, there is an intense fight to become a winner by any means. But many times, such a winner is not clearly chosen by the voters. Absence of leaders in a society create power vacuums, which typically do not remain so for a long time. It is often seen that whenever such a vacuum is created say, due to lack of majority for a particular party, politicians use their network forgetting ideological differences, and form governments of alliances. Sleeping with the enemies is justified for a share of power. Many a time, these opportunistic alliances are against the spirit of voters' mandate. *That gain, is a practical logic.*

Voters have the right to get verified and verifiable information, especially from political leaders and parties. Truth and politics cannot and should not be separated in a fair democracy. However, many political parties either do not bother to verify the information or deliberately spread mis-information, euphemistically called alternate facts, that could improve their winnability. Some tell voters what they want to hear, and not what is good for them. *This practice as well, is purely based on practical logic.*

People's memory is short. Occurrent memory (short memory) only mattes in politics and not the dormant (long term) memory. Hence politicians do not mind indulging in inappropriate or corrupt practices as people tend to forget them over a longer period. *That is a practical logic politicians rely on.*

Preferential policies aimed at benefitting certain cultural segments or groups in societies are major reasons for social disorder. The rules of resource allocation in a fair governance model must not be partisan. This is a central hallmark of a modern democratic nation, though there could be exceptions in the policies, like providing protection or benefits to weaker sections or physically challenged members of the society. When policies based on culture dominates the political game, or when one cultural group dominates, in order to ensure social order, independent institutions will have to come forward and enforce fair treatment of all segments. In the absence of such neutral institutions, or in cases where such institutions are weak, the nation will face conflicts and violence. When the institutions lose power or will, political entrepreneurs will make nonnegotiable resource demands on behalf of identified cultural groups. This is a major reason for continued civil conflicts in many nations. Defeating the deliberate activities aimed at creating sectarian conflicts is a big challenge in nations. Stopping the efforts to perpetuate ancient hatred, and promoting an inclusive society requires a better understanding of society in general and the real drivers of economic welfare.

Liberal, neutral institutions, well supported by human and material resources, are required for spreading the above basic awareness. Economic and social welfare must dominate politics rather than sectarian interests. However, this is sadly absent in many democratic countries, where *politicians allow this to happen, based on their practical logic.*

Goal-based Logic

Political systems are not short of thinkers. But they have become highly liquid in the sense that they take opportunistic shapes at will, just to grab power. Most of the time, the politicians are preoccupied with or focused on building their own image or on demolishing opposition image. Their energies are not channelled for creative purposes. The first step, therefore, is to have a clear vision for the society. A good society, in a democratic set up, must:

1. Be knowledge seeking and knowledge respecting one;
2. Create decentralized, autonomous institutions closer to people.
3. Have respect and promote logic-based decisions;
4. Have members who are willing to sacrifice for their fellow living beings;
5. Keep religion and politics separate;
6. Be aware of the longer-term repercussions of political decisions to the society in general; and
7. Be aware that economic development, many times, comes at the cost of nature and culture. A balance, therefore, is both required and inevitable.

Let the political logic be people-centric.

Chapter 11

<u>MYTH OF GLOBAL PLAYERS</u>

Man's progress is built on his received wisdom and knowledge accumulated by him and his predecessors over the past many centuries, across various tribes, societies, and cultures. In the process, most of the tribal cultures and values got changed from the ancient, so-called mafia cultures to much wider, universal cultures. Over these periods, people realized that self-sufficiency of an individual or an isolated society, is an illusion. They also reckoned that they need to get out of their caves and dingy rooms to look at the starry sky, enjoy the fresh fragrance of blooming flowers and get new experiences. An expansion of playing field allowed them to enrich their lives in many ways. People became aware of the criticality of relationships with the outer world, and their inter dependency. That awareness created a wandering tribe and the first set of global citizens were born. Indeed, it also created the dilemma of being in a new territory, under an unknown chief. But such a dilemma possibly existed ever since lands and rulers became part of human lives.

In almost all societies, globalization trends were preceded by internal migration to nearby prosperous urban cities. These centuries-old trends are recorded in many documents. References have been made to the existence of 120 towns and 3,200 *qasbas* or village towns in north India during the 16th century, including cities like Delhi, Agra, and Lahore, which acquired a size equal to cities like Paris or London[19]. Many of these villages had primary village assemblies, which were attended by 'mahattaman' in Uttar Pradesh, 'mahattaras' in Maharashtra, 'mahajanas' in Karnataka and 'Perumakkal' in Tamilnadu, all indicating great men of the village.

During Mughal rule in India, the villages had headmen, who were the local chiefs. About 15% of the population later came to live in towns and cities including qasbas. The historiography of India shows a period of decay of urban cities as well, in the early medieval period. The reason attributed for deurbanization was the practice of land grants by rulers, to brahmins. Cities lost prominence broadly during 300 to 1000 AD in India. But the migrations in the earlier centuries undoubtedly expanded the horizons of human knowledge, for sure.

Arthur Schopenhauer, the German philosopher, wants us to distinguish between the things that promote human happiness and those that only appear to do so. That distinction and advantages derived from it would be lost if man is not allowed to go beyond a pre-determined territory, for any reason. Human beings have historically made progress by going beyond man-made restrictions and borders. Nationalistic barriers and isolated geographies put constraints on experimentations. From an economic point of view, a global market can create advantages in terms of larger scope and scale of operations, which a stand-alone, island nation cannot. In today's interlinked world, an individual cannot economically prosper beyond a limit, unless he or she accepts and experiences the challenges, opportunities, and consequences of globalizations, manifested in the form of migrations, urbanizations, exports, imports, cultural exchanges, etc.

Globalization has historically been considered both as an opportunity and a threat. Countries with comparative advantages, in terms of labour, natural resources, technology, etc., benefit more from it. It is a process of expanding the scope for exchange of goods and services, interactions, and integration of ideas between people, governments, and firms across the globe. Globalization puts global interests ahead of national interests. It impacts international trade, technology transfer, capital movement, migration, cultural exchanges, etc., among others. The encounters between ancient civilizations, mass migrations, colonization, etc., were all, in a way, part of globalization. Industrial and technological advancement in the 19th century actively promoted the idea of globalization. The international economic agreements created after the Second World War accelerated this process. After the fall of Soviet Union, the process became even faster.

Types of Globalizations

Globalization broadly covers three major categories that relate to economic, social, and political segments. The economic globalization covers both trade and financial globalization. It gives private capitalists more freedom, and goes by the simple idea of a single global market. Globalization, in that respect, is seen as an economic model based on global consumption where the consumers are expected to maximise their material and economic self-interest. The unbridled reach, expansion, and domination of global products, brands, and companies are its key features. Economic globalization is justified in terms of its ability to manufacture cheaper products and services, enabled by higher and arguably fairer levels of competition helped by larger volumes. Capital, under this arrangement, flows to places where it can reap higher returns and multiply faster.

One problem with the economic globalization is the fact that weaker countries with shortage of capital, poorer basic infrastructure facilities and smaller number of consumers tend to suffer. Smaller nations and their governments also tend to lose bargaining power as multinational corporations are too strong for them to effectively regulate. For example, the much-desired idea of 'de-platforming' is just beyond the control of small sovereign nations. Economic globalization is accused of dumping unwanted products and services into unsuspecting, weaker, external markets. Another major problem under globalization is the use of tax havens by rich, multinational corporations and individuals, for avoiding tax. Sovereign states are unable to tackle tax avoidance as there is a lack of willingness on the part of few nation states that facilitate and promote such tax avoidances by helping establish legal structures and tax havens in their territories.

The whole talk about sustainable globalization, is a myth. What is euphemistically called sustainable is what suits some nations. The multinational corporations create strong global networks systems to promote standardised consumption patterns across nations. They connect economies using a complex array of supply chains, trade links, capital flows, data analytics, and movement of good, machinery, and men. The globalists and anti-globalists are playing their cards close to their chests, to win themselves. A win-win, unfortunately, is not in their menu.

The social globalization includes three sub segments of inter personal globalization, informational globalization, and cultural globalization. The socio-cultural globalization is the process of exchange and transmission of values, ideas, philosophies, arts, and other forms of cultural expressions. In an era of mass communication and social media explosion, writers, thinkers, and artists can interact each other easily, sharing their knowledge and experiences. Multiculturalism and cosmopolitanism are to some extent, manifestations of cultural globalization. People can get access to global information and can take decisions on issues like say, their lifestyles, based on the global cultural and consumption trends. A society can also showcase, spread, and defend its own values and ideals globally.

Political globalization is a new segment of globalization. The emergence of supra national institutions like United Nations, World Bank, International Monetary Fund, European Union, Organization for Economic Cooperation and Development, World Trade Organization, Association for Southeast Asian Nations (ASEAN), etc., are now powerful actors in deciding domestic policies of various governments. They contribute to global peace, notwithstanding the fact that in many conflicts, including the recent Russian war with Ukraine, they were ineffective spectators. These supranational bodies promote universal values like freedom, fair treatment of women, etc. However, they are accused of using their money power to subjugate smaller and weaker nations, thereby threatening their sovereignty. Since most of these institutions are controlled by big countries, there are accusations suggesting that they tend to protect the interests of 'big brother' nations.

The country specific hurdles in globalization are continuing. China, for example, is engaged in global trades and liberal reforms, but is in no mood to embrace democratic values. It maintains the domination of the Communist Party and pursues a nationalistic agenda. Globalization goals of China do not extend to personal choices like freedom of expression. Most Islamic countries continue to reject the Western models of civilization and follow laws, regulations, dogmas, and practices related to their religion in governance. Few of them, however, follow liberal political systems. Policies of nations such as Turkey and Pakistan are getting increasingly influenced by the West.

In the 2000s, globalists faced many problems that were 'civilizational' in nature. Since the late 1990s, world faced no new, political, or economic ideologies that could challenge neo liberalism or globalism. These principles have apparently been accepted by almost all societies in varying degrees. The idea of abolition of nation-states in favour of a World Government, however, got stalled due to many reasons.

Globalization Winds

Formal, recorded human migrations started centuries ago. From 16th century onwards, granting of travelling papers and use of the term 'passport' became prevalent. Whether it originated with the idea of people using ports or city gates for entry into new territories or locations, remains a matter of debate. As per historians, passports were not generally required for international travel until the first world war. It was in the early 20th century that passports as we recognize them today began to be widely used.

Modern globalization started with relatively safe voyages. Based on historical developments, the modern globalization trends are broadly categorized into four distinct phases by some historians. The first phase saw use of caravel, which was first developed around 1450, as the preferred vessel for trade. International trades were at that time mainly conducted under the sponsorship of Empires. This phase of 'Globalization Under the Flag of Empires,' was between 1492 to 1914. The second phase was a reversal of this system leading to a kind of de-globalization, from 1914 to 1945. The third phase was after the World War II, from 1945 till 2016, when global trades expanded. This period witnessed the domination of United States of America in world trade, higher levels of exports and imports, and creation of many bilateral and multilateral trade agreements. The third phase witnessed both the formation of European Union and the disintegration of USSR. The current 4th phase has started from 2017 and continues. There are clear trends now that suggest the beginning of another era of deglobalization.

Globalization was equated with progress and economic growth by the capitalist leaders as economic growth was the main aim of globalization. Globalization was credited with efficient use of raw materials and it expanded as a result of efforts of nation states to reduce the negative effects of war with a liberal model. The economic, social, and political integration of societies was expected to create collective prosperity for entire mankind.

Deglobalization Winds

Many people dislike globalization as they believe that it can lead to loss of their values and that it corrupts their unique cultures. In Europe there were protests, against large scale immigrations, though Europe has historically been a beneficiary of immigration. Some societies there saw movements that started as mere protests on a local issue like fuel rise, which then got catapulted into revolts against inequality, globalization, and against authorities. The 'yellow vests' protest in France was one such movement. The 2016 elections in the USA were fought by some using high dose of nationalistic ideologies. Though they were criticized, it is also true that they were supported by a sizeable population in the US.

Anti-globalization trends threaten economic liberalism, which is recognized as the best governance model in a democratic set up. One of the supporters of globalism, Charles Krauthammer, declared that the 'unipolar moment' was over and that the globalists had failed to take advantage of it. Anti-globalization waves have picked up now, mainly in developed countries. Both left-wing anti capitalists and conservative nationalists oppose globalization as they feel it leads to unemployment, inequality, terrorism, and cultural homogenization. Globalization is accused of destroying local businesses in smaller countries, and eliminating independence of nation states.

It is argued that social protection gets weakened by globalization as welfare activities get less attention under neoliberal policies. Acting as an external power, globalization forces restructuring of nations, leading to reduction in socially oriented policies. Another criticism is that the super profits made by expansion of markets enriched only the multi-national corporates, who never passed on the benefits of scale of operations to consumers. There was a view that capital would be cheaper in a globalized world. This was also proven wrong. Return expectations on equity investments are much higher, specially from developing country projects. Interest rates on debts to such countries are also 'marked up' considering country risk, exchange risk, etc. In all these developments, no global level interventions were initiated.

There are other tailwinds for deglobalization. A major one is the prevalence of high level of national unemployment. When that happens, politicians tend to promote job protection policies in their home states, especially in nations that import a lot of goods and services. The workers' anger is mainly against imports, offshoring of production, and immigrants taking jobs, though as per reports, more jobs are lost in developed countries due to automation, robotics, machine learning, and other productivity enhancers within the nations. One of the factors driving reshoring of supply chains in developed nations, is the expectation that it would create domestic jobs. Another tool used for protection of jobs is import tariff. The G7 imports of goods and services have not been increasing since 2008, the year of global financial crisis.

Reincarnation of Tribalism

In many countries, nationalism is a critical symbol, when it comes to political allegiance. Nationalistic political leaders often play down the benefits of globalization. Nationalists and activists try to create discontent by blaming outsiders or other cultures for poor economic conditions of their countries and citizens. When it comes to economic matters, ours is not a group of relationship-based societies. They are, in that respect, mostly consumption-based. In the cultural sphere as well, there is a strong argument that it is not possible to have relationship-based societies, especially of larger size. Larger size of societies is, however, a key determinant for markets as it affects the viability of products and services. It should be possible for humanity to balance both these factors and develop a civic culture that understands and appreciates the relationships between local, and national interests, as also their international linkages. The absence of such a balance can be quite critical. Tribalism or 'group narcissism' can get developed in such situations, which could be dangerous, as the perceived winners in a culture-dominated community may tend to promote the interests of their 'own' tribe, at the cost of national welfare. It is debatable whether nationalism is intended to protect the interests of 'few' groups. Many realise that in an economic sense, the scale of operations would turn problematic when all nations become protected islands. They also realise that the high degree of deglobalization fever with the spread of blind nationalism can adversely affect the economic health of all nations in the longer run.

Deglobalization could be disastrous for the global human welfare. A near term casualty, for example, could be the much-publicized Electric Vehicles (EVs). EVs need aluminium, lead, lithium, chromium, rare earths, silver and gold, as raw materials, among others. No country has all these raw materials in required quantity, and all depend on each other for production of EVs. In a deglobalized world, supply chain bottlenecks can kill their business models. Another set of groups that could face severe problems would be the smaller countries, which would be hit from both supply and demand sides. Scale of operations is extremely critical in high investment businesses. Small nations generally do not have the required domestic resources or technology (from supply side) or the large enough number of consumers (from demand side) to justify investments in high technology ventures domestically. Disintegrated or tiny markets are hardly the ideal ones for such investments or experiments. The smaller countries are therefore dependent, by default, on global supply of goods and services. In technology and capital-intensive businesses, the world certainly needs more cooperation.

So, what next? The local sense of belonging still prevails. In some cases, the nationalistic themes are driving people to go back to their tribal days. Race, culture, nationality, etc., are all strong concepts that hold people together, but they can also lead to symbolic dismemberment of the marginalized sections. This is a dangerous mind set. In a post-industrial, knowledge-based economy, there is no merit in going back to concepts like isolationism and protectionism. Cultural homogenization is possibly a negative by-product of cultural globalization. It is a fact that many communities are today less insulated against cultural invasions due to the impact of globalization. The existential threats of small cultures remain, as the likelihood of their getting assimilated into stronger cultures is high. These cultures, like the bigger ones, are in continuous transition.

Future of Globalization

In order to counter the increasing trend of nationalistic rhetoric, modern nations must find out new models of solidarity, that can be borderless and tradition-neutral. Urbanization, digital networking, etc., could be some of the possible platforms for such a solidarity. Unity can be achieved if nations can turn away from their narrow nationalism and look at cultures and traditions that promote human welfare. In most countries, people want to hold on to their local or national traditions, arts, culture, languages, etc., which is quite understandable. An interesting observation here is that certain laws and restrictions are not made applicable uniformly. The powerful and rich get to go abroad, interact with alien cultures, and get newer, varied experiences. Their off springs live and study abroad. But the common men are asked to look back, and be happy, ruminating on the nations' past glories.

Social identities are mixed. In a globalized world, some loss of identity is unavoidable for an individual, for a society, and even for a nation. In return, globally connected citizens stand to gain by way of varied experiences and newer forms of knowledge, which are beneficial and rewarding. A multidimensional, cubist view is always preferable for the modern man. We all could be very much a part of world cinema or world literature. It is an entirely different question as to whether we can or should be converted to, or desire to be, cultural citizens of the world.

History tells us that communities that are hostile to outsiders, dissenters and immigrants can hardly innovate or experiment. Such societies are less creative. They tend to prefer stability over dynamic progress, which warrants continuous experiments. Even within a nation, the market economy can prosper on a sustained basis only if all sections of society participate in it, and more importantly, work as a team. As Kropotkin said, "the species that co-operate rather than compete survive more."

A global sense of belonging could be more rewarding in coming days for a different reason as well. The trends in labour movement are changing, globally. Hard labour is getting replaced slowly and steadily by soft labour which uses communication as a major tool. Here, cross border communication is critical. While the world is becoming much more chaotic and inter dependent, it is also turning out to be more plural in its outlook, and that can create its own disorders. In a community that is pluralistic in many aspects, it is extremely important to create space for diverse voices and to find an acceptable balance, to counter such disorders.

It is a proven fact that creation and sharing of new knowledge with diverse peoples globally, does result in newer forms of human culture. The Indian concept of unity in diversity is relevant in such situations. In large developing countries, there could be internal migration from underdeveloped to developed and more peaceful locations within the nation. In the absence of a collective approach, these migrations can create related political and cultural turmoil. India faced the 'sons of the soil' agitations in the 1970s. The same trend can make a comeback.

One possible option for nations is to replace hard nationalism and hard religiosity with soft nationalism and soft religiosity. That could preserve and promote both nationalistic and religious spirits without offending other cultures. Nations can also focus on other value additive areas like say, education. If the perceived standards of education are low in a nation, the segments that can afford foreign education will send their children abroad. The sufferers would be those from the lower strata of such nations. An added problem these nations face is the trend of most students who go abroad for studies staying back after completion of their studies. The foreign education of students will not benefit the countries of their origin in such cases. India is facing currently a challenge in educational standards and many colleges and universities are criticized for their lack of commitment to education, which allegedly create too many unemployable youths. Focussing on quality in education and promotion of innovative, original research in universities should be a national priority. Excellence in universities could be a highly inspiring, and forward-looking nationalistic policy. It can improve productivity of the nation in the longer run, for sure.

A nation that does not promote education or skill development, or skill upgradation of its current and future work force, is indirectly playing into the hands of profit maximizing global businesses. These workers can only perform jobs as told to them, or as mere onlookers (watchmen, guards, mall / shop attendants, etc., to name a few) who just show up in offices and places of work without any significant personal value addition. The situation feeds itself and deteriorates, as the absence of unskilled or semi-skilled labour in an economy justifies increased use of mechanization by businesses, leading to further job losses. It also has potential to depress the wages for all, including the already employed.

In 2020, at the forum in Davos, the forum's founder Klaus Schwab and Charles, the then Prince of Wales, talked about a new course for humanity, the Great Reset. It included capturing the imagination and will of humanity, plans for an economic recovery to put the world on the path of sustainable employment, livelihoods and growth, redesigned systems, advancing towards net zero transitions, promoting scientific and technological innovations, etc. The main idea of the 'Great Reset' was the continuation and strengthening of globalization. The first waves of modern globalization led by technology, were probably in the age of railroads, steamships, and telegraphs. Today, the international trade is driven mainly by both geopolitics and technology. However, globalization is firmly on a reverse gear now and efforts to improve it are, at best, seen as a series of half-hearted, unfinished attempts.

In the current era of the digital globalization, the international movement of information and data are critical. An increasing number of services are being offered using digital platforms and applications. Even at the individual level, there is a strong incentive for people to use these platforms and international network to offer their services globally. Small entrepreneurs can use the network to reduce their costs of operations. Global digital networks, satellites, undersea cables, etc., are all strong pillars of globalization. Any fragmentation in these could be disastrous for world economy and the worst affected could be poor economies.

A blended culture is very much a part of human living now. Cities typically have a multi-culture, as they embrace different languages and traditions of immigrants. A workable culture across various groups is, therefore, an absolute necessity there. In a borderless world, the global cultures are shared on invisible, easily accessible networks that connect persons living in far-away places. People can today appreciate the traditions of alien communities without physically interacting with them. This is less threatening, politically, and culturally. In addition, immigrants who are forced to interact with strangers assimilate, partly out of sheer necessity and partly out of passion, their cultures, and values. In turn, they also influence the local population. As a result, identities are getting changed and redefined.

Globalization affects a person's identity with migrations, shorter job-related stays, assignments, journeys, platform jobs, and shorter relationships. It creates a portfolio of relationships and transnational identities, which transcend the bounds of nations and traditions. The new realities change the way a person creates, and shares his services and ideas.

Shrinking Head Counts

World population growth is slowing down. The population explosion of earlier decades is attributed to increased longevity of people, which in turn, was driven by better health care systems. Population growth is declining now and a reversal in the trend is not expected. Many developed countries and even some developing countries would face low to high population decline, going forward. A larger proportion of aged in communities will lead to reduced economic productivity, as decline in population would reduce the working population.

Longer periods of continuous economic degrowth and higher levels of dependents, are both dangerous situations for any nation. The shrinking working population can be partly addressed by technological innovations. But beyond a limit, most greying nations will have to attract younger workers from other countries in future, if they are to keep growing economically. With the trend of depopulation continuing, nations would be forced to encourage migration of non-nationals. World is also likely to see new trends like Virtual Migrants and Digital Workers rather than physical migrations, in future. In any case, compensating for the decline in population by alien nationals could be the new trend in the second half of twenty first century. Nations will have to put in place policies to attract talented youth from less developed locations. There could be policies that would encourage immigrations from locations of 'friendly' cultures. Given the trend, it is almost certain that the developing and underdeveloped countries stand to lose their scarce capital and best talents to the better off nations.

Depopulation will sooner or later hit developing countries as well. When that happens, the shrinking, low base of population pyramids in such countries cannot support the expanding, dependent, aging, top of the pyramid segments of the population. These countries would then face the double whammy of losing talent on the one side and increasing dependents on the other side.

Another driver for higher future migrations would be the issue of over built cities. When population declines, the sub optimal level of replacement of population due to lower growth rate would lead to unoccupied houses and offices. Nations in such situations would be forced to encourage migrations from under developed countries or other nations with relatively higher unemployment rates. This would drain the top talents of the underdeveloped and developing countries. Culturally tolerant people would be ready to migrate to multicultural locations and countries. The migrant receiving nations will have to then take a hard look at some of the 'acceptable' alien cultures and review their nationalistic theories.

Under the above assumptions, the benefits of globalization will have to be reevaluated. It may be possible that migration policies in future are driven primarily by non-economic factors like cultural fit, social cohesion, etc. Economic migration, especially of those with skill sets or capital, is beneficial to the recipient nations' economies. But some nations may still prefer a lower rate of economic growth in order to avoid potential cultural conflicts. In an EU-wide opinion survey in 2016, respondents stated that the commitment of immigrants to the way of life of countries of destination must be the most important factor in deciding immigration policies. Other factors, including those traditionally used in migrant selection, such as the language or occupational skills and educational qualifications were deemed secondary. Many countries require immigrants to sign an integration contract, committing them to adhere to host-country traditions and values. Most OECD countries have civic integration tests for naturalization.

One Way Valves

National economies, globally, are both integrated and disintegrated, and their degree of integration would broadly depend on the criticality and need for sectoral alliances, political and cultural alignments between the nations concerned, history of wars and conflicts, etc. A strong argument for globalization is that it can be instrumental in uniting human societies across the world by efficiency and integration of markets. However, markets are neither integrated nor efficient anywhere in the world.

There are market forces acting for and against globalization all the time, driven mainly by their own commercial and political interests. Corporates with excellent products and services would like to encourage globalization as it expands their addressable markets. Same would be the case with new technology products that can address global consumers. On the other and, producers of low-end goods and services for local consumption would like to insulate their domestic markets against competition from foreign, superior, rival products and services.

There are strategic areas and sectors where nations need to be more secured. These can include areas like defence, food, healthcare, telecommunications, transportation, key raw materials needed, etc. Companies are also unlikely to delink from countries perceived as 'big' markets for their products, as that would hit their global sales. A balanced approach to globalization must be market-friendly that takes care of these realities. Greater regionalization of supply chains is fine in some cases. The alliances between friendly countries, and trustworthy corporates can have their own socio -political challenges.

World As a Family
The ancient Indian collection of animal fables, 'Panchatantra' (3rd century BCE), says "Only small men discriminate saying that one is a relative and the other is a stranger. For those who live magnanimously, the entire world constitutes but a family." ("ayam bandhurayam neti ganana laghuchetasam, udaracharitanam tu vasudhaiva Kutumbakam.") A similar message is also contained in 'Hitopadesha' or 'Good Advice' written by Narayana in 12th century AD. Hinduism believes in the concept of world as a family and universal brotherhood.

The pre modern societies were organized around religions, myths, and tribal practices. Later it was built around the means of production. In the process, the devil fetishism of primitive world got transformed into commodity fetishism of the industrial world. This was, in many ways, an improvement in human social outlook. There are concrete reasons to appreciate the fact that human beings have a shared history. The scientific or technological progress have happened not due to the efforts of one community or one nation. These were achieved by the joint efforts of different communities and nations.

This is where the forces of nationalism clash with world-as-a-family concept. The economic choices between globalization and national self-sufficiency are quite tricky. Today, there are nationalistic voices pleading for 'reshoring,' 'friendly shoring,' and 'just at home' relating to key supply chains. The European Commission recently adopted the concept of 'open strategic autonomy' which seeks a new balance between open trade and efforts to reduce dependency and strengthen security of supply. As part of this move, the Commission is exploring a future legal instrument to address the issue of subsidies. That can possibly create a new set of disputes as many countries consider these subsidies as 'trade distorting.' To handle such situations, nations need to redefine the product classifications in better ways or do away with some of the discriminatory classifications.

Globalization is not an unmixed blessing. It has quite a few dark areas which must be tackled in a manner that its negative impacts on various players and members of the communities are minimized. Sovereign governments will have to consider the vulnerabilities of various players in the economy and create regulations in the best interest of all. They can possibly encourage big corporates to fight globally on their own, for market penetration. Medium size players will need to be supported by state agencies on merits, while the smaller domestic units must be actively protected from the onslaught of global competition, till they reach a medium size.

One Way Valves

Globalization is indeed beneficial in many ways. But it does show an increasing tendency to focus on material growth, favour certain groups and ignore many others. Globalization is impacting economies and economic factors like labour, capital, etc. In the process, the non-economic global goals like peace, human and animal rights, environment protection etc., do not get properly addressed.

While there are many valid and strong arguments for a connected, globalized world, there are equally serious concerns and opposing views as well. A major reason for the same is the *'one way valve'* approach by pro globalists. Let us examine some of the *'one-way valves'* more closely:

Right to Live; Right to Kill: Under globalization, corporates are allowed free entry in any market. Such entries, however, can be destructive for local businesses that are relatively smaller or less technologically advanced. Multinational corporates with huge money power can kill any emerging, potentially competitive businesses identified by them. These are *One-way fights*.

Costs Down; Margins Up: One of the major anticipated advantages of globalization is the fact that under such a system, global producers can use cheap offshore labour, raw materials etc., so that they can offer cost efficient products and services. In practice, however, the cost benefits are not being passed on either to ultimate consumes or to labour class. These advantages are getting translated into higher profit margins for the multinational corporates. Profits get priority over customer care or employee welfare. These are unjustified, *One-way gains*.

Fair Markets; Unfair Competition: Opening the local markets for entry of global players was expected to increase competition, which would then lead to availability of varied and arguably better global goods and services for the consumers. However, it is observed that the global level competition is grossly unfair, given the advantages of big corporates in terms of their deeper pockets, better technologies, more efficient networks, larger reach, ability to buy out or eliminate competitors, tax benefits, etc. There are cartels of big corporations as well. The business focus is on capturing markets by any means. And in the market, the number of consumers and their life long dollar spendings matter more than the actual needs of the individual consumer or their affordability of products. In the absence of fair competition, businesses are *one-way dominations*.

Co-operation not Operational: Global co-operation is one of corner stones of globalization. But many nations provide subsidies to domestic producers, levy custom tariffs, impose anti-dumping duties, etc., which work against free movement of products and services. Then there are multilateral and bilateral trade pacts which create preferential treatment for exchange of goods and services between friendly nations. These are hurdles in globalization, as the system under such conditions do not promote the best products and services. These are *one-way regulations.*

Touch Me Not: Another critical component of globalization is the flow of capital 'freely' into and out of nations. But capital is choosy. It does not go where it is really required. Instead, it flows to places where it is taxed minimum and where it can multiply faster. Capital owners do not want their income to be taxed at normal rates. So, they go to so-called tax havens and make it difficult for nations to tax their income. In the entire process, common people are discriminated against. The owners of capital are undeserved beneficiaries. These are *'One-way benefits.'*

Secret Inventions; Hidden Knowledge: Technological inventions are generally patented and kept secret. The general public do not have access to them. These inventions and innovations get monetized or are commercially exploited, for the benefit of those who engage the inventors. We do not celebrate the knowledge by sharing them freely with the outside world. We need to defocus on monetizing patents and knowledge. To begin with, the research institutes that are funded by charitable organizations and the ones using public resources like tax breaks, can allow the general public free access to their knowledge libraries and inventions. That would be value added charity.

May be, we need to learn from nature here. The benevolent acts of the Sun or Moon or Wind, are worthy of emulation. They give away their wealth free, for the benefit of all. In the case of inventions, let the efforts be compensated by a reasonable profit. But super profits must be barred. If everything is commoditized and commercialized, only the *one-side winners* will survive in the long run.

Fragmented Standards: There are benefits of global standardization. Common utilities like say, GPS, underwater cables etc., could be shared by the whole world, rather than by few nations. However, the recent Ukraine war has created a frenzy for 'owning' key utilities by each big nation, as the fear of blockage and sanctions have increased. The recent weaponization of financial transactions against Russia was a major push factor for anti-globalization. Reshoring, and friendly shoring have since then become preferred options in supply chain management. This is a major tail wind for deglobalization. Each major country is now going for its own standards in areas like GPS, payment systems, etc., which can potentially fragment the global system.

May be, these nations can work together and arrive at a standard platform, owned jointly by the human kind. The supra national institutions can have a say in blocking and pricing these facilities. There could be an international law that can stipulate, for example, that in cases where a product has more than 25% of its customers outside its registered nation of origin, it cannot unilaterally stop supply of goods or services, without getting a majority approval from such foreign customers, measured in terms of value of such services availed by them in the past say, two years. The idea of taking care of own side or *one side,* only, is a dangerous one.

Islands of Growth: Globalization was expected to lead to overall global growth. Instead, we are witnessing islands of growth. The thinly populated regions, remote villages, and tribal belts are yet to see the full benefits of globalization. This is because their population is not 'big enough' to attract flows of capital or goods or services. They do not have the 'critical' size. They are the *neglected side.*

Living for the Community: To be effective, globalization must be oriented more towards the welfare of common men. The social waves generated by globalization should be visibly humane, truly sympathetic, and not necessarily limited to just material comforts and progress.

Let all of us live *for* and not *off* the community.

Select Bibliography and References:

1. Adhikari, Kishor; Krippner, Stanley; Pitchford, Daniel B; & Davies, Jeannine A: "The Search for Universal Values" IOSR Journal of Humanities and Social Science (JHSS), Volume 2, Issue 1 (Sep-Oct. 2012).

2. Alina Polyakova, Torrey Taussig, Ted Reinert, Kemal Kirişci, Amanda Sloat, Melissa Hooper, Norman Eisen, and Andrew Kenealy, The Anatomy of Illiberal States: Assessing and Responding to Democratic Decline in Turkey and Central Europe, (Washington, DC: The Brookings Institution, February 2019), https://www.brookings.edu/wp-content/uploads/2019/02/ illiberal-states-web.pdf.

3. American Phycological Association: "Beyond the 'East–West' Dichotomy: Global Variation in Cultural Models of Selfhood" (2016).

4. Anastasia Aldelina Lijadi, "What are universally accepted human values that define 'a good life'? Historical perspective of value theory" Working paper – International Institute for Applied Systems Analysis.

5. Andrew Miles & Catherine Yeh, Department of Sociology, University of Toronto: "Do demographic predictors of personal values vary by context? A test of Schwartz's value development theory."

6. Aravacik, Esra Dundar: "Social Policy and the Welfare State," Public Economics and Finance Edited by Bernur Acıkgoz.

7. Boaventura de Sousa Santos: "Governance: Between Myth and Reality," RCCS Annual Review [Online], 2009, http://journals.openedition.org/rccsar/95.

8. Caruso, Loris: "Theories of the Political Process, Political Opportunities Structure and Local Mobilizations. The Case of Italy."

9. Eco, Umberto: "Holy Wars, Passion and Reason, Scattered Thoughts on Cultural Superiority"

10. Encyclopedia Britannica, www.britannica.com

11. Escude Carlos, Professor of Political Science, Senior Researcher at CONICET and Director of the Centro de Estudios Internacionales y de Educacion para la Globalizacion (CEIEG): 'Reflections on Cultural Superiority and the Just War: A Neomodern Imperative.'

12. "Ethics and Globalization in the Light of Hinduism." Maya Mainkar, University of Pune, India, The Asian Conference on Arts & Humanities 2013, Official Conference Proceedings 2013.

13. "Exploring Universal Basic Income: A Guide to Navigating Concepts, Evidence, and Practices": By Ugo Gentilini, Margaret Grosh, Jamele Rigolini, and Ruslan Yemtsov (Editors).

14. Fitzgerald, Kathleen J., Department of Sociology, University of North Carolina, Chapel Hill, NC USA: "Creating an Ideal World: A Review of Work, Love, and Learning in Utopia: Equality Reimagined" (Review 2021).

15. Fourie, Carina: "What is Social Equality? An Analysis of Status Equality as a Strongly Egalitarian Ideal."
16. Hag-Min Kim and Ping Li Department of International Business and Trade, Kyung Hee University, Seoul, Republic of Korea, and Yea Rim Lee International Commerce, Finance, and Investment, Kyung Hee University, Seoul, Republic of Korea: 'Observations of deglobalization against globalization and impacts on global business.'
17. https://jkrishnamurti.org/content/causes-war
18. Internet.
19. Mannheim, Karl, The London School of Economics and Political Science, (University of London). "Ideology and Utopia - An Introduction to the Sociology of Knowledge."
20. Natarajan, Ashok, Secretary and Senior Research Fellow, The Mother's Service Society, India, Fellow, World Academy of Art & Science: "A Values-based World Order"
21. National Academy of Sciences (Biographical Memoirs - www.nasonline.org/memoirs.
22. Parmar, Pooja. "Undoing Historical Wrongs: Law and Indigeneity in India." Osgoode Hall Law Journal 49.3 (2012) - http://digitalcommons.osgoode.yorku.ca/ohlj/vol49/iss3/3.
23. Piff, Paul K, Stancato, Daniel M, Cote, Stephane, and Keltner, Dacher: "Higher social class predicts increased unethical behavior." Edited by Richard E. Nisbett, University of Michigan, Ann Arbor, MI.
24. Schwartz, Shalom H. "An Overview of the Schwartz Theory of Basic Values" The Hebrew University of Jerusalem.
25. Stiglitz, Joseph E. University Professor, Columbia University, Chief Economist at the Roosevelt Institute: "The Welfare State in The Twenty-first Century." (June 2017).
26. Storm, Servaas: "Why the Rich Get Richer and Interest Rates Go Down"
27. "The Calculus of Consent: Logical Foundations of Constitutional Democracy" : by James M. Buchanan and Gordon Tullock (1962).
28. World Bank. Poverty and Shared Prosperity 2022: Correcting Course. Washington, DC: World Bank. doi:10.1596/978-1-4648-1893-6. License: Creative Commons Attribution CC BY 3.0 IGO.

ENDNOTES

1   Daniel Hojman & Alvaro Miranda, 2015. "Agency, Human Dignity and Subjective Well-Being," Working Papers wp398, University of Chile, Department of Economics.

2   Min, Tong-Keun, 'A Study on the Hierarchy of Values' Chung Nam National University.

3   Inglehart, r & c. Welzel. 2005. "Modernization, Cultural Change and Democracy: The Human Development Sequence. "New York: Cambridge University Press.

4   "Higher social class predicts increased unethical behaviour", by Paul K. Piff, Daniel M. Stancato, Stephane Cote, and Dacher Keltner. Edited by Richard E. Nisbett, University of Michigan, Ann Arbor, MI.

5   "Cultural identity is subjective, On the political role of culture in multicultural societies" by Lisen Stenberg, Lund University, Department of Political Science.

6   The Mother was born Mirra Alfassa in Paris on 21 February 1878. She was an accomplished artist, pianist, and writer. When the Sri Aurobindo Ashram was formed in November 1926, Sri Aurobindo entrusted its full material and spiritual charge to Mother.

7   Definition of culture provided by the 19th-century English anthropologist Edward Burnett Tylor in the first paragraph of his *Primitive Culture* (1871).

8   Professor Andrew Whiten, School of Psychology & Neuroscience, University of St Andrews, St Andrews, UK.

9   "The Myth of Ethnic Conflict: Politics, Economics, and Cultural Violence." Editors: Beverly Crawford and Ronnie D. Lipschutz, University of California at Berkeley.

10 "A revealing map of the world's most and least ethnically diverse countries" By Max Fisher, The Washington Post (May 16, 2013).

11 "Civil Wars & Global Disorder: Threats & Opportunities," Publication by the American Academy of Arts & Sciences (2017).

12 Timur Kuran, "Ethnic Dissimilation and Its Global Transmission" as quoted in "The Myth of Ethnic Conflict: Politics, Economics, and Cultural Violence," Edited by Beverly Crawford and Ronnie D. Lipschutz

13 Federal Reserve Bank of Kansas City's annual Jackson Hole symposium, 2022. The title of Economic Policy Symposium was "Macroeconomic Policy in an Uneven Economy."

14 Scientific American, "Ancient Teeth Reveal Social Stratification Dates Back to Bronze Age Societies" October 2019.

15 Tilly, Charles: "Coercion, capital and European states, AD 990-1990" (Cambridge, 1992), Mann, M. "The sources of social power" (Cambridge, 1986; 1993) 2 vol.

16 Weber, Max ([1921] 1978). Economy and Society: An Outline of Interpretive Sociology, translated by Guenther Roth and Claus Wittich. Berkeley: University of California Press.

17 Scientific American, "Ancient Teeth Reveal Social Stratification Dates Back to Bronze Age Societies" October 2019.

18 Peter F. Drucker, "The Age of Social Transformation" https://www.theatlantic.com/past/docs/issues/95dec/ chilearn/drucker.htm.

19 History of Science, Philosophy and Culture in Indian Civilization (Centre for Studies in Civilization), various volumes.

About the Author

Dr. Pushpangadan Mangari retired as Chief Executive of L&T Capital, a Wealth and Portfolio Management firm owned by Indian multinational, Larsen & Toubro Limited. Prior to that he was Managing Director of UTI Securities Exchange Limited, a public sector broking / wealth management / consulting firm. He was also the Managing Director of the first electronic stock exchange of India, the OTCEI. He is currently an independent Director in an Indian Non-Banking Finance Company and in another Public Sector Indian Mutual Fund Trustee Company.

Dr. Pushpangadan has published many articles on social and financial topics, in both English and in his mother tongue, Malayalam. In book form, he has published a collection of his various articles on social subjects and 2 poetry collections, both in Malayalam. His article "Impact of Financialization: View from India" was included in the book titled "The 2008 Crisis Ten Years On: in Retrospect, Context and Prospect" edited by Arturo Hermann & Maria Alejandra Madi, under the World Economic Association Conference Book Series, in 2020.

Email: pushpangadan@hotmail.com